Putin's Trolls

PUTIN'S TROLLS

ON THE FRONTLINES OF
RUSSIA'S INFORMATION WAR
AGAINST THE WORLD

Jessikka Aro

IG PUBLISHING
New York, NY

Ig Publishing
Box 2547
New York, NY 10163
www.igpub.com

ISBN: 978-1632461-29-2

PRINTED IN THE UNITED STATES OF AMERICA

FIRST EDITION | FIRST PRINTING

This book is dedicated to the strong women in my family.

To my grandmother Mannukka, who volunteered to monitor the skies as a teenager, and protected Finland from the Soviet warplanes.

To my other grandmother Hilja, who escaped the Soviet occupiers from Karelia and never let her mind be occupied.

To my mother Hilkka, who is so full of love.

To my sister Pipsa, the Supreme Being.

To my aunts Kaisu and Ritu, who showed me how Finnish freedom of expression ought to be used.

CONTENTS

1.

Escape

I FLED MY HOMELAND OF FINLAND in February 2017. Just before my escape, I gave a presentation on the dangers posed by Russian propaganda and fake news at the National Police Board of Finland in Helsinki.

In school I was taught that Finland was one of the safest countries in the world. But for me, an ordinary journalist for Yleisradio, or Yle, the Finnish national public broadcasting company, the basic right to safety in my home country had been severely compromised simply because of my profession.

By the time of my forced departure, I had endured a two-and-a-half-year campaign of death threats and libelous news articles. Online hate sites had brainwashed even some of my friends, turning them into enemies. These same sites portrayed me as a criminal, a liar, and mentally ill. Anonymous users suggested various methods of killing myself. One stranger proposed that I hang myself, while another recommended a "Russian suicide": someone would push me under the metro, but in a manner staged as self-inflicted. A third individual wished that someone would put a "bullet in the whore's head, Russian style." Each time I opened my laptop, or glanced at my phone, I was forced to read snuff fantasies about me produced on an assembly-line scale. I was afraid that the psychological violence would spill out of the internet into the physical world. I installed an alarm system and other security measures in my home.

I had become the target of such vitriol for one reason only: I was a journalist investigating Russian social media information warfare.

ooooo

When I launched what would become my world-famous investigation into Russian online propaganda trolls in September 2014, I was thirty-three years old. My life was serene, and I dreamed of starting a family. I had no enemies that I knew of, and aroused no interest from anyone in the online world.

As a journalist, I specialized in Russia and extremist groups. Earlier in my career I had lived in Russia, and throughout President Vladimir Putin's time in office, I had kept an eye on the pressure exerted on journalists, including retribution via violence and murder. The reporters who risked their lives investigating his regime's wrongdoings were my professional idols.

While I had previously investigated jihadists' recruitment activities on social media, as well as organized crime, it wasn't until I began examining the Kremlin's tools of international information warfare that a hate campaign was launched against me. The harassers wanted to exhaust me psychologically, hoping that I would ultimately decide to protect myself and cease investigating and publicly discussing Russian operations.

In my work as a journalist, I had become accustomed to extreme and violent material. I had reported on wars, natural disasters, plane crashes, and human rights crimes. But nothing had prepared me for the uncontrollable online spread of thousands of defamatory memes, threads, pictures, and videos—all about me![1]

Before I left Finland, I did everything in my power to put an end to the witch hunt, or at least limit its crippling impact on my life. I reported to Facebook, Twitter, and YouTube those accounts that violated the community standards outlined in their terms of service. The companies' automated responses declared that the content did not violate their community standards—even though it was crystal clear that it did. In effect, these media giants were happy to offer their services as platforms for what amounted to state-sponsored propaganda and hate speech.

I implored Finnish security officials for help. I cried my frustration out to a police officer, who told me that no legislation provided the tools to stop the crimes I was enduring. The only avenue available was filing criminal complaints, which would take years to process in court. Online propagandists skillfully abuse Western laws and legal systems, which are inadequate for meeting the challenges of organized online hate dissemination. I anticipated that even police scrutiny would not guarantee an end to these crimes.

Unfortunately, I was right.

As the police launched their investigation, many of the officers themselves were libeled and targeted online. Confidential police documents were published, and as the investigations continued, fake news sites accused *me* of launching a bogus investigation, which incited more angry attacks. I tried lobbying the Finnish government, and proposed legislative changes to more effectively counter the Russian information warfare. As a result, I was again abused and shamed.

In addition to the police, I turned to my employer, Yle, for assistance. The employer's responsibility is to protect its employees, while the duty of the police is to solve crimes. I trusted both. I believed that one day the propagandists would be held accountable. All I had to do was stay safe until then.

ooooo

Time passed, yet nothing stopped the Mafia-like internet gang or their mission to destroy my credibility, professional reputation, and life. The alarm systems in my home couldn't protect me from the parade of online slander, which had succeeded in influencing thousands of people against me.

I was left with two options.

Either continue investigating Russian information warfare and educating people, and, in so doing, remain subject to stalking—both physical and online—and other crimes.

Or stop investigating the topic, withdraw from public life—and likely be left alone.

I understood that the architects of my persecution were manipulating me toward the latter option. However, out of respect for the journalistic profession and my home country, I chose to continue my work. Had I ceased to report on Russian online propaganda, I would have broken my fundamental promise to the public. A journalist's duty is to convey factual information to readers, listeners, and viewers. If, out of fear, I had halted my investigations into Kremlin trolls and fake news, I would have denied my audience its universal human right to receive the truth.

ooooo

I discovered that Russian social media disinformation threatened civic discussion and national security in several countries. I therefore tried to warn the public of Russia's ambitions to shift the political atmosphere in its favor, as well as showing how it was taking advantage of social media companies in order to meddle in the affairs of the West.

Events following my warnings proved that I was right. In 2016, Russian social media trolls attacked the US presidential election and Britain's referendum to leave the European Union;

promoted Catalan independence from Spain; and fueled violence in France during the yellow vest protests.

After that, I received a steady stream of gratitude and positive feedback for my work. My research was widely quoted. I was invited to conferences around the world, and gave interviews to the international media.

But when I walked down the street in Finland, I was forced to look over my shoulder. My biggest fear was that a mentally unstable consumer of fake news might become incensed enough to physically attack me. The police conducted a threat assessment and came to the same conclusion: in Finland I was a target for impulsive violence, should I find myself in the wrong place at the wrong time. But abroad, where no one knew me or read the sites where I was attacked, I was safe.

Finland was—and still is—one of the world's safest and freest countries with regards to the media; just not for me.

Because I wanted to continue my work, share information, and educate the public—and get back to leading an ordinary, boring private life in which my biggest dream was to get pregnant and become a mother —I had to leave Finland.

I gave away my extra belongings, packed the rest, rented out my home, and booked a one-way flight out of Helsinki.

∞∞∞

The day of my emigration in February 2017, I finished my presentation at the National Police Board and informed them I would be leaving the country. The Finnish National Police Commissioner shook my hand and wished me safe travels.

Two hours later I boarded a plane. I didn't know whether I would be granted work and residence permits in my new country. But I was hopeful that the move would give me back my freedom, and for that I was prepared to pay any price.

I cried throughout the whole flight.

A VILLAGE BANDIT

As a Finnish journalist, I had enjoyed liberties that most of the world's reporters can only fantasize about. Finnish criminal codes and employment laws, strict ethical guidelines for journalists, and the institutional self-regulation of the media coalesce to create a safe and supportive environment for reporting and publishing stories.

Or so I thought.

Beginning in late 2013, I had reported on the people's uprising in Ukraine against the corrupt president, Viktor Yanukovych. As the pro-Kremlin "separatists" started to take over television stations and administrative buildings in the spring of 2014, conveying confirmed, factual information became a challenge. The situation was muddied by the Russian media and a variety of odd websites, which pushed accusations of Ukraine as the aggressor in the conflict, as well as the false idea that the country was experiencing an internal conflict, when in fact Russia had started the warfare against Ukraine.

Earlier, I had covered another particularly propaganda-infested conflict, the five-day war between Russia and Georgia in 2008. But the number of international and fake social media information campaigns surrounding Russia's secretive operations against Ukraine in 2014 was astonishing.

I had always been intrigued by the concepts of nonmilitary malicious influence, psychological operations, and propaganda targeted at civilians. Nazi Germany and the Soviet Union had taught the world how political leadership could gain control over the minds of the people and condition them into being loyal servants of the government. In order to maintain power and fulfill outsized political ambitions, all a dictator needed to do was to take over the free media and turn it into a megaphone of the regime—gradually or by force.

Historically, one of war propaganda's most efficient methods has been dehumanizing the enemy. After the enemy is demonized, war against it is justified and the soldiers are motivated to fight for a seemingly legitimate cause.

Neuroscience shows why dehumanizing is effective: human brains are wired to divide and thus discriminate. Racist language and hostile images arouse strong mental responses and drive bias. The discriminative propensity of the brain was demonstrated in a 2006 study, where test subjects evaluated photos of homeless people and were prone to categorize them as "subhuman."[2] Historically, demonization has led to genocide and crimes against humanity; as such, many Western countries have laws forbidding the incitement of hatred against minorities or ethnicities.

In 2014, the Russian state-controlled media systematically portrayed Ukraine as a country governed by historically well-known enemies: fascists and Nazis. According to the Kremlin's narrative, the Ukrainian people needed to be liberated.

As I read the conspiracy theories about Ukraine spreading across the internet, I became interested in Russia's information warfare against the greater international community.

In the autumn of 2014, I interviewed Andrei Illarionov, a former close aide to Vladimir Putin, who had provided insightful information to the international media about Russia's activities in Ukraine. Illarionov had revealed, for example, that the Kremlin had planned the operation against its neighbor over a decade earlier. Illarionov left Russia in 2005, stating publicly that the country was no longer a democracy. He moved to the United States to become a senior fellow at the Cato Institute.

Illarionov described how in modern Russia, psychological warfare is taught at schools and universities as well as to government officials. He explained how the Russian media is not independent, but part of the state-run machinery supporting the Kremlin's political interests. Illarionov pointed out that in the digital era, disseminating online propaganda is cheap and efficient, crossing borders in a split second.[3]

When I asked him why the Russian government conducted information warfare, he told me that it wanted to justify to both the Russian people and outsiders why it was waging war in Ukraine. It also wanted to show who was boss.

And there was another explanation.

"For the Kremlin," he said, "it is most important to show that it *can* wage information war. Just like a village bandit, Russia wants to show the world that it can do as it pleases."

MODERN WEAPONS OF MASS DESTRUCTION

A so-called "troll factory" had been exposed in St. Petersburg, Russia, in 2013. Independent Russian journalists had infiltrated the office and worked there as "trolls," as the propaganda workers called themselves. The trolls were paid a monthly salary for pretending to be unaffiliated citizens posting their real opinions on social media. They built and updated fake profiles and filled the social media space with comments praising Putin and mocking Russian opposition figures and the United States.[4] According to a strategy paper obtained by BuzzFeed, the aim of the factory was to "change the balance between pro-Russian and Russia-critical commenting online."[5] In practice, the mission was to manipulate online discussion about Russia.

In Finland, the trolls were already on the upswing in the summer of 2014 when I interviewed Jarno Limnéll, a Finnish cybersecurity expert and visiting professor at Aalto University, about the concept of hybrid warfare.[6] Limnéll told me that Russian-language Twitter trolls regularly denounced and commented on the information he tweeted. In addition, the then Finnish Defense Minister, Carl Haglund, stated that he had received hundreds of anonymous messages under his Facebook and Twitter postings concerning Ukraine.

I became concerned about the potential threat that the army of fake Putin fans posed to the general public. Many could unwittingly follow troll accounts and become influenced by false information originating from propaganda agencies in Russia. More than 70,000 people in Finland speak Russian as their first language, and this group, I feared, were especially at risk of opinion molding.

Research has shown that people's brains do not process the information they get from social media very critically. Social media content is agitating, provocative, addictive—perfect for state-sponsored psychological operations. Many of the features of social media work well in the service of international propaganda operations. Any user can establish a personal bot network or a farm of private harassment accounts on sites like Facebook and Twitter. In the hands of Russian political technologists, these social media platforms are transformed into psychological weapons of mass destruction.

I wanted to investigate this matter in cooperation with Finnish internet users. So, I began with a very basic journalistic method: I asked people questions. I described the modus operandi of the Russian troll network, and asked people to share their experiences of anonymous or fake profiles spreading aggressive Russian propaganda online. I specifically wanted to find out how the trolls impacted real people.

Knowing that Finland still suffered from a Soviet-era legacy known as Finlandization, the official appeasement of the Kremlin in order to secure trade and maintain a peaceful relationship, I expected my project would raise some backlash from extremists, communists, conspiracy theorists, and Putin sycophants.

However, when Yle published my first article in September 2014, I was not prepared for the possibility that my life as I had known it would be over.

A ONE-TO-ONE SECRET

As soon as my article was published, my social media and professional communications channels melted down. I received threatening text messages, phone calls, and emails from Russia, Kazakhstan, and elsewhere in the Russian-speaking world. The anonymous messages, written in Russian or poor English, accused me of various crimes and said I should be "imprisoned." Someone called me from a Ukrainian number and played the sound of a shooting gun.

I had never experienced anything like it, and neither had any other journalist in Finland. The ensuing wave of online propaganda was so similar, it appeared as if someone had sent a press release to the media. "Journalists" at approximately ten different fake news sites seemed to have copied and pasted the same information in the articles they wrote against me. No evidence to back up their allegations was ever provided.

Some of the articles lacked the name of an author. Most troubling was that many included my email address and phone number—enabling countless people triggered by the lies to harass me directly. As I tried to respond to the outrage, I learned how online disinformation was strategically used to drive people to take hostile actions.

Four days after publishing my article, I alerted my supervisor as to what was happening. He said that we should consult with Yleisradio's security department.

ooooo

As I investigated the misinformation against me more closely, I discovered that a Finnish citizen named Johan Bäckman had disseminated false allegations about me on several Russian fake news sites. Bäckman is notorious for disseminating Russian propaganda. He doesn't even try to hide his connections with

Russia, openly posting photos of himself in the company of top Kremlin officials and members of the Duma, the Russian parliament.[7] He publishes his military adventures with Russian forces on his YouTube channel.[8]

Bäckman is frequently interviewed by Russian state-controlled media outlets. In one of his most famous interviews, broadcast on the Russian state-backed international propaganda network, Russia Today (RT), Bäckman declared that the killer of Anna Politkovskaya, the Russian investigative journalist and Kremlin critic assassinated in Moscow in 2006, was the "Western media."[9] He also regularly tours Russia and Russian-annexed Crimea, speaking to soldiers, civil servants, and the public about the "Western hybrid war against Russia." Bäckman's message has efficiently penetrated Russia: according to the Levada Center, an independent Russian polling organization, 80 percent of Russians believe their country is the target of information warfare coming from the West.[10]

In 2014, Bäckman declared himself the Finnish "representative" of the Donetsk People's Republic, a self-declared and unrecognized pro-Russian state in the Eastern Ukrainian region occupied by Russia.[11] Another Finnish citizen who traveled to Eastern Ukraine to fight on the Russian side told the Finnish press that Bäckman had covered his travel expenses and arranged for his visa to the conflict region.[12] In Ukraine, Bäckman is labeled as a terrorist supporter.[13] In early 2019, the Ukrainian government denied his entry into the country, along with three other Finnish pro-Kremlin extremists. Estonia has also forbidden his entrance, reportedly for fueling pro-Kremlin conflict during the Bronze Soldier clashes in 2007.

At the time of his attacks against me, Bäckman represented a Putin administration policy think tank called the Russian Institute for Strategic Studies (RISS), based in Moscow. The institute states that it provides "recommendations and analytical materials" to the

Russian president, government, and parliament. The employees at the institute are former KGB and current Russian security services officers appointed by Putin. In 2014, the leader of the institute was Leonid Reshetnikov, the lieutenant general of the SVR, Russia's foreign intelligence service.

While Bäckman presents himself as a pro-Kremlin village idiot "who should not be taken seriously," he has filed nearly 100 criminal complaints against journalists and researchers who write and discuss Russia.[14] This has created an atmosphere of fear for many Finnish journalists. In some newsrooms, coverage of Bäckman has been suspended, as many editors think it easier not to report on his activities than to be forced to allocate resources answering his many complaints and responding to his potential smear campaigns. One well-informed Finnish journalist called Bäckman a "one-man troll factory."[15] Even government officials have avoided public discussions concerning his activities, which has allowed Bäckman to continue his promotion of Kremlin aggression.

As soon as Bäckman started to vilify me, I called him and asked why he was doing it. He told me that it was "politics." When I asked him to specify—"politics on behalf of what and against what?"—he hung up.

Over the course of the following year and a half, I asked Bäckman to correct fake news about me on multiple occasions. As many times as I asked, he declined. Instead, he bombarded me with private messages. He manipulated me, mocked me, sometimes flattered me, invited me to his conferences in Moscow, St. Petersburg, and Crimea, and pressed me to divulge personal information. He vigorously demanded and tried to cajole me into meeting him face-to-face, promising to cease writing social media posts about me if I met him. He said he would keep our meeting "a one-to-one secret." His messages implied that it was my research on the Kremlin's trolls that specifically troubled him.

If I had met him, he would have tried to force me into cooperating with him or tried to compromise me in a manner that could jeopardize my career.

I rejected his proposals to meet, and instead responded to his online intimidation with silence or the demand that he correct the false accusations he had spread about me. To this day, none of the accusations have ever been corrected.

∞∞∞

Four years later, I sat as the plaintiff in front of three judges in the Helsinki District Court. The prosecutor had described my case as an exceptional example of hostile information influence.

When my lawyer asked me how my life had changed since Johan Bäckman entered it, I broke into tears.

2.

The Diplomat

THREE YEARS AFTER LITHUANIAN DIPLOMAT Renatas Juška lost his job as ambassador to Hungary in 2013, the police investigation into the illegal tapping of his phone came to a dead end.

Even forensic scientists couldn't provide an answer to the burning question: Who had secretly listened to and recorded phone conversations between Juška and a Vilnius-based colleague, edited the tapes, and published them on YouTube? It certainly wasn't "Zydrunas Gerintas," the supposed uploader of the videos. Zydrunas Gerintas might strike one as a Lithuanian name, but he doesn't appear to exist outside of the internet.

The Lithuanian police found out that the tapes had been uploaded by a mobile device that operated through an unidentified IP address. They sent multiple requests to YouTube for more information, but the company never replied.

Forensic research analysts combed through the files with special software. They identified a thud sound at the beginning of one call, which they interpreted as a "device being switched on or off." The technical investigation confirmed what Juška had been saying since the beginning of the scandal in the summer of 2013: the recordings had been edited together from several phone calls with his colleague. But on YouTube, they were presented as one call.

The videos were clearly aimed at an international audience, as they were accompanied by sensationalistic English-language headlines and subtitles, portraying Ambassador Juška as reckless and undiplomatic, and therefore unsuitable for a position of such responsibility. Simultaneously, two other phone calls were uploaded on YouTube. These were recordings of the conversations of another Lithuanian ambassador, based in Baku, Azerbaijan, with a colleague in Vilnius.

This wasn't the first time Juška had been targeted by *kompromat*, a Russian term meaning "compromising material." He had been able to escape nearly untarnished from previous scandals over the previous seven years because his employer, Lithuania's Foreign Ministry, publicly supported and protected him. But the manipulated videos, erroneously characterized as "leaks" by the sloppy Lithuanian media, were too much. After a month of public pressure and parliamentary hearings, Juška's superiors ordered him to leave his post in Budapest and return home.

Ambassador Juška wasn't targeted by mere coincidence: He was targeted because he had always fought for democracy.

ooooo

A human rights champion and visionary, Renatas Juška was a trained historian. He began his career with the Ministry of Foreign Affairs of the Republic of Lithuania in 1995, when he was only twenty-three years old. Five years earlier, Lithuania had regained its independence after a violent Soviet occupation. In the Ministry of Foreign Affairs, Juška mostly specialized in Belarus, Lithuania's southeastern neighbor, a former Soviet republic that was—and still is—heavily influenced by Russia.

As a young diplomat, Juška worked first with the Organization for Security and Co-operation in Europe, and then as an adviser for the Lithuanian ambassador in Minsk, the capital of Belarus.

That was when Juška experienced intimidation for the first time. In a stunt typical of Russian secret services, someone entered his home and left cigarette ashes in the kitchen sink. Neither Juška nor any of his family members smoked. "I found it unpleasant, but accepted it as part of my job," Juška told me.

While in Belarus, Juška saw firsthand how elections were rigged to ensure that the Kremlin's protégé president, the authoritarian Aleksandr Lukashenko, remained in power. At first, Lukashenko's election was ensured by corrupt election officials. Later, the country's constitution was changed to allow Lukashenko, in office since 1994, to continue as president indefinitely.

Lukashenko was ever present on television, offering himself as the only option to rule the country. He would also regularly mock Western Europe and the United States. As early as 1999, Belarusian opposition activists and journalists critical of his government started disappearing. Those who followed Belarus closely understood that Lukashenko was fashioning himself into a dictator, with Moscow's blessing.

Unlike today, back then it was uncommon for Western diplomats to openly support opposition politicians or civil rights activists in former Soviet republics. Instead, Western governments would veil their support by using nongovernmental organizations (NGOs) or foundations as proxy forces. But Lithuania, as a recently reborn Western democracy with the Soviet Union's oppression tactics a fresh memory, directly communicated with pro-democracy activists within the former Soviet states.

After Juška returned from Minsk to Vilnius in 2003, his job at the Ministry of Foreign Affairs was exactly that: to stay in contact with and provide support to the fragile Belarusian opposition groups, the NGOs, as well as marginalized politicians. He was behind the idea and implementation of the Lithuanian government's decision to provide refuge for the European Humanities University in Vilnius. The school had been the only independent university in Belarus before Lukashenko closed it down in 2004. Today, this unique educational institution, which focuses on humanities and social studies, operates in exile in Vilnius. Many young Belarusians study there and receive European-standard diplomas. "The Lithuanian Foreign Ministry was one of the first, if not the very first, to get in touch with the democratic opposition of Belarus directly," Juška shared. "This was a brave move, and we all understood that it might bring many complications. But it makes me proud that I was a part of those first steps."

While Belarus was pushing the Kremlin's messaging and interests in the international arena, in their relations with Russia, most Western European governments at the time were optimistic. They waited patiently for Vladimir Putin to lead Russia toward reform and democracy. The West sincerely wanted to build mutually beneficial ties with the regime of the former KGB and FSB agent, who had risen to the presidency in 2000.

In the early years of his reign, Putin signaled that he was willing to cooperate with the West. Officially, Russia was the European Union's strategic partner, and after the 9/11 attacks, it vowed to fight international jihadist terrorism with the Western coalition led by the United States. In those days, rare were the public concerns about covert Russian operations or fake news. If such views had been pushed, they would have quickly been dismissed as conspiracy theories.

But Juška and his colleagues within the Lithuanian Foreign Ministry saw that Belarus was being used as a testing ground for Russia's intelligence services and political manipulators. If Putin's aims of isolating Belarus from the Western information space and value base were successful, the Kremlin could use similar techniques within its own borders, and beyond.

ooooo

Less than twenty-five miles from the Lithuanian capital of Vilnius, the human rights of the Belarusian citizenry were being violated, and the state of the nation's democracy was deteriorating. Juška watched these developments with concern. In response, he connected pro-democratic activists in the region, including those from the Georgian Kmara, Ukrainian First Maidan, and Serbian *Otpor* ("Resistance," in English) youth movements. His team assisted Belarusians with donor relations, organizing meetings, and brainstorming campaigns promoting human rights and European values.

The next presidential election was to be held in 2006, and they would almost certainly be rigged. Lukashenko's regime had introduced an early voting system, through which fraud was easy to implement. With a strong mandate from the Lithuanian Foreign Ministry, Juška tried to strengthen the fragile opposition groups working to steer Belarus toward a modern, Western-style democracy. He exchanged ideas with the pro-democratic presidential candidates Aleksandr Milinkevich and Aleksandr Kozulin. International NGOs and Western donors were banned from working inside Belarus, so they regularly met in Lithuania for coordination. "We gave advice, created pro-European slogans and initiatives, thought of ways to print material and to distribute it to people throughout the country," Juška said. "We also worked hard to get the Belarusian people's voices heard in the international media."

Georgia and Ukraine had recently witnessed the so-called color revolutions: widespread peaceful protests, where citizens loudly vocalized their desire to integrate with the European Union and the West, and to distance themselves from the corrupt regimes in the Kremlin's pocket. "If the Belarusian opposition wanted to achieve results, they would have to go to the streets and protest. It was the only option to not let a fake election, organized in plain sight and in the heart of Europe, pass by unnoticed," Juška explained.

The election was held on March 19, 2006. The election committee, a puppet of the Lukashenko regime, claimed that 92.6 percent of Belarusians had voted. The committee also claimed that Lukashenko had won in a landslide, receiving an astonishing 82.6 percent in the first round of voting. The opposition candidate, Aleksandr Milinkevich, was said to have come in second, with 6 percent of the vote.[1]

The opposition immediately questioned the result. An independent research center said the accurate turnout for Lukashenko was 40 percent. This would mean a second round of voting was required.

Shocking the regime, activists staged mass protests. The evening of election day was freezing cold. But thousands of people, mainly students, gathered in Oktyabrskaya Square in Minsk, climbed atop the roofs of buses, built a small tent village, gave speeches, and chanted, "Motherland! Freedom! Luka out!" The square was full of protesters for five days and nights. Lukashenko's entourage sent KGB security police to film the students. When that didn't scare them away, they were attacked by aggressive provocateurs and an organized group of angry old ladies, *babushkas*, who accused the students of "working for America."

On the fifth day, special police forces drove trucks into the square. They isolated the reporters covering the unrest, dragged the protesters into the trucks, and drove them to prison. The protesters' banners, tents, grills, and kettles were demolished. In the meantime, President Lukashenko was rumored to be sitting in safety at a military base in Grodno, Western Belarus.

That was the end of what was known as the Jeans Revolution.

Those protests were the reason Renatas Juška became the target of Russian special information operations for the first time.

INITIAL ACCUSATIONS
In the aftermath of the protests, the Belarusian KGB held a press

conference. (The Belarusian KGB was the only national branch of the infamous organization which hadn't reorganized or rebranded itself after the collapse of the Soviet Union.) In a live interview on Belarusian television, the agency claimed that the United States as well as neighboring countries had organized "terrorist attacks" in Belarus, which Belarusian security services had supposedly warded off. The KGB then listed the people behind the alleged terrorist plot: Renatas Juška, his diplomatic colleague from Lithuania, and two US citizens working with pro-democracy donor organizations. Juška's designation as a "terrorist supporter" was circulated in the Lukashenko-controlled Belarusian media. Quoting directly from the Belarus KGB, the Lithuanian media reported that Juška and the other Lithuanian diplomat were "meddling with the Belarusian elections."

That was only the beginning.

Minsk then sent an alert to Interpol, the international police organization, requesting Juška be added to its list of internationally wanted criminals. Lithuanian security officials processed the politically motivated alert, found it groundless, and refused to arrest Juška. Despite this, Juška was advised not to travel to Russia or Belarus.

∞∞∞∞

One month after the accusations, in April 2006, the next fabricated scandal concerning Juška broke internationally. Russian television channel ORT, now known as Pervyi Kanal (Channel One), published recordings of several phone conversations said to be between Givi Targamadze, Chairman of the Committee on Defense and Security for the Georgian Parliament, another Lithuanian diplomat, and Juška. According to the infamous Russian political commentator Mikhail Leontyev, who aired the phone calls on his television program, and an article published on the ORT website, the recordings "proved" that Juška and the others had discussed assassinating the Belarusian opposition politician, Aleksandr Milinkevich. (Juška and the Lithuanian Foreign Ministry had, in fact, supported Milinkevich.) ORT claimed to have obtained the file from "sources close to the Georgian security services." "This file simply proves who organizes 'orange' revolutions and how," ORT lied. To add even more so-called evidence, ORT published the phone numbers from which the alleged intercepted calls had been made, as well as the dates of the calls.[2]

The faked transcripts can still be found on various Georgian, Russian and Belarusian news sites. They claim that Juška, his Lithuanian colleague, and Targamadze had discussed an agreement with Targamadze's brother-in-law to kill Milinkevich for either $10,000 or $20,000.[3] According to the fake transcripts, Targamadze, who at the time was serving in the administration of pro-Western Georgian president Mikheil Saakashvili, said that he would "swear in the name of my own child, that I dream every night only about [the killing]." On his television show, Leontyev mocked Targamadze as "sentimental" and called the participants on the phone call "opponents who were not just criminals but degenerates."[4]

In reality, Juška and the others had indeed talked on the phone. But they never said the things that Leontyev claimed they did. "They fabricated the stories, first in Russia and then across borders," Juška said to me. "I believe this was one of the first such projects by the Russians, at least vis-à-vis Georgia and Lithuania. And being a novelty, it worked quite well."

The fake story about the plot to kill Milinkevich spread to the local news in Lithuania and Georgia. Juška and the others who were falsely implicated had to defend themselves from the accusations and tell journalists that they were a provocation coming from Russia. "I'm sure that not a single normal person is capable of taking seriously the stupidity fabricated by Leontyev. In the next show, he will accuse me of assassinating Kennedy and attempting to dig a tunnel from London to Bombay. This does not deserve a more serious comment," Givi Targamadze told the media.[5]

At least one of Targamadze's political opponents exploited the scandal, demanding that Targamadze "prove his innocence." In the Lithuanian press, the case was in the headlines for several weeks, sparking questions about the security of government officials' phone communications. "Even though we told the media that it's all falsified and it's a provocation from Russia, many didn't believe us. They asked, why would the Russians do that, and thought there must be something behind it," Juška shared. It was becoming clear that fake news originating in Russia, including illegally recorded and doctored private phone conversations, were being used to sow distrust among carefully targeted groups—in this case, Georgian and Lithuanian decision makers and local media—as well as the general public.

Georgian government officials told the press they suspected that Russian security services had wiretapped their calls using two Russian military bases that were located in Georgian territory. Thus, it was reasonable to assume that the manipulation of the tapes was also conducted by Russian agencies, who then handed them over to the Russian media. Lithuania had spent decades under Soviet occupation, and top-level officials in the government were fully aware of Russia's interference attempts.

Among Juška's peers, his commitment and expertise in promoting democracy were duly respected. He was seen as continuing the tradition of Lithuanian resistance. As a result, the scandalous stories didn't initially cause friction or mistrust between him and his superiors. At the time, Juška felt fully protected by the state, even though the risks of his work were obvious. "Real human beings, opposition figures and civil activists suffer from oppression, persecution, or jail and need concrete support," he told me. "And real people, diplomats or NGO activists, ordinary 'soldiers' or 'freedom fighters' who are in charge of the support projects, are perfectly aware of their risk of being blackened or smeared. All these soldiers can hope for is that their 'generals' protect them when the shit hits the fan. So, I was that soldier."

Juška's colleagues sometimes jokingly called him a revolutionary. But as time passed and one scandal followed another, some started to question him. Behind his back people asked whether he was doing something a diplomat shouldn't be doing, or going beyond his duties. "I can only laugh at that," Juška told me. "Today the European Union, as well as my own country, is organizing public meetings to openly support the Belarusian opposition leaders. And rightly so."

Unfortunately, Juška's stalkers weren't finished with him.

CYBER PURGES

Lithuania had likely vexed Russian political manipulators for some time—perhaps since it declared its independence from the USSR in March 1990, becoming the first former Soviet republic to do so. Vladimir Putin later characterized the collapse of the Soviet Union as the greatest geopolitical catastrophe of the twentieth century.[6]

After decades of economic and societal regression, Lithuanians had chosen to tie their future to the West. The country of over three million voted to join both the European Union and NATO in the spring of 2004. During the same time period, as Putin's Russia started to implement aggressive policies against its neighbors, Lithuanian diplomats repeatedly demanded that their Russian counterparts respect Western democratic processes and human rights and that they observe the Partnership and Cooperation Agreement between the European Union and

Russia, as well as other international agreements. Lithuania was probably the country that was most vocal in raising hard questions about Russia in the international community. And Russia didn't appreciate that, regarding Lithuanian diplomats as troublemakers who were capable of influencing opinion in the EU and NATO.

And so the Kremlin attacked.

As often happens with well-planned Russian-origin online attacks, the hostile takeover of the public debate seemed to emerge organically, unattached to the Kremlin. The connections of cyber operations to the Kremlin are often well-hidden. Especially well-hidden are their connections to the FSB and other Russian security services. If the perpetrator is unseen, the Kremlin can hide behind plausible deniability.

As early as 1971, in his book *Information War and the Free Person*, Finnish academic and member of parliament Kullervo Rainio described a central technique of information warfare: the manipulation of the meaning of concepts, which leads to the distortion of people's thought processes.[7] Through methods of information warfare, the word *democracy*, for example, can be redefined to mean "socialist system."

The corruption of the meaning of the word *statesman* in Lithuanian was such an operation. The *Merriam-Webster Collegiate Dictionary* defines a *statesman* as "a wise, skillful, and respected political leader." But on the Lithuanian internet, *statesman*, or *valstybininkas*, was redefined to mean the opposite: a member of a sinister, clandestine, perverted, and corrupt elite conspiracy.

The scandal surrounding "statesman" began in 2005, as lists started mushrooming throughout the Lithuanian online sphere that included the names and titles of high-ranking Lithuanian officials and politicians, current and former leaders of security and military services, and national media journalists. These "statesmen" were portrayed as suspicious characters through vulgar descriptions and repeated baseless accusations of corruption. According to the online trolls, most of the Lithuanian statesmen were gay. In a conservative society, such as Lithuania, an effective method of blackballing someone is to call that person a homosexual, engaged in secret sexual activities.

Over time, the trolls' stories about "blue statesmen" ("blue" means gay in Lithuanian) evolved. Secret society members were said to have suddenly become rich. Their conspiratorial fraternity was said to be pulling the strings of everything that went on in the country's politics. This conspiracy theory, which was later echoed by parts of the traditional media, accused the statesmen of controlling the Lithuanian Foreign Ministry, too. Online trolls claimed that Juška served the statesmen. Some were convinced by the online slander that this deep state jeopardized the country's national security—that, in fact, Lithuania needed to be protected from such a "dangerous" group.

Many of the maligned statesmen had actually pushed for reforms since the beginning of Lithuania's restored independence. They had long voiced critical views about the actions of Putin and Lukashenko, as well as presenting pro-Western ideas. But in online forums and comment sections of the traditional media, they were said to merely "pretend to fight against Russia." *In reality*, the trolls wrote, these statesmen were nothing more than *Russian agents* who served the Kremlin's interests.

∞∞∞∞

The defamation and name calling wasn't restricted to the internet.

In August 2006, a respected security officer posted at the Lithuanian consulate in Grodno, Belarus, was found dead under suspicious circumstances while on a work trip. The first reports were conflicting. Some sources said he might have been stabbed or poisoned by Russians or Belarusians. Others claimed he fell— or was pushed—from the window of his ninth-floor hotel room.

The deceased officer was quickly defamed, on and offline.[8] One conspiracy theory claimed that the officer was killed because he had received too much confidential information about the alleged wrongdoings of the statesmen, and had conducted his own investigations into the alleged theft in Vilnius of millions of American dollars belonging to the Belarusian opposition.

The problem with this theory was that the Belarusian opposition never had millions of dollars. But according to the fake news, "the statesmen were able to steal $40 million either by themselves or in cooperation with the Belarusian opposition and the case had to be investigated." The story of the "stolen millions" was taken up by Lukashenko's propaganda arm in Belarus, as it helped the regime's narrative by smearing the opposition as "bought by Americans."

In Finland, Russian media expert Jukka Mallinen exposed how the FSB was employing paid online trolls, or "opinion torpedoes" as early as 2006. According to Mallinen's Russian contacts, FSB provincial school students earned money by targeting people online.[9] "A simple Google search revealed that the same rancid and propagandistic filth comments against opposition politicians were posted on different platforms as mass production," Mallinen wrote.

At the time, however, few in Lithuania spoke publicly about the possibility of Russian information warfare or smear campaigns. Solid evidence of Russian participation in hostile internet operations wasn't systematically gathered anywhere in the world until Robert S. Mueller's special counsel investigation in the United States in 2017. Thus, there was no proof that the corruption of the Lithuanian concept of *statesman* or the accusations against the dead officer were connected to the Kremlin's international disinformation apparatus. But these operations nevertheless served the Kremlin's goals: to create distrust and division in Lithuania, undermining the people's confidence in their Western-minded political leadership.

Thus, the Lithuanian public debate was partly fueled by hostile web brigades as the country entered the parliamentary elections of 2008 and presidential elections the following year. One well-informed former Lithuanian official recalls the massive amount of online lies: "Similar fake articles with troll comments that we nowadays see on Facebook and Twitter were orchestrated all around Lithuanian portals during the mid-2000s." Many Lithuanian officials speculated that the messages originated from Latvian Street—where the Russian Consulate in Vilnius is located.

THE AFGHANISTAN PARK SCANDAL

In the spring of 2009, Renatas Juška was appointed ambassador to Hungary. At that time, he was also in charge of the Foreign Ministry's Department of Development Cooperation and Democracy Promotion, which he had created in late 2006. "I was particularly proud of the department's title: Democracy Promotion," Juška shared with me. "Some still doubted whether supporting democratic processes in other countries was going too far, or whether the ministry was 'walking on thin ice.' But I was convinced we had to continue."

As soon as the announcement of Juška's ambassadorial post in Budapest went public, a new scandal, about oak trees being planted in Afghanistan, was launched against him. The story first aired on Lithuanian television and hinted that Juška might be responsible for misusing taxpayers' money. On the broadcast, a journalist interviewed an expert in forestry, who, in response to a question, said, "No, I don't think oak trees will survive in Afghanistan. It's very wrong, trying to plant them in Afghanistan."

The story condemned a project that didn't exist, as the Ministry of Foreign Affairs never intended to plant oak trees in Afghanistan in the first place. "It was unbelievable to see that item on the news," Juška remembered.

The department Juška headed was indeed in charge of helping to rehabilitate central Afghanistan's Ghor Province. The project included building a park and planting trees—not oaks—that could thrive in the country's climate. In Afghanistan, parks symbolize peace, and Lithuania wanted to provide a peaceful, quiet place for people in Afghanistan to spend their free time. During the Soviet invasion of the country, wood had been burned by military operations and later used by the locals as fuel, which resulted in many trees being cut down. In the international community, building parks in war-ravaged Afghanistan was a common gesture of goodwill.

Oak was chosen to add an extra layer of hysteria to the scandal. The national tree of Lithuania, Oak is a symbol of strength and statehood. The most famous Lithuanian oak, Stelmužė, estimated to be 1,500 years old, has a saying associated with it: a strong man is said to be as strong as Stelmužė oak.

Some journalists connected the oak allegations to the statesmen conspiracies and the Belarusian opposition's supposed stolen millions and demanded that Juška be held accountable. A handful of members of parliament asked for an inspection of his department's projects. Recognizing that the public debate had been derailed by fake news, Juška requested a thorough investigation into the spending of the whole department. "Once allegations against you are public, the only proper way out is a full investigation," he explained to me. "That provides the answer to every question. How else do you fight this?"

Parliament conducted its own research, while the Lithuanian state office in charge of spending investigated separately. Questions were asked, and documents and transactions examined over almost four months. The day-to-day work of the department was nearly paralyzed. Some employees grew anxious over the intense public criticism and became scared about the possible outcome.

A handful of journalists and politicians used the scandal in a calculated attempt to dig up and reveal the names of Belarusian opposition organizations and figures supported by the Ministry of Foreign Affairs. Lukashenko's regime had criminalized and banned citizens from receiving foreign funds; disclosing names could have resulted in Belarusian activists being sent to jail. "I was pressured by individual MPs and ministry officials to open all the files," said Juška. "They argued that it was public money, and everyone is supposed to have access to the projects." Juška managed to keep the names from going public. Only a limited number of MPs and state finance regulators were provided access to the information, after declaring that the data would remain confidential.

A delegation of MPs and investigators, accompanied by a group of journalists, also traveled to Chaghcharan, the capital of Ghor. There they found the Lithuanian-financed park under construction, as it was supposed to be. But there were no oak trees. Instead, what was being planted were Afghan trees, suitable for the country's climate. "The same politicians who had attacked me baselessly participated in the public ceremony planting the trees," recalled Juška. "Ultimately, they made a personal PR campaign out of the scandal, using the same Afghan trees for which they wanted to fire me. After months of stress, that day was finally some good fun for me." As well as the absence of oaks in the park in Chaghcharan, it was also established that there was no misuse of taxpayer money or corruption within Juška's department. The scandal stalled Juška's appointment as ambassador to Hungary for several months. But finally, the investigations were concluded, and Juška was cleared.

In June 2009, Juška stood before President Valdas Adamkus to receive his ambassador's credentials. During the ceremony, the president thanked Juška for his promotion of democracy in Belarus and Georgia, and the continuing projects in Afghanistan.[10]

"I looked into your story. You're so young and went through so much," Adamkus said.

"That made me very proud," shared Juška. "Especially when that was said in front of my family and my parents, who were present at the ceremony."

Juška was thirty-seven, becoming the youngest Lithuanian ambassador up until that time.

THE LAST STRAW

As ambassador, Juška took the same precautions to secure his work as he had throughout his career. He frequently changed his computer passwords, had multiple email accounts, and never used Facebook, Messenger, or Twitter. He also didn't engage in activities which could have resulted in the dissemination of damaging videos.

In Hungary, Juška also kept in regular contact with democracy activists from Serbia, Ukraine, Georgia, and Russia, several of whom were under surveillance in their home countries. Many Russian activists wanted advice on how to organize peaceful street protests, so they approached Juška, who met with them a few times.

After the sham presidential elections in Russia in 2011, massive protests were organized around the country opposing Putin. In the aftermath of the protests, Russian security services went after those whom they claimed were responsible "for the unrest sowed by the West." As a result, Juška's name appeared in Russian-fabricated stories about alleged protester training camps in Lithuania, which had never existed.

∞∞∞

Juška couldn't have imagined that at the same time he was reading fake news about his alleged participation in organizing protests in

Moscow, someone had begun secretly recording his phone calls. On July 8, 2013, an unknown operative behind the fake name Zydrunas Gerintas uploaded doctored versions of Juška's phone calls to YouTube. "Gerintas" had never published any videos before, and never did again. The timing was carefully chosen, as Lithuania had started its half-year turn chairing the European Union that month.

The two twelve-minute videos are titled, "This Is How Lithuania Really Treats Azerbaijan. Part 1" and "This Is How Lithuania Really Treats Azerbaijan. Part 2." In the videos, a still photo of Juška is shown, beside which is appended an anonymous male figure. The only moving visual elements are the English-language subtitles. The audio is comprised of intercepted private telephone conversations between Juška and a colleague working in the Lithuanian Foreign Ministry in Vilnius. Although parts of their conversations are manipulated, authentic discussions are presented as well. Juška and his colleague speak in Lithuanian about a variety of political developments concerning Azerbaijan, Armenia, Lithuania, and Hungary. Putin and Russia are also mentioned. While the conversations are portrayed as one uninterrupted phone discussion, in reality, they are a collage of multiple, completely unrelated phone calls which have been cut and pasted together. Lithuanian speakers can tell that the English "subtitles" include many mistakes.

The manipulated conversations were published in order to stir outrage, particularly in Lithuania, Azerbaijan, and Armenia. For the Lithuanian public, the most interesting part was Juška's comments about the then Lithuanian prime minister. In the videos, Juška is told by his colleague that he is preparing for a visit by the Lithuanian prime minister to St. Petersburg, where he will be meeting his Russian counterpart, Dmitry Medvedev. Juška responds by jokingly raising the possibility of putting a pack of chewing gum in the pocket of the Lithuanian prime minister before the meeting. He was referring to an earlier incident where Lithuania's president had met President Putin in Helsinki for the first high level government meeting between the two countries in many years. During the meeting, Putin had been constantly chewing gum. "It was impolite, to say the least," said Juška. "So, on the phone I made a joke: 'Why don't you put chewing gum in the pocket of our premier, so he too looks cool.' In the original call, I had referred to the Putin gum-chewing episode right after that sentence, but that had been cut from the YouTube version." In Lithuanian slang, "chewing gum" means being stupid or dumb, unserious. Because the context was removed, the Lithuanian prime minister interpreted Juška's comment as criticism and disrespect, which it wasn't meant to be.

In the edited video, Juška also refers to Armenia's and Azerbaijan's long-disputed territory, Nagorno-Karabakh by its original, Armenian name, Artsakh. In early 2017, the Armenians officially adopted the name. On the phone call, Juška tells his colleague that he passively supports Armenia in the dispute "because the borders were drawn by Stalin, so why should we defend Stalin's decisions."

ooooo

The Azeris were the first to discover the manipulated videos, with Azeri journalists frantically reporting about "diplomatic leaks" and calling Vilnius for comment.

Simultaneously, another made-up person uploaded a second set of similarly incepted phone calls between the Lithuanian Ambassador to Azerbaijan and a colleague in Vilnius to YouTube. The two-part set was headlined "This is how Lithuania Really Treats Turkmenistan."

The well-planned YouTube operations hit their target. Many media outlets republished the illegally obtained and manipulated discussions and quoted them as factual "leaks," which they claimed revealed "total incompetence and stupidity," on the part of the diplomats, who had "gossiped irresponsibly" over the phone. However, no journalist inspected the videos before writing about them. The videos were also aired on television talk shows.

The main narrative condemned Ambassador Juška and his colleague in Azerbaijan, accusing them of engaging in improper behavior. Hardly anyone asked how it was possible that the diplomats' supposedly secure phone conversations had been hacked.

While many journalists and readers of the scandalous stories believed that the diplomats should be held accountable for their actions, some in the media defended them. One of the supportive views came from Nerijus Maliukevicius, a Lithuanian political scientist from Vilnius University, who stated that "[t]he information leaked of the alleged discussions of the Lithuanian diplomats might be useful for those who want to portray Lithuanian diplomacy in a bad light That's why I see the fingerprints of the Russian security services in the story."[11] Despite this, the general consensus was overwhelming: the diplomats should be removed from their positions.

The Russian media also published several slanderous articles about the diplomats. One such operation appeared on August 5, six days after the scandal broke in Lithuania, when three shady Russian-language websites published an identical article about the case. The three sites—two small so-called news sources[12] and a fake LiveJournal blogger,[13] who had previously published insider information about Russian security services—seemed to have received a coordinated press release that attacked Juška and the other diplomat for being unprofessional.

The Russian stories were served up as the "scandal around the Eastern Partnership." This narrative revealed one of the goals of the YouTube operation: to undermine Lithuania's attempts to boost EU policy vis-à-vis the Eastern Partnership countries during its term as chair of the European Union. All six partner countries—Armenia, Azerbaijan, Belarus, Georgia, Moldova, and Ukraine—were heavily under the Kremlin's influence, which would have loved to see them sever ties with the EU.

Maliukevicius, the political scientist, followed the case closely. He noted that the timing of the operation was well planned. Lithuania was slated to chair the Eastern Partnership Summit, which is seen as one of the most important duties of the chair of the European Union. "The idea was to put Lithuanian diplomats in a bad light right before the summit," Maliukevicius said.

The "diplomat scandal" also broke in Hungary,[14] where Juška was posted as ambassador. Some papers predicted his "sacking" and referred to him and the other diplomat as "offenders."[15]

The Lithuanian Foreign Ministry, Juška's employer, was also dragged into the epicenter of the scandal. In 2013, the general political attitude toward the Kremlin was much more tolerant in Vilnius than it would be a year later, when Russia started its military operations in Ukraine. Lithuania wasn't the only country in the European Union that had "forgotten" Russia's military aggression toward Georgia in 2008. Officially, Vilnius wanted to normalize its relationship with Moscow.

As journalists frantically called for comment, the Lithuanian prime minister started issuing statements without consulting the diplomats to get their side of the story.[16] YouTube trolls and an army of gullible local media had evidently convinced him that his own diplomats were laughing at him. "Our then prime minister thought my bubble gum joke meant that we weren't taking him seriously," said Juška. "He got offended. This is how the manipulation works."

Lithuania's then president also commented on the videos, calling it a provocation. But she also said that the diplomats' conversations were unprofessional.[17]

Even though it was clear that Russia was behind the operation, all three of Lithuania's top leaders—the president, prime minister, and the foreign minister—had difficulty admitting it publicly. Much easier than blaming Russia was to accuse their own diplomats of poor behavior.

ooooo

After three weeks of continuing public pressure, Lithuania's foreign minister declared that he had lost confidence in the diplomats.[18] As a result, it was proposed to the Foreign Affairs Committee of the Lithuanian parliament that the diplomats be called home. However, after hearing out Juška and the other ambassador, the majority of the committee members supported Juška and voted not to recall him. Nevertheless, the ambassador to Azerbaijan decided to resign his post.[19] Two days later, on August 28, 2013, the foreign minister told the government that he had decided to propose that the president recall Juška—despite the committee's recommendation.

Juška said he was happy that he was at least able to finalize his last important project in Budapest—a monument built on the grounds of Buda Castle to honor the Lithuanian and Polish king Jagiello and the Polish queen and Hungarian princess Hedwig, who lived in the fourteenth and fifteenth centuries, respectively.[20] The monument was officially inaugurated by the foreign ministers of Hungary, Poland, and Lithuania in October 2013.

ooooo

After his removal as ambassador to Hungary, Juška moved back to Vilnius and continued to work at the Ministry of Foreign Affairs. He gave interviews in which he defended his actions and criticized the government for its hasty decisions. In response, his employer issued him an official warning.

But Juška refused to let it be.

No one had requested a thorough investigation into who had planned and implemented the illegal operation. The question of how it was possible to intercept phone calls between diplomats in two NATO countries, Lithuania and Hungary, was likewise left unanswered. "I decided to fight and find out the truth," Juška said. "Probably it's because of my rebellious and stubborn character. But mainly because I felt disappointed about the government's reaction to the scandal. It was me, not the state, who filed the criminal report with the police. The state didn't do that, even though it was the state and its diplomatic corps that were hit."

Juška contacted YouTube several times, asking the company to remove the illegally obtained and published videos. YouTube never responded to his requests. The videos are still there today, and have since been republished on another channel. Revealingly, after the ambassador to Azerbaijan resigned, the smear videos about him on YouTube were removed the next day.

Six months after Juška's "scandalous and undiplomatic" comments about chewing gum, Russia started its war in Ukraine. Following that, criticism of Russia's policies became acceptable within the Lithuanian leadership. The Lithuanian president went as far as calling Russia a "terrorist state" and used the nickname "Putler" to refer to Putin.

∞∞∞

In 2014, the Lithuanian secret service went public with the results of its investigation into the hacked phone calls. In the Lithuanian State Security Department's *Annual Threat Assessment 2013*, the entity in charge of the YouTube operation against the diplomats was finally identified as Russian intelligence services:

The leakage of Lithuanian diplomats' telephone conversations in July 2013 was the operation of Russian intelligence services aimed to discredit the Lithuanian presidency of the Council and the Eastern Partnership program, as well as to create new tensions in Lithuanian domestic politics. It should be noted that a part of international calls from Lithuania to Western countries and the rest of the world is channeled via networks of Russian telecommunication operators. Russian intelligence services have every means to control the international calls from and to Lithuania that are transmitted through Russian telecommunication networks.[21]

It appeared that the phone calls between Hungary and Lithuania had been rerouted through the Russian Federation. According to an insider source, sending Lithuanian calls through Russia was "cheap." This revelation sent shock waves through Lithuania.

In the summer of 2014, Juška resigned from the Foreign Ministry and gave his last major interview concerning the incident, in which he spoke critically about the state of Lithuanian diplomacy. He then moved to Brussels, where he spent the next five years working as an adviser to a Lithuanian member of the European Parliament. "Brussels was my voluntary banishment," he told me. "Not an easy one, as I am very homesick and would prefer to have my family with me."

ooooo

The YouTube operations against Ambassador Juška and his colleague were the first known cases of Russian security services combining intercepted phone calls with online video. However, it wasn't the last. In early 2014, the phone calls of Victoria Nuland, then US assistant Secretary of State for European and Eurasian Affairs, were intercepted and published on YouTube. On the calls, she was reported to say, "Fuck the EU." The incident created a stir in the media, and many fake news sites still refer to it today. But that hacking didn't lead to Nuland losing her job. As a matter of fact, she was appointed by President Biden as Under Secretary for Political Affairs in 2021.

"IT'S A HOSTAGE SITUATION"

The experiences of Renatas Juška have taught us a lot, says Nerijus Maliukevicius. "This was a classic active measure," he shares. "Russia stole confidential information, conducted psychological operations, and threw the material out to the public. The messages were spread to the media and caused discussions about the diplomats' 'inability to protect their communications.'"

Maliukevicius works in Vilnius University's Institute of International Relations and Political Science, specializing in societal resilience, the ability to defend against disinformation. "It's a hostage situation," he says. "The blackmailer shouldn't be paid the money that it tries to extort." In order to stay vigilant against these types of operations, Maliukevicius says that states must do everything they can to protect the targets of active measures. The complex, often privacy-breaching cases must be handled with discretion. Careful counterintelligence is also needed.

ooooo

Renatas Juška wished that the YouTube scandal had never happened. But because it did occur, he wanted to share his experience in order to help others in the future. "This is the way to never even come close to being mentioned by those propagandists as a 'failed state,'" he said of his homeland. "I humbly hope that my story helps others to make the right decisions." Juška told that me he was proud that since the Russian aggression against Ukraine, Lithuania has become one of the leaders in the EU and NATO on educating others against cyber and propaganda warfare launched against the West.

Juška also wanted to talk about the issue because dictators are quick to learn from each other. "It is my view that all regimes, and in particular the ones trying to ruin Europe by selling their corrupt partnerships, deserve the same tough treatment, be it Putin in Russia, Lukashenko in Belarus, or anybody else."

∞∞∞

Renatas Juška passed away on September 3, 2019.

Two months later, the newspaper *Lietyvos Rytas* published an article about Juška and the phone-tapping scandal. In the article, several former colleagues paid their respect and described him as a true example of what a Lithuanian diplomat should be. Žygimantas Pavilionis, a former Lithuanian ambassador to the United States and Mexico, called Juška "one of the bravest, most creative, most strategic diplomats," adding that, "Renat did everything he could to make Belarus, Russia, Sakartwell and our other eastern neighbors free and democratic, for which he was blacklisted by Russia and Belarus."[22]

Juška's close friend Vytis Jurkonis, a lecturer at Vilnius University, eulogized him for this book, saying that

> Ambassador Juška was a bit unconventional, but I believe that a true European diplomat needs to take the initiative and be creative as well as being principled about freedom, human rights and democracy, as this is the essence of what Europe is. Renatas Juška was informally called Mr. Belarus because of his steady commitment to these principles. Despite several diplomatic postings, Belarus remained his

mission and passion and he was the institutional memory regarding the tricks and manipulations of the authoritarian regime in the country. Ambassador Juška also worked with democrats in other countries in the region, for example Georgia, Moldova and Ukraine, supporting them in distancing themselves from the negative pressures of the Kremlin as much as possible. And yet he also believed that a democratic Russia was possible, and encouraged the Russian freedom fighters to never give up.

3.

Psyops

IN SEPTEMBER 2014, A FEW DAYS after I published my first article about the influence of the Kremlin's trolls, a second front was launched against me on social media.

Again, Johan Bäckman's Finnish network of pro-Russian collaborators were behind the attacks. They produced an outwardly professional-looking complaint, addressed to the Finnish parliamentary ombudsman, and shared it on Facebook.[1] According to the complaint, both me and my employer, Yleisradio, had violated Finnish law and caused "persecution and discrimination targeted at real citizens" because of my article. The complaint demanded that the ombudsman investigate the legality of both my activities and those of Yleisradio.

In Finland, the parliamentary ombudsman monitors the legality of the actions of government officials. Neither the complainant nor those sharing the "legitimate" complaint on social media were interested in the fact that the ombudsman's responsibilities do not include inspecting the content of journalistic articles, or their legality. Nevertheless, over 100 real people and fake profiles shared the complaint on Facebook, labeling both me and Yle as criminals. Over ten official complaints copy-pasted from Facebook were sent to the ombudsman's office by either real or fake personas supposdely enraged by the alleged crimes.

The ombudsman investigated the complaints and concluded that Yleisradio hadn't violated any laws. The campaign was solely designed to harass me and undermine my credibility, and further spin the fictitious story that I was investigating real people instead of fake trolls.

Simultaneously, a Finnish-language pro-Kremlin conspiracy site named Verkkomedia (Web Media) published a piece claiming that Yleisradio's "troll hunt" had caused a flood of complaints to the ombudsman. The aim of the story was to raise additional suspicion over both my personal integrity and that of my employer. I watched powerlessly as a made-up story about how I had labeled real people as paid trolls took on a life of its own, despite the fact that in my article I hadn't labeled anyone; to the contrary, I had carefully defined Russian social media trolls as anonymous or fake profiles. Moreover, I had specifically asked my audience not to call out any individual fake profiles.

The story of the editor in chief of Verkkomedia is a telltale example of how the Kremlin's propaganda architects recruit foreigners to serve in their global information war. A layer of credibility is added to deception operations when the visible leaders are seemingly harmless and well-reputed foreigners, instead of Russian intelligence officers.

Verkkomedia was run by a respected Finnish citizen, a former theater director named Janus Putkonen. According to several of his former acquaintances, Putkonen had always been interested in Russia. In a 2014 interview with a local Finnish newspaper, Putkonen openly disclosed that he conducted information operations on behalf of the Kremlin.[2] He also said that he had burned his Finnish military pass, the identification document used for conscripts in the Finnish Defense Forces. Putkonen also administered a network of Finnish Facebook sites and groups, focusing on spreading false information, memes, and Russian propaganda.

Putkonen later scored an international job in the field of information warfare when he was assigned as director of DONi News,[3] an outlet funded by Russia's shadow government in Eastern Ukraine[4] and charged with camouflaging the Kremlin's messaging so that it appears to be real news.[5] On top of spreading propaganda, Putkonen's office built an information blockade around the war region in Eastern Ukraine. Leaked documents later revealed that DONi News monitored and outed Western journalists trying to report developments in Eastern Ukraine.[6] Fact-based and critical journalists were labeled as "Russophobes," and their entry to the region was prevented.[7]

Putkonen has personally conducted interrogations and harassed Western journalists trying to travel to Ukraine's Donbas region to cover the war.[8] In Eastern Ukraine, he was photographed with another Finn, who is wearing a military uniform with Russia's military intelligence insignia, a black bat on a yellow circle.

Putkonen also cooperates with Johan Bäckman, who frequently visits East Ukraine,[9] representing Russia.[10] The two men have produced videos for YouTube, brainwashing their audiences into believing that the war in Ukraine was the fault of the United States and the West. In one video, posted on YouTube by Bäckman, Putkonen smiles happily as he receives a loaded handgun that came from the late Donetsk separatist leader Alexander Zakharchenko, who partook in the armed occupation of Donetsk city council offices in 2014 and was killed in a bomb explosion in 2018.[11]

As Putkonen's Russian-funded career evolved internationally, he began smearing me on DONi News and on Facebook. According to him, my troll investigations had broken up marriages and caused people to lose their jobs. These accusations might have been humorous if they had not come from a person who was engaged in psychological operations and hung out with Russian military intelligence.

MENTAL VIOLENCE

After I published my article in September 2014, someone established a Facebook group called Russian Troll Army.[12] The public goal of the group was to protest against "Yle's attempt to label citizens as trolls." I was added to the group without my permission and was actively tagged in aggressive discussions insulting me.

The group's internal dynamics were fascinating and revealing. The administrators set the group's discussion agenda and provided examples of accepted discourse. All critics and dissidents were blocked or bullied. The group was loaded with fake news from the Kremlin and smears targeting me, other reporters, and Russia analysts.

The most active spinners in the group were fake profiles and professionals including Bäckman and Putkonen and their pro-Kremlin network. Die-hard communists, far-right activists, Putin worshippers, and people with extreme anti-establishment tendencies also found a home in the group. Many real citizens who happened to join the group or were added by a friend followed the administrators' lead, and thus became influenced. Russian Troll Army and an international network of similar Facebook groups are set up for one purpose only: to normalize Russian propaganda and the persecution of anyone who criticizes or uncovers information about the Kremlin.

While monitoring the activities of Russian Troll Army and other similar communities, I came to understand that one especially vulnerable target group that is easily manipulated by the Kremlin's disinformation are those individuals who spend a lot of time on social media. Because of the way social media algorithms work, membership in one hate community offers endless possibilities for drifting into a network of similar groups. Radicalization through Facebook is practically one click away.

On Russian Troll Army, I was labeled a liar and a Russophobe, and accused of "spreading hatred against Russians." There were comments fantasizing about my death, hoping for a nuclear attack on my newsroom, and questioning my mental health. There was also an impressive amount of deliberately nasty writings focused on my gender, looks, and private life. The group administrators justified their mental violence against me by claiming that they were "protecting freedom of speech." According to them, *I* was the one who had destroyed it. Not once did anyone remind the members of the group that according to legislation in Finland and the majority of Western countries, much of their threatening content was potentially criminal. However, the more outrageous the accusations the Facebook trolls posted about me, the more likes and comments the post received.

Over time, I watched the group evolve. My public appearances and reports were systematically stalked and linked to the group for ridicule and spin. One of the goals of Russian security services is to marginalize the psy-op target not just in public debate but also within the person's professional community. Thus, the troll group members united in an effort to find the email addresses of 260 of my colleagues and supervisors. The people on the list were then sent an email claiming that I wanted "to destroy freedom of speech." The aim was to create friction between me and my employer and colleagues by presenting me as a troublemaker.

I never actually participated in the group's discussions. Once I watched as four mocking threads were opened during a one-hour radio interview I was giving. In the threads, fake profiles and actual people tried to tear apart my every word. I was shocked at the unmitigated viciousness. I realized that if I kept reading the hateful content, I myself might start to believe in the systematically demonized image they built about me. In the worst case I might become afraid of giving public interviews and presentations— exactly what the group was aiming for.

I blocked the most hostile people tagging me and reported

the group to Facebook. The social media giant's community standards forbid fake profiles, bullying, and hateful content. Facebook responded that the group, which shared fantasies of me being poisoned, didn't violate their community standards.

∞∞∞

Only one week after publishing my troll article, I was exhausted. I met my supervisors and the head of security of Yle. As we reviewed the events following my story's publication, Yle's security director inquired whether I really wanted to continue investigating Russian trolls. When I said "yes," he sighed. In that case, he said he would contact the police.

As police officials familiarized themselves with the campaign against me, they warned that if I was planning a trip to Russia in the near future, my communications might be tracked.

I was, in fact, planning a trip there, which I didn't mention. I was about to go investigate the troll factory in St. Petersburg.

4.

The Volunteer

ROMAN BURKO, A UKRAINIAN JOURNALIST LIVING in Crimea, received an urgent call on March 2, 2014. On the phone, local journalists asked him to grab his camera and head over to the base of the 191st Training Detachment of the Ukrainian navy.

Three days earlier, fifty miles to the northeast in Simferopol, the capital of the Crimean Peninsula, Russian soldiers in unmarked uniforms had started seizing administrative buildings. Many in Ukraine, and the world, were confused. No one knew what was happening or who was to blame. And now, soldiers without insignia had entered the coastal city of Sevastopol and infiltrated the navy base.

Burko hurried to the base and began filming. Thirty men in green uniforms, their faces hidden by black balaclavas, were shouting orders at Ukrainian officers. They shot their automatic rifles in the air for emphasis.

As a youth, Burko had served in the Ukrainian army. He was thus able to identify the intruders as Russian special forces.

When Burko pulled out his camera, one of the green-clad men pointed his machine gun at him. "If you don't put away the camera, I am going to kill you!" the man said.

Burko continued filming, and the masked men rushed toward him. "I ran away and exited the area. I managed to flee because I wasn't wearing a heavy bulletproof vest, unlike them," he recalls.

When he got home safely, Burko posted his video on YouTube. In less than twenty-four hours, the video had been viewed over one million times. This made Burko realize that it was possible to fight back against Russian aggression by bringing information into the daylight. "In a way, I'm grateful to the Russian soldier who pointed his gun at me: he enraged me, and I realized I had to do something about it," Burko says.

∞∞∞∞

Along with several friends, Burko continued collecting and publishing information about Russia's military activities in Crimea. He watched as Russian military personnel seized strategic facilities and took over communications channels around the peaceful peninsula by the Black Sea. Back then, no one guessed how quickly after the infiltration of the first soldiers Russia would escalate its hybrid warfare into a manipulated referendum and then the annexation of Crimea.

In the beginning, Burko and his associates were unaware of the severity of the situation, so they didn't bother hiding their IP or home addresses. But then a friend of Burko intercepted the Zello Wi-Fi-activated walkie-talkie conversations of Russian soldiers, who were pretending to be locals, deceitfully calling themselves "Crimean self-defense forces." The soldiers' conversations revealed that they knew where Burko and his friends lived, and were threatening to come and kill them.

Burko and his compatriots immediately left Crimea. Burko tucked several T-shirts into a backpack and headed to Kyiv, the Ukrainian capital, 430 miles away. All of a sudden, he was a refugee.

Before resettling in the capital, Burko stayed at a friend's place, where he launched his project: an international network of volunteers to investigate and expose Russia's illegal military operations and influence attempts in Ukraine, Syria, Georgia, and other countries. "One night we were sitting on the roof, watching the stars. We decided to build a resource where we could publish information about Russia's crimes and identify Russian war criminals," Burko shares.

Less than a month after masked Russian military bands had threatened to kill him, and two weeks after the United States, the European Union, and Canada imposed travel bans and asset freezes against the Russians behind the invasion of Ukraine, Burko launched InformNapalm[1] with the help of an IT expert from Crimea named Volodymyr Kolesnykov.

The volunteers behind the site spend their time waging information warfare against the Russian Federation. Their primary goal is to win the war. And while at it, they gather and publish enough evidence to ensure that the Russian criminals terrorizing their homeland will one day end up in the tribunal in The Hague, the International Criminal Court, to account for their war crimes. "The earth can be contaminated, air and water can be polluted, but fire can be used to purify. Information-wise, we want to burn down and reveal the secrets of the Kremlin," Burko says of InformNapalm.

∞∞∞∞

The Ukrainian man using the pseudonym Roman Burko was born and raised in Donbas, Eastern Ukraine, on the Russian border. He is between twenty-five and forty years old. Like many other InformNapalm investigators, Burko conceals his true identity for his own safety. "Conditions of hybrid war demand the use of hybrid strategies and hybrid tools. Anonymity is one of those tools," he says.

Anonymity also adds an extra layer of security by reducing the number and efficiency of propaganda attacks against community members. Staying under Russia's radar protects the volunteer's families. too. "If my name were made public, my relatives and friends could be linked to me. Their safety could be endangered," Burko explains.

Conspiracy theories swirling in the Russian information space claim that Burko is a military officer serving in a special unit of the Ukrainian Ministry of Defense, working in close cooperation with NATO. One pro-Kremlin propaganda website published a photo that it claimed was of Burko and hus family. As I compare the photo to the man called Burko I've met, I can confirm that the picture is of another person.

According to the UN, the Russian-led war in Ukraine has killed over 14,000 people,[2] while more than two million people have been forced to flee their homes.[3] Human rights organizations have report extrajudicial killings, torture, and discrimination against minorities in the occupied territories. Twenty percent of the schools in Donbas have been damaged by the fighting; homes are looted and destroyed. Occupation forces have imposed censorship, established checkpoints, and ordered curfews.[4]

Russian operations in Donbas are conducted with full plausible deniability, with no official connection to the Kremlin. Withholding information and conducting secret operations is a traditional Soviet-era technique of information warfare, designed to paralyze the target and its capability to make decisions. It is difficult to defend oneself when the attacker is unknown and denies the basic rules of warfare.

To this day, the Kremlin strictly denies the very presence, as well as any specific actions, of its military troops in Ukraine. Russian state-controlled media has systematically built up the image of a Ukrainian internal crisis, and a civil war with "mostly locals" fighting against each other. Russian officials have classified all details concerning its military's presence and operations in

Ukraine as top secret.

Roman Burko and his friends seek to expose those secrets.

ooooo

According to InformNapalm, the most effective way of countering the Kremlin's tactics is to expose Russian intelligence. By publishing verified, factual data about the country's actions, InformNapalm is often able to provoke a strong reaction from the Russian government. "Maybe, one way or another," Burko hopes, "the Russian regime will be forced to spend so many resources to downplay and negate InformNapalm's activities that we might contribute to getting rid of Vladimir Putin's regime."

As soon as Ukraine launched its defensive operations against Russia in the spring of 2014, InformNapalm began focusing on gathering information that they thought could be useful for the Ukrainian troops fighting the Kremlin. "We realized the war was not going to end soon," explains Burko. "And because it was going to last for a long time, people had to combine their efforts to fight back. Different forms of this war can be spread elsewhere in Europe, so people had to be educated about the different types of hybrid war."

Some of the volunteers behind InformNapalm lived in the conflict zone. Based on their eyewitness accounts, the site started listing the heavy weaponry smuggled into Ukraine by Russia: grenade launchers, armored vehicles, air defense systems, and drones. Russian checkpoints, roads, and other infrastructure used by the military units were geolocated, mapped, and published online. During the summer of 2014, as Russia began full-scale military operations in Donbas, Burko and another volunteer ran a detailed daily update from the battlefield.

As word spread of an online group exposing the Kremlin's

secret warfare tactics, the InformNapalm volunteer network expanded. The group also gained respect among experts, with diplomats, policy makers, researchers, and the Ukrainian defense and intelligence communities using their findings. Today, the InformNapalm community includes professional journalists, open-source investigators, analysts, military experts, IT engineers, graphic designers, and translators. The volunteers operate around the world in Ukraine, Scandinavia, Central Europe, the Middle East, the United States, and South Africa. Articles on the site are translated into twenty different languages. None of the community members receive financial compensation for their work.

Ukrainian media outlets regularly quote InformNapalm reports. The group is also celebrated by the general public. For example, the site's spokesperson often receives special treatment in Kyiv's markets and stores. Sales clerks recognize him and offer him discounts as thanks for his efforts. Much of the Ukrainian government approves of what InformNapalm is doing as well. However, acceptance from Ukrainian or foreign governments isn't what's important, Burko explains. "We rely on the support of regular people: the support of Ukrainians, not on the support of any government," he says. "We stay away from all official organizations—we are not part of any system."

Unsurprisingly, the Russian state-controlled media takes a much less favorable view of InformNapalm, with the most influential and popular outlets publishing smear articles about the group, referring to it as a "citizen project," without mentioning its name. Roman Burko believes the name is intentionally omitted to prevent the Russian public from accessing the information on the site. "Our investigations might demoralize young Russian men, who are brainwashed by propaganda and called to join Russia's hybrid army and travel to Ukraine to fight the 'fascists,' as the Russian media calls the Ukrainian ruling class," he says.

However, the attitude of the pro-Kremlin trolls toward the

group's volunteers is straightforward: They want them dead.

DIVIDE AND CONQUER

After InformNapalm accounts were established on Twitter, Facebook, and YouTube in 2014, the channels were quickly flooded with murderous threats. Experts at InformNapalm analyzed the comments and the locations from which they had originated. Part of the traffic came from the Russian troll factory in St. Petersburg, while the rest came from real people who had been turned into true believers by the Kremlin's propaganda machine. "Those people have an ideology," Burko explains. "They hate the information we publish because it contradicts Putin's words. Thus, they despise us, and attack us."

The pro-Kremlin social media accounts would often adjust their messaging based on the content posted on InformNapalm, accusing the contributors to the site of working for the security services of Ukraine, Israel, or other countries, for example. They would also often implement a mirror strategy: for instance, when InformNapalm posted a story profiling Russian military intelligence officers who had been spotted in Eastern Ukraine, the trolls replied, "But YOU yourself work for the Ministry of Defense of Ukraine!" "There is only one reply to that," says Burko: "Well, there are still Russian troops in Ukraine."

The online harassers operate according to a frequent Russian strategy in Ukraine: divide and conquer. The Kremlin had begun undermining Ukraine with targeted information warfare well before 2014. Using disinformation and influence agents, Russia tried to create support for the upcoming invasion, especially within that segment of the population that for historical reasons self-identified more as Russian than Ukrainian. A variety of different theories attacking the government in Kyiv were cultivated in the information space. Separatist sentiment was fueled through social media and pro-Kremlin fake news sites.

The goal of the pre-invasion information attacks was to split Ukrainian society into smaller, more easily controllable and manipulable groups. Through carefully targeted messaging, a portion of the population was lured to favor Kremlin policies. For example, groups in the eastern oblasts of Donetsk and Luhansk were induced to support the region's "independence," which meant separation from Ukraine into "people's republics." As Russian servicemen put their boots on Ukrainian soil and took over television stations and administrative buildings, they renamed regions of the country, declared them independent, and replaced the local governors with Russian "people leaders." Primed by the information warfare, many citizens warmheartedly welcomed the regime change—unaware of who in fact was running the show. "Ukraine, like any other democratic society, is more or less divided," Burko says. "The Kremlin is trying to split the population into smaller ideological groups and set them against each other. That's the most dangerous aspect of these operations." The troll's coordinated attacks against InformNapalm's social media channels is similarly intended to influence ethnic Russians and Russian speakers in Ukraine and Russia.

The volunteers at InformNapalm investigated the accounts that commented on their social media posts and the website's comments' sections, trying to put an end to the vitriol. Once, they were able to trace a person who had threatened to come to Ukraine and stab an InformNapalm editor to death. Within an hour, the person's IP address, home address, last name, and patronymic (father's first name) were identified. The individual was discovered to be located in the Caucasus, near Chechnya. "We told him: 'Hey pal, we know who you are,'" recounts Burko. "Then we published a statement saying that trolls are welcome to post their threats, because we will find out where they live and pass their personal information to the Myrotvorets Center to be published." Myrotvorets (Peacekeeper) is another Ukrainian website, specializing in tracking down Russian terrorists and anti-Ukrainian separatists. After that statement, the number of people making threats decreased significantly.

The volunteers also employed a strategy of utilizing the flood of negative comments to boost the popularity of their own articles. Back in 2014–15, Facebook's algorithms increased the visibility of a post in a user's news feed if they attracted lively comment responses immediately after publication. Thus, each hateful comment resulted in greater visibility for InformNapalm articles; volunteers intentionally provoked negative troll comments in order to gain a wider reach. "We only publish articles with solid facts, such as numbers, which are difficult to challenge," says Burko. "We also keep some information up our sleeves. So, when the trolls try to provoke us, we strike back at them with still more information."

The volunteers found out that the most effective method against Russian trolls was to put them on the defensive, which often led to retreat.

THIS FUCKING SHIT

Throughout the summer of 2014, the war in Ukraine raged. In September, the first ceasefire agreement, known as the Minsk Protocol, was finalized. This agreement did not improve the situation, so it was later followed by a second accord—Minsk II, which was signed in February 2015. Like the first agreement, Minsk II also failed to stop the fighting.

Whenever Russia smuggled new military equipment and units into Ukraine, InformNapalm was the first to expose these activities. The group has tracked infantry mobility vehicles, armored personnel carriers, battle tanks, military trucks, command vehicles, infantry vehicles, rocket launchers, multiple rocket launch systems, tactical surface-to-air missile systems, anti-tank guns, and howitzers that have been sent by Russia into Ukraine.[5] As of this writing, InformNapalm has identified over fifty different pieces of weaponry brought into Ukraine by Russia. Of course, the Kremlin denies everything.

Beginning in July 2014, InformNapalm began investigating the downing of Malaysia Airlines flight MH17. The plane had been shot out of the sky by a Russian surface-to-air Buk missile launcher,[6] but the Kremlin aggressively denied any involvement.[7] Burko and his community gathered evidence of the Kremlin's role in the crash and sent it to the international team that was officially investigating the downing.

In Eastern Ukraine, InformNapalm has also collected evidence of the efforts Russia has invested in electronic warfare, which the Kremlin defines as a form of information warfare. Jamming radars and disrupting communications is harder to trace than physical attacks and is therefore difficult to respond to or to prosecute in war tribunals. InformNapalm was the first group to spot cutting-edge Russian weapons in Ukraine: radio proximity jamming stations and other electronic warfare systems designed to monitor airwaves. They have also traced the smuggling into the country of well-equipped unmanned drones, designed for air surveillance. In 2015, InformNapalm identified the headquarters of Russia's electronic warfare forces in a captured tax office building in occupied Luhansk.[8] The transmitting center was interrupting the area's radio communications, and was several times more powerful than the regional television tower.

InformNapalm also discovered a video of Russian soldiers bragging about "protecting this fucking shit."[9] By "this fucking shit," they were referring to a sophisticated Russian-manufactured Borisoglebsk-2 weapon system, which is the mainframe system used for electronic warfare by the Russian army.[10] In addition to many other tricks, it can block GPS and mobile phone systems, extensively collect radar data, and jam and identify radar locations. In the video, one of the Russian soldiers says, "Take a look! We take the bearing of the Ukies, point at a target, and fucking fire.

And this is our position. This is our invisible man watching. And he is looking in the direction of Ukropia." "Ukies" is a demeaning slur referring to Ukrainians; "Ukropia" is a derogatory term for Ukraine.

Russia also uses Ukraine as a testing ground for its units dedicated to electronic warfare and signal intelligence.[11] The units are constantly jamming, intercepting, and interrupting the Ukrainian army's control units and attacking them electronically. In 2015, Ben Hodges, then commanding general of the United States Army Europe, described the quality and sophistication of Russian electronic warfare as "eye-watering." Hodges shared how US troops learned about Russia's jamming capabilities from the Ukrainians.[12]

PERSONAL INFORMATION MADE PUBLIC

Roman Burko and his associates at InformNapalm collect a lot of their evidence directly from Russian servicemen. Some Russian soldiers post photos of themselves engaging in warfare to Facebook and the Russian social media networks VKontakte and Odnoklassniki. The volunteers at InformNapalm then sift through the social media accounts and harvest the names, military ranks, and other personal information of the soldiers. Occasionally, InformNapalm publishes individual soldier's contact information, such as their phone numbers and home addresses.

I asked Burko about the ethics of publishing this kind of information. He says that InformNapalm has ethical standards that guide what they post publicly. But, at the same time, he believes they have more freedoms than regular journalists because their agenda is different, as they are also fighting back against Russian warfare. "For example, when we publish the telephone number of a terrorist," Burko says, referring to Russian soldiers, "then a journalist or anyone else can call up the terrorist and ask him directly what he thinks about the information published on the InformNapalm website."

After the Russian Air Force bombed civilians in Syria in October 2015, killing women and children, InformNapalm published information about crew members of the Air Force group who were responsible for the air strikes. Simultaneously, they published an ultimatum addressed to the Russian military command: every time Russian forces violated the ceasefire in Donbas, InformNapalm would release more personal information about the Russian pilots killing civilians in Syria.

The Russian media immediately accused InformNapalm of endangering the lives of the pilots and attributed the group's reports to "Ukrainian information warfare against Russia." Denis Denisov, director of Ukrainian branch of the Institute of CIS Countries, a pro-Kremlin institution, gave an interview in which he stated that Kyiv had opened a "Syrian front" against Russia.[13] Contrary to the facts, he attributed the publication of the pilot's details to Ukrainian "officials." According to Denisov, the Ukrainian authorities were believed to be conducting a hybrid war against Russia. "Therefore, we see how they try to excite the public with the help of lies and falsified facts," he said.

Denisov went on to say that publication of the personal data of Russian pilots in Syria was "absolutely unacceptable, and it seems Moscow will have to respond to this provocation." The article also reiterated the Kremlin's typical talking points depicting Russian strikes in Syria as part of fighting Islamic terrorism and ISIS, adding that, "The international community should take action against Ukraine to prevent further similar incidents." The killings of civilians by the Russian Air Force was not mentioned, even though human rights organizations had already brought them to light.

On October 15, 2015, Vladimir Putin's press secretary, Dmitry Peskov, responded to InformNapalm's ultimatum, declaring it "hostile activity" toward Russia.[14] He said that Russian special services were monitoring the situation, and would take all necessary measures to ensure the safety of the Russian military. The statement confirmed what InformNapalm had suspected: they were being watched by Russian intelligence.

ooooo

As the ceasefire violations continued in 2015, InformNapalm published infographics revealing the names, military ranks, military units, facial photos, military education, graduation years, and dates of birth of thirty-two Russian Air Force pilots and navigators who had bombed Syria.

Soon after, Russia started applying diplomatic pressure.

The InformNapalm website had been registered in Ukraine, but was hosted on servers located in Canada. In December 2015, the Russian embassy in Canada sent an official request to Global Affairs Canada, the Canadian foreign ministry, asking the Canadian government to remove the "sensitive information, published on Canadian servers." The spokesperson for the Russian embassy told the media that "the Canadian side was duly informed on this matter. The Russian side expects appropriate reaction on this security-related issue."[15] Global Affairs Canada replied that they had heard Russia's concern and had forwarded the request to the police. The Canadian police, when contacted by journalists, refused to comment.[16] At the present time, Burko is not aware of any police investigations of InformNapalm in Canada or other countries.

Burko and his fellow volunteers are well aware that their site could face take-down requests. To prepare for this, they have set up mirror servers in different countries. Thus, if the website were to be taken down in one country, it could be instantly reopened in another. "Russia cannot pressure all of the countries in the world. It's not difficult to set up such a system, when you're an expert," Burko says.

∞∞∞

The Kremlin's condemnation of the publication of the names of its pilots were taken up by a handful of international media outlets,[17] with some speculating that exposing the pilots' personal information would make the Russian aircrews vulnerable to attacks by Islamist extremists in Syria. However, elements of the Russian media took the discussions to a new level, accusing InformNapalm of supporting ISIS terrorists.[18] As the accusations were publicly aired, social media trolls spread them further. InformNapalm reported receiving death threats from Russian security services.

Then, a surprising new front popped up to support the attacks against InformNapalm. These attacks were conducted by a trilingual website called Military-Political Review,[19] which is run by Belarusian military reserve officers. The website claims to be the answer to the "one-sided and inadequate media coverage over military and political issues concerning Belarus." In December 2015, the site labeled InformNapalm contributors "friends of ISIS" and employees of the Ukrainian Ministry of Defense. Military-Political Review claimed to be conducting an "investigation" of a Belarusian InformNapalm volunteer. The same volunteer had previously been intimidated by the Belarusian KGB for his human rights activities. Military-Political Review published his name, birth date and multiple photos, as well as the names of his parents, and unverified details about their family history. The volunteer's partner's photo, name, and link to her Facebook profile were also published, as were the couple's home address, and phone numbers. Details about their co-owned company were also disclosed, attached to accusations that the business was as "lousy as the military equipment of the Kyiv junta." In addition, the article speculated that the volunteer was paid by InformNapalm. It also traced his family all the way back to his great-grandparents, making racist guesses about the nationalities of his ancestors and concluding that "there is most likely Jewish, Russian, Polish and Ukrainian blood running in his veins." At the end of the article, the authors stated how studying this specific subject had caused them feelings of "disgust."

After invading the privacy of the volunteer and his family, the Belarusian reservists behind Military-Political Review next went after Roman Burko. They bragged that they had conducted "open-source investigations" of the person supposedly behind Burko's pseudonym. Referring to evidence that wasn't provided, they declared Burko to be a Ukrainian officer with "suspicious connections" to a random but named American soldier. The article included private information and photos of the alleged wife and alleged son of the alleged Burko. Again, I have seen Roman Burko, and can confirm that he is not the person in the photos. The authors of the article claimed their motive as "defending Belarus from people like Burko and the named Belarusian volunteer." InformNapalm, according to the article, was nothing more than a special project led by the Ukrainian Ministry of Defense.

From Military-Political Review, the stories circulated further in the pro-Kremlin online ecosystem, including being published by a popular Russian propaganda site called Russkaya Vesna (Russian Spring).[20] Russian Spring is the name the propaganda masterminds gave to the 2014 pro-Kremlin unrest and violent demonstrations in Ukraine, organized by Russian special forces. The name is a reference to the Arab Spring, the people's uprising against dictators in Libya, Egypt, and Syria in 2011. The site was launched in 2014 and is owned by a "private person." According to web traffic counters, Russkaya Vesna has over two million daily page views. It is read in Russia, Ukraine, Germany, the Netherlands, and the United States. The site publishes Kremlin propaganda and fake news, though it claims to publish only "verified information."

Despite the rampant lies about Burko and other volunteers, InformNapalm remained up and running in all its languages and continued to publish personal and military information about Russian soldiers.

PATRIOTIC HACKTIVISTS

A distributed denial-of-service (DDoS) attack can be executed in several ways, including by directing so much fake traffic to a website that the server becomes unresponsive and crashes.

InformNapalm coders have spent many sleepless nights countering the numerous DDoS attacks (ddossing) launched against their website. "Sometimes the attacks are quite a headache, because they are massive," Burko shares. "Often multiple attacks are directed at our site simultaneously." InformNapalm volunteers study the methods used in the attacks, in order to counter them more effectively in the future. Once, they managed to reroute an attack to the servers hosting the FSB's website. "We hope they found out it was we who did it," Burko says.

Ukraine is the homeland of many skilled hackers who defend their country in the raging cyber war against Russia. Four groups, who call themselves hacktivists, are particularly active. Their names are Trinity, CyberHunta, Falcons Flame, and RUH8. When they join forces against the Kremlin, they dub themselves the Ukrainian Cyber Alliance. These patriotic hacktivists often send the data they have acquired to InformNapalm. Burko and the other volunteers then produce reports and articles based on the hacktivists' disclosures.

In April 2016, InformNapalm published several stories based on thirty gigabytes of hacked email and social media accounts of key Russian officials who were involved in "coordinating [the] activities of mercenaries, Russian soldiers, and militaries in Donbass and Syria."[21] The hack revealed a large network of Russian influence agents commanding and advising various groups who were sabotaging Ukraine. One leader of a seemingly independent civic organization in Donbas was unmasked as a former Russian

FSB officer. The data also proved that Russia gave visas to foreign fighters who wanted to join the Kremlin-backed militants in Eastern Ukraine. According to Ukrainian law, crossing the border through any checkpoint that is not under control of the Ukrainian government is illegal.

The emails also showed scans of the passports of Indian, Italian, and Finnish fighters, as well as their tourist and business visas, which had been issued by Russia.[22] InformNapalm attached the passport data to other evidence that proved that foreign fighters were engaged in combat in Eastern Ukraine.

ooooo

April 2016 was a busy month for the Ukrainian hacktivists. Two of the hacker groups, Falcons Flame and Trinity, penetrated a pro-Kremlin propaganda site called Anna News and destroyed its content.[23] The hackers then posted their own content on the site: links to InformNapalm and a video message, which was delivered by a man wearing a Guy Fawkes mask: "If you're watching this video," he declared, "we have cleared the information space from another site of Russian terrorists." He also revealed that the hackers had obtained confidential information about the website's administrators and users. Finally, the masked man asked viewers to unite in the fight for victory against the Russian aggressor: "Stop buying Russian products, and stop trusting Russian media." Instead, he encouraged people to support each other as well as the Ukrainian army: "Our weapon is the mind, faith, and free will. Each of you is capable of inflicting damage on the enemy. Help those who are in need of assistance and protection. Together we are the force that will win the war."

The hacktivists handed the data over to InformNapalm and Ukrainian security services. Roman Burko's community of volunteers published stories about the fate of Anna News and described the administrators' attempts to restore the site. "Normally, when a site goes down, IT guys use a ready backup copy. But the hackers managed to install their own files as the backup. So, the admins used that backup file twice, but it was faulty. So, they couldn't replace the site," says Burko.

The patriotic hackers had one more trick up their sleeve. They copied the original backup files, then proposed an exchange to the Anna News admins: the hackers would hand over their copy of the backup file if, in return, Russian forces would release Ukrainian prisoners of war.

I asked Burko whether some of the actions performed by the hackers might run counter to Ukrainian laws, including those pertaining to data breaches and internet crimes. He acknowledges this, but added that, "On the other hand, our constitution states that it is the citizen's responsibility to stand up for the independence and territorial integrity of Ukraine. If the patriotic hacktivists were prosecuted, Ukrainian civil society wouldn't accept it. Most likely, it would trigger protests and rallies."

THE SURKOV LEAKS

Federanoye Agentstvo Novostei (Federal News Agency), also known as RIA Fan, claims to be a local news site run out of Ukraine. In fact, it is administered by the troll factory in St. Petersburg. In September 2016, the site went after Roman Burko.[24]

In a smear piece that it claimed was based on electronic correspondence between "military personnel working for the Special Operations Forces in the Ukrainian Ministry of Defense," RIA Fan alleged that Burko had ties with Ukrainian government officials. The correspondence had supposedly originated from a Ukrainian female hacker group called Beregini. I asked a Ukrainian diplomat whether such a group existed. The diplomat had never heard of Beregini.

RIA Fan also accused a specifically named Ukrainian army

captain of being the real person behind Burko's pseudonym. It also claimed that the same Ukrainian captain who had been "unmasked" as Burko might also be the real person behind another one of InformNapalm volunteer pseudonyms. "The person who is alleged to be me is in fact not me. The same shopworn Soviet-style accusations are still used everywhere," says Burko.

∞∞∞

In the autumn of 2016, the Ukrainian Cyber Alliance cracked open the office email account of Vladislav Surkov,[25] a political adviser to Vladimir Putin, as well as the account of an advisor to Surkov.[26] The hacktivists gave the content to InformNapalm, which combed through the emails to confirm their authenticity. They then published a story presenting evidence that Putin's inner circle had participated in engineering the conflict in Ukraine. The emails proved that Surkov had driven Russia's interests in both Kremlin puppet states established in Eastern Ukraine, and that Russian agents and warlords in charge of the mercenaries in Donetsk and Luhansk were reporting their sabotage activities to Surkov. The emails also discussed instructions for specific media operations, and listed the names of suggested candidates for top-level posts in Luhansk.

The data breach, referred to as the Surkov Leaks, broke internationally. "I'm so happy that our organization could help to promote important information obtained through the operations of the Ukrainian Cyber Alliance. That brings us closer to victory," Burko shares.

The Kremlin denied any hack ever took place, and asserted that Surkov didn't even use email. However, in early 2017, the advisor to Surkov whose email account had been hacked was fired.

∞∞∞

Soon after publishing the Surkov emails, InformNapalm was smeared by Putin's inner circle. This time the information attack was carried out through a website owned by Alexander Dugin, the "odd philosopher and occult fascist" often referred to as "Putin's Brain."[27]

Dugin is known for the unique wording of his attacks against Western liberalism and democracy. He advocates and fosters the idea of rebuilding Eurasia, which is basically the region of the former Soviet Union. Dugin lectures at international disinformation conferences organized by Putin sycophants and Russian state-employed propagandists like Johan Bäckman, who brought Dugin to speak in Finland.[28]

Dugin's small and, according to web traffic counters, unpopular Russian-language propaganda platform, Evrazia (Eurasia), labeled two InformNapalm contributors as propagandists for the "Kyiv junta." The same article also attacked respected international security experts and researchers, calling them "NATO-prepared cadres to occupy Russia."[29]

In reality, the international community has long applauded InformNapalm's findings. For example, both the European Council and NATO have relied on InformNapalm analyses when drafting resolutions on how to counter Russian aggression.

"THESE VIDEOS ON YOUTUBE ARE *VERY IMPORTANT*!"

Throughout 2017, the Ukrainian hacktivists helped InformNapalm uncover the owners and admins of several Russian propaganda websites, evidence of the Kremlin's meddling in Poland,[30] and use of the infamous Russian mercenary Wagner Group and other private military companies in Ukraine.[31] They also identified over 2,000 Russian military personnel in Donbas, as well as exposing an FSB-supported bomb hoax.[32]

The hacktivists also identified multiple pro-Kremlin groups spreading propaganda on the Russian social media network VKontakte. In particular, they were able to gather evidence of ordinary citizens receiving orders from Russia. After reviewing the hacks, InformNapalm concluded that Russian citizens had engaged in systematic information warfare against Ukraine,[33] which had been coordinated and paid for by Russian politicians, intelligence agencies, businessmen, and the like.

One remarkable revelation was the case of the Belarusian pro-Kremlin saboteur Alexander Usovsky. The Ukrainian hacktivists accessed Usovsky's computer and monitored his communications for several months,[34] uncovering his correspondence with the Kremlin-led Institute of CIS Countries. The Institute is headed by Russian State Duma deputy Konstantin Zatulin, who is a member of Putin's United Russia party.

In emails, Usovsky told Zatulin's people that he was eager to create a "citizens' association" that would advertise "Russian world" concepts in Poland, the Czech Republic, Slovakia, and Hungary.[35] He calculated the budgets he would need for the projects, and asked for funding from Russia. Usovsky also wrote memos for Zatulin, as well as appearing on Russian television as an expert. In addition, Usovsky also ran many parallel projects, including trying to organize a pro-Russian party in Poland and strengthen various anti-EU groups, among other activities designed to create an anti-Ukrainian atmosphere in Eastern Europe.

The hacktivists accessed Usovsky's Facebook Messenger messages as well, which showed that he had received large sums of money, including at least €100,000 from a Russian oligarch,[36] to organize pro-Kremlin rallies promoting the propagandistic idea of *Novorossiya* (a large swathe of southern and eastern Ukraine that became part of imperial Russia) in Poland, the Czech Republic, and Slovakia. One of his projects included discrediting and destroying a Ukrainian monument in Poland.[37] For his dirty work, he employed paid Polish nationalists. As soon as Usovsky had transferred €2,000 to the bank account of a Polish activist's daughter, a monument was painted with pro-Kremlin slogans. A handful of people also waved banners and picked a fight at the monument.

From Usovsky's communications, it was also revealed that the Kremlin expected to see public YouTube videos as proof of a successful project that was worth funding.[38] "Moscow is waiting for the report of Hruszowice and Budapest, the further financing of the project depends on it. These videos on YouTube are VERY IMPORTANT!" Usovsky wrote. His messages made multiple mentions of Western Union payments to Slovakia and elsewhere, which were spent on organizing events that the Kremlin wanted to happen.

The hacktivists also uncovered a connection between Usovsky and Mateusz Piskorski, a Polish politician and former member of the Sejm, the lower house of Poland's national legislature. Piskorski was detained in the summer of 2016,[39] the same summer that Warsaw hosted the NATO summit meeting attended by President Barack Obama. Piskorski was suspected of cooperating with and accepting money and job assignments from Russian intelligence services. He was also listed as the Polish representative of the Russian-funded fake human rights organization World Without Nazism on the organization's old website. This is the association that Johan Bäckman has operated as Finnish representative of, and from which he has publicly admitted receiving money.

Piskorski tried to return to the Polish parliament in 2015 (he had previously served from 2005 to 2007) with a political party named Zmiana (Change), which he had established. The party was said to consist of self-styled anti-capitalists and anti-imperialists. In the party's first meeting, pro-Kremlin representatives of *Novorossiya* presented their views about the war in Donbas—that is, about pro-Kremlin information operations.

Usovsky and Piskorski had kept in close contact through FB Messenger since 2014, and had organized protests in support of lifting the sanctions against Russia. Usovsky had even applied for funding from Moscow to "help Mateusz Piskorski develop his new structure," most likely referring to Piskorski's pro-Kremlin political group. The day before Piskorski was detained, Usovsky had discussed with him their plans for joint political events and the organizing of Polish tourists to Donetsk, East Ukraine. The hacks revealed that Usovsky had had similar discussions with other political activists around Eastern Europe. Whenever they could be used to benefit the Kremlin, Usovsky started sending money.

InformNapalm analyzed the material and stated that Usovsky's correspondence gave a completely different perspective on recent events, revealing that Pro-Russian protests in Poland and other Eastern European countries had often been backed by Russia.

EVIDENCE

Over the years, InformNapalm has presented its findings to Ukrainian security officials and policy makers, local and foreign journalists, and to the international diplomatic community. Their efforts have greatly contributed to both Ukraine's[40] and the international response to Russian aggression. For example, in 2017, InformNapalm published 313 investigations in 2,470 translated foreign language versions, identified eleven new types of Russian weapons in Ukraine, educated the public at conferences in Europe and the US, and met with over 120 journalists, experts, and diplomats. In February 2018, Ukraine's deputy minister of justice confirmed that some of their data regarding special weapons categories, locations, and photos had been received from InformNapalm.[41]

In April 2018, InformNapalm published a massive database detailing all their findings since their founding four years earlier.[42] According to the Ukrainian media, this is the biggest existing database of evidence of Russia's undeclared war.[43]

VIOLATING COMMUNITY STANDARDS

Throughout the spring of 2018, anonymous attackers used Facebook to launch a campaign against InformNapalm. On the social media platform, anyone can report another user or page for violating its "community standards." According to its rules, Facebook prohibits certain content, for example hate speech and bullying. Although InformNapalm hadn't posted any type of forbidden content—unlike the Russian trolls—some person or group submitted user reports about the group to Facebook. As a result, the accounts of three volunteers were suspended for thirty days. Roman Burko's profile was suspended, too, for a few days.[44] An investigation later revealed that the volunteers had been suspended for comments they had written several years earlier.

Burko assumed that InformNapalm was being targeted by automated Kremlin bots or Russian government–supported groups. Such attacks are difficult to counter or prevent. "Apparently, Russian bot farms had developed software that automatically searches for specific keywords in all content posted by popular Ukrainian journalists and bloggers and reports them to Facebook admins," Burko explains.

The volunteers at InformNapalm tried to search through their accounts and comments to clean up any possible violations. The problem was that the comments didn't show up on Facebook's activity logs, or as part of a search. Roman Burko wrote to Facebook to try and solve the issue, but didn't receive a satisfactory answer. He then decided to appeal to Facebook publicly.[45] "Current Facebook policies are only beneficial to the Russian authoritarian regime and Russian propaganda," he wrote.

Burko's appeal went unanswered.

ooooo

In 2017, Ukrainian human rights groups reported that since the beginning of the Crimean occupation, there had been forty-four cases of forced disappearances on the peninsula.[46] Most of the disappearances occurred from March to May 2014 and were individuals declared to be dangerous by the Russian authorities. The disappeared included members of the Crimean Tatars (the Turkic ethnic group who are an indigenous people of Crimea), journalists, local activists, and visitors from mainland Ukraine. Some of the disappeared were locked up, while others were found dead. Some are still missing.

One can only speculate whether Roman Burko would have disappeared had he stayed in Crimea. However, having been threatened with a gun by a Russian soldier made the truth about Russian aggression brutally clear to him. "The most important thing is to try focusing on the established facts, to analyze and compare information," Burko says. "Also, you might get a Russian soldier's gun pointed at you, and only then believe that what you previously read in the news is in fact true. I had a gun pointed at me by a Russian soldier. That convinced me a lot, probably forever."

Burko believes that the reason the Kremlin's information warfare has been so successful to date is because Russia has mastered the new rules of war, unlike the West—mainly because Russia invented the whole game. "The Russians are currently winning only because they know the new rules," says Burko. "Europe is still trying to apply the old rules to an updated situation. The EU is losing because there is not enough will and effort to adapt. You must get used to the new rules. And the sooner the better. It's a hybrid war, and we need to unite and counter it together. We should pay back Russia with their own currency."

Burko has a plan for how to win the game, which requires digging up information and spreading it to a wide audience. "We will win, if and when we have lots of honest journalists bringing all the information to an international audience," he states. "This is when we get it noticed and make it heard. After that, the governments will have no other option but to step up and put diplomatic pressure on Russia. Because you simply cannot tolerate what Russia is doing." Burko also wants to disabuse others of the notion that the reasons behind his actions are because he somehow hates Russia. "Maybe you think I'm anti-Russian," he says, "but I am not. I'm 50 percent Russian. But 100 percent of my soul belongs to Ukraine, and it is calling for justice."

5.

Millions of Views

THE DIGITAL ABUSE AGAINST ME CONTINUED throughout the winter of 2014–2015. At the same time, my crowdsourcing was going well, as internet users were sending me tips on Russian trolls who were spreading propaganda on multiple platforms.

On Twitter, fake accounts posted brutal YouTube videos that showed Russian-supported militias mistreating captured Ukrainian soldiers. In one video, Russian militia members cut the Ukrainian flag from a bound soldier's uniform sleeve and forced him to eat it.[1] The trolls shared the video widely, celebrating the violence, which was potentially a war crime.

The Russian network RT also used YouTube for propaganda means. Among the videos it published was one in which an RT reporter stood by the side of Russian soldiers firing GRAD missiles on Ukraine.[2] As the first rounds were fired, the reporter celebrated.

The pro-Kremlin-YouTube videos that tend to go viral are those that are professionally directed in the style of Western music videos. One of the most horrific of these showed Ukrainian soldiers being sent to their deaths in East Ukraine, and others having their limbs amputated.[3] By showing this type of violence, the video aimed to cripple Ukrainians' will to defend their country.

The video also reinforced the common Russian conspiracy

theory that accuses the United States of being the root cause of the war in Ukraine. In this manipulative video, an actor dressed as a high-ranking American officer hands a medal of honor to a badly injured Ukrainian soldier suffering in a hospital bed. Between the cuts, the video flashes short messages framing Ukraine as the "real aggressor."

Together, these videos gathered millions of views in just a few days, as the troll and bot accounts spread them internationally, with the help of YouTube and Twitter.

The skillfully manufactured videos reminded me of a previous investigation in which I had researched how jihadist terrorists used social media as a propaganda tool. In 2008, during the wars in Iraq and Afghanistan, I worked as a foreign affairs correspondent for the biggest daily newspaper in Finland, *Helsingin Sanomat*. With the help of experts, I analyzed al-Qaeda jihadist recruitment materials and agitation techniques from online open sources. Even back then, it was easy for terrorist groups to motivate people into joining their global jihad or a local conflict through social media. All they needed to do was upload an extremist speech or an exciting combat video spiced up with catchy battle songs to YouTube. Anyone with internet access could watch the video, become radicalized, and join the cause.

Analyzing jihadist propaganda and its impact revealed how the makers manipulated the use of symbols, language, music, and illustrations to imprint a permanent psychological mark in people's minds. The pro-Russian videos spread by Twitter bots use precisely the same technique. Videos also appeal to audiences who may lack reading skills.

Historically, moving images and movies have been an important tool in building and sustaining regimes, for example in Nazi Germany and the Soviet Union. That's why Vladimir Putin took over Russian television early in his presidency.

RT, in particular, has long understood the power of viral

social media. They were among the first networks to upload their televised content to both Facebook and YouTube. In addition, they skillfully launched brand new social media products, such as In the Now, which produces emotion-inducing popular videos, usually totally unrelated to politics, in order to gain an international audience.

As I browsed through the Russian state's invasion of the most popular social media platforms, I learned how propaganda conveyed through digital means was a fascinating, cheap, and dangerous weapon. Especially at risk were those audiences who felt let down by society. For them, digital hate communities built by malicious actors provided a place to speak out without censure, and have their anger, disillusionment, and frustration reinforced by others.

Ultimately, as my investigations continued, I could see that jihadists, the Kremlin's digital propagandists, and neo-Nazis all used the same platforms—namely, Facebook, Twitter, and YouTube—and had the same goals: to attack and undermine Western democratic systems, spark regime changes and conflicts, endanger civilians, and create wider acceptance of their extremist ideologies. The reason these groups are so successful is because the social media companies don't regulate their platforms well enough, and the US government doesn't regulate the social media companies. Some of the most vicious pro-Kremlin YouTube channels are monetized—meaning that their owners earn money from their content. I found various American advertisers promoting their products and brands on troll channels. Facebook, too, profits from extremists by selling them ads and visibility. Google, for its part, doesn't moderate its search results based on factuality. Trolls can buy ads that serve fake news on the first page of a Google search, for example, about Eastern Ukraine.

Thus, it is easy to see how the social media giants enable the meddling of the Kremlin's trolls.

6.

The Businessman

AS THE US PRESIDENTIAL CAMPAIGN HEATED up in May 2016, the *New York Times* published an article about my troll investigations and the Russian fake news campaign that had targeted me.[1] At that time, the Kremlin's social media influence operations weren't high on the agenda of the mainstream American media.

Soon after the *Times* piece ran, I received a message from Bill Browder, the well-known investor and businessman. Browder, who had famously run into trouble after managing an investment company in Putin's Russia, wanted to encourage me to continue my work, which he found valuable.

I traveled to London to meet him. His company, Hermitage Capital Management, was headquartered in Mayfair, in the center of the city. Framed newspaper articles about his life and work hung on the walls of his office.

An investment pioneer, Browder in recent years has dedicated himself to investigating and exposing Kremlin-connected international money-laundering and human rights crimes. Because of this, he has become one of the largest targets of Russian disinformation during the Putin era. And he hasn't just been the subject of filth online, as lawyers, lobbyists, PR officials, investigators, and process servers have all been recruited in an organized manhunt against him. Russia has also tried to initiate several groundless warrants for his arrest via the international police organization, Interpol. "The Kremlin actually believes in what they're saying," Browder told me that first time we met. "There are people who know that I'm not a CIA agent, but a lot of people have said it to each other so many times that it's become firmly lodged in their brain that I am." He estimates that the Kremlin spends around $100 million a year to smear him.

To understand why Bill Browder is such a pressing concern for Russia, one must examine his history with Vladimir Putin.

∞∞∞

The American-born financier Bill Browder founded Hermitage Capital Management in Russia in 1996. The firm invested in undervalued companies in the promising post–Soviet environment, quickly becoming the biggest portfolio investor in Russia. It had an international clientele, both institutional and private, and in its most successful year, managed over $4 billion in assets. In 2006 it paid more in taxes than the country's national airline and many banks.

Russia's business atmosphere back then was challenging. Corporate crime was exploding, and crooked oligarchs were stealing from newly privatized state companies. Browder was forced to fight against this high level of corruption. In addition to managing his own company, he investigated fraud and the pillaging of assets in Russian companies, such as the state-controlled energy giant Gazprom and the country's biggest bank, Sberbank.

When Vladimir Putin rose to power in 2000, Browder had been working in Russia for four years. Initially, their interests coincided because Putin was fighting the same oligarchs as Browder. The oligarchs threatened the new president's power. As a result, Putin appreciated Browder's work in uncovering irregularities. "When we published our investigations, Putin would regularly step up and act on the information we provided," Browder shares. "He would fire someone or issue a presidential decree."

By 2003, Putin had succeeded in subordinating the Russian oligarchs to his command. The richest of them all, Mikhail Khodorkovsky, owner of the private oil company, Yukos, and funder of political parties opposing Putin, was arrested and convicted of alleged tax evasion and embezzlement. He was sentenced to prison; his company, Yukos, was sold for a fraction of its value. Photos and TV coverage of the pro-democracy oil tycoon sitting in a cage in court, answering political charges, was a message powerful enough to force the rest of the oligarchs to strike deals with Putin. According to Browder, after the trial, many oligarchs agreed to give 50 percent of their income to the Russian president. That was the price of freedom.

From that moment on, Browder recalls, Putin focused on securing his own economic interests. For Browder's company, Hermitage, Putin's policy change manifested itself in a violent crackdown.

ooooo

In late 2005, Browder was detained at the Russian border, declared a threat to the country's national security, and deported. His visa was also revoked. Browder resettled in the United Kingdom and started running his business from London.

Two years later, twenty-five Russian Interior Ministry officers raided Hermitage's Russian offices and the office of its American law firm in Moscow. As one of the lawyers tried to prevent the illegal raid, he was assaulted by the officers. According to Browder, Lieutenant Colonel Artem Kuznetsov supervised as the officers confiscated the company's computers, servers, and confidential documents. The policemen also took the company's original certificates of registration, as well as the seals.[2]

Browder hired a young and talented lawyer named Sergei Magnitsky and entrusted him with investigating the raids. "Sergei Magnitsky was the smartest lawyer I knew," Browder says. Magnitsky discovered that Russian officers used the confiscated certificates and company seals to illegally reregister three companies under the Hermitage umbrella—Parfenion, Makhaon, and Rilend. Parfenion had been transferred to a firm in Kazan, a city in southern Russia, and registered to Viktor Markelov, a recently convicted murderer. Makhaon and Rilend had new directors appointed, with the help of forged documents. Those new directors were also convicted criminals. The transfer of the companies' ownership was validated by a court in Kazan. But Magnitsky's investigations revealed that the courthouse didn't even exist.

A month after the raid, the Hermitage companies were sued in a court in St. Petersburg, accused of breach of contract. No one informed the genuine Hermitage management about the charges, even though they included a demand for $376 million in damages. All of the plaintiff's documents presented in the trial were forged.[3]

The accusations had been presented by a company which had never signed contracts with Hermitage and thus wasn't even in a position to ask for damages. The most shocking detail was that Hermitage was represented in court by unknown lawyers who hadn't been hired by the actual company. The fake lawyers fully acknowledged and accepted the plaintiff's claims, including the damages. The judge ruled that the alleged breach of contract was so clear that the plaintiffs weren't required to prove it. He ordered Hermitage to pay the plaintiffs the precise sum they demanded: $376 million. Similar ghost judgments were passed in arbitration courts in Moscow and Kazan against the two other illegally reregistered Hermitage companies. In total, Hermitage companies were ordered to pay damages of $973 million. That sum equaled the companies' actual profits for the previous year.

Matching the judgments with the companies' profits allowed the new owners to apply for a tax refund from the Russian authorities. In 2006, Hermitage companies had paid $230 million in taxes. After the court judgment, in December 2007, the fraudulent new owners applied for a tax refund—worth $230 million. Within a day, the Moscow tax service had approved the massive refund. The Russian Treasury paid the sum to the fraudulent owners' bank accounts, which had been opened less than two weeks before. The money was then hidden in a complex maze of money-laundering bank accounts and shell companies.

The scheme was unearthed by Magnitsky, who also identified the high-profile perpetrators. Hermitage and its trustee, HSBC, filed a criminal complaint with Russian officials, based on Magnitsky's findings. The 255-page complaint documented the thefts of the companies and fake damage claims, singling out the involvement of Russian Interior Ministry officials Artem Kuznetsov and Pavel Karpov.

Copies of the complaint were sent to Russia's prosecutor general, Yuri Chaika, the head of the Internal Affairs Department of the Russian Interior Ministry, Yuri Draguntsov, and the head of the Russian State Investigative Committee, Alexander Bastrykin. The Investigative Committee is practically the Russian equivalent of the FBI in the United States. If the authorities had acted on Hermitage's complaint, they would have had enough time to prevent the theft of $230 million from the Russian taxpayers.

None of the officials took any action.

The Russian State Investigative Committee did open one case, and even questioned some of the named suspects. But in June 2008, Artem Kuznetsov, who had led the illegal raid, was appointed to *run* the investigation. Additionally, another key suspect, Pavel Karpov, a police officer with the Russian Interior Ministry, received the complaints, becoming the second official "investigating" a case in which he himself was a suspect.[4]

The Russian State Investigative Committee heard Magnitsky on three different occasions. In the first hearing, held in June 2008, the lawyer named police Kuznetsov and Karpov as the perpetrators of the crime. In October of that year, Magnitsky again identified the same group as being involved in the embezzlement of the $230 million. But the Investigative Committee didn't believe any crimes had been committed.

As soon as the real Hermitage learned about the fraudulent tax refund, it filed eight more complaints. Instead of investigating the crimes, the Russian Interior Ministry retaliated, stamping Hermitage, and its trustee, HSBC, as the guilty parties in the fraud. Hermitage's American lawyers were accused of crimes, and cases were opened against them. Many lawyers connected to the company were threatened with arrest and had to flee the country.

Undeterred, Sergei Magnitsky, continued his investigation. His perseverance would result in fatal consequences.

ONE HOUR AND EIGHTEEN MINUTES

In November 2008, the Russian police raided Sergei Magnitsky's home in Moscow and arrested him. The Interior Ministry charged the lawyer with conspiracy to commit tax fraud in cooperation with Hermitage.

Magnitsky was locked up. The guards at Butyrka, the infamous Moscow prison, wanted him to change his testimony, in which he had named the suspects of the crimes as Russian state officials. Magnitsky refused, so the guards tortured him. He was deprived of food and kept awake at night. His cell was overcrowded and freezing and lacked working plumbing.

Magnitsky fell ill, and his condition quickly worsened. Once, when he managed to get an appointment at the prison infirmary, the doctor told him, "You should have gotten treatment when you were free."

Magnitsky constantly wrote letters complaining about his

inhumane treatment to the head of the prison and its medical unit.

His complaints were ignored.

After Magnitsky had been tortured for almost a year in prison, he was taken back to court. Again, he testified against the same police officers, reaffirming their participation in the crimes against Hermitage—and the misuse of Russian taxpayer money.

Two days after his testimony, on November 16, 2009, Magnitsky was beaten in prison so severely that he died from his injuries. Investigations launched by his family revealed that the prison guards had hit him with rubber batons.[5] The coroner's photos showed injuries to his hand, knuckles, wrist, and knee. The official death certificate is devastating to read: Magnitsky had suffered severe brain trauma. Further investigation revealed that the guards had kept the ambulance staff outside the prison for as long as it took for Magnitsky to die on the floor of his cell: exactly one hour and eighteen minutes.

◌◌◌◌◌

When I met Bill Browder for the first time in London, he told me that his life's work was to bring Sergei Magnitsky's murderers to justice. "First, we tried to get justice inside Russia, because everything was well documented there," he shares, "but we couldn't." The criminals who performed the operation and the Russian government officials exposed by Magnitsky have never been prosecuted. Instead, some of them have been awarded promotions.

As soon as Browder realized that justice wouldn't be served inside Russia, he began to think of ways to find it outside the country. He came up with an idea for new legislation bearing Magnitsky's name. If it was passed into law, the United States could impose visa sanctions and asset freezes against the officials who had killed Magnitsky and engaged in other human rights abuses. The sanctioned officials would be banned from entering the US, and their illicit money stored overseas would be frozen. "It started out as a small idea, but it got bigger," Browder says.

Browder met with American politicians such as Senators John McCain and Ben Cardin. He told them about his experience in Russia and Magnitsky's fate and presented his idea for legislation targeted directly at the perpetrators.

Simultaneously, Browder and his employees at Hermitage continued investigating the crimes back in Russia. One whistleblower, Alexander Perepilichnyy, confessed to his participation in the money laundering and gave Browder bank records and documents that tied a senior Kremlin official to the scheme. Two years later, Perepilichnyy died at the age of forty-four under suspicious circumstances. Browder believes he was poisoned, just like many others whom the Kremlin has labeled as traitors.

Based on their findings, Browder and his team initiated money-laundering investigations in eleven countries—Cyprus, Switzerland, Estonia, Latvia, Moldova, Lithuania, Poland, Spain, France, Luxembourg, and the United States. "We're interested in going after them hard to get the police to take away their money," Browder explains. "That's the one thing that really hits them right between their eyes."

In the United States, the Departments of State, Treasury, and Justice, as well as the National Security Council, launched their own investigations into the Hermitage case and came to the same conclusions as Magnitsky. As a result, then US president Barack Obama signed the law bearing Magnitsky's name on December 14, 2012, as part of a broader piece of legislation known as *The Russia and Moldova Jackson–Vanik Repeal and Sergei Magnitsky Rule of Law Accountability Act of 2012*. The Act prohibits the Russian officials who were responsible for or who financially benefited from the detention and abuse of Magnitsky from entering the United States.[6] The law also authorizes the government to freeze the sanctioned individuals' property and financial transactions in the US. In addition to the officials involved in the Magnitsky case, the Act authorizes the sanctioning of other Russians responsible for extrajudicial killings, torture, and other human rights violations.

President Putin was outraged by the Magnitsky Act, and immediately retaliated.

For a long time, American families had adopted disabled, HIV-positive, and other severely ill children from Russian orphanages. After the Magnitsky Act was passed, Putin banned the adoption of Russian children by families in the US.[7] As the ban took effect in January 2013, nearly 100,000 Russians protested by marching in the streets of Moscow. "The implementation of the Magnitsky Act made Putin furious," shares Browder. "There's nothing that touches him more profoundly than the idea that the assets that he stole inside Russia can be frozen outside Russia. The fact that the Magnitsky Act exists is an existential threat to his reason for staying in power, which is to steal money."

Russia's then prime minister, Dmitry Medvedev, was so angry that he threatened Browder at the World Economic Forum in Davos, Switzerland. When journalists asked Medvedev about Magnitsky's death, he replied, "It's too bad that Sergei Magnitsky is dead, and Bill Browder is still alive and free."[8]

ooooo

Soon after, the Kremlin launched a robust propaganda attack against Bill Browder.

In March 2013, NTV, a television channel owned by the state-controlled energy company Gazprom, broadcast a film that accused Browder of stealing billions from the International Monetary Fund.[9] The real story on which the accusation was based dates to Russia's financial crisis in 1998, when the country borrowed $4.5 billion from the IMF—money which indeed disappeared. According to the program, it was Browder who took the money.

The fake documentary also accused Browder of being the biggest beneficiary of the death of Edmond Safra, his billionaire former business partner. It further claimed that Browder himself benefited from the death of Sergei Magnitsky, and that Magnitsky hadn't uncovered any crimes, but was instead a crook himself.

Five days after airing the film, Russian officials prosecuted Bill Browder in absentia and Sergei Magnitsky posthumously. The Russian media was filled with images of an empty cage in a courtroom—meant for Browder and Magnitsky. Amnesty International condemned the trial as "deeply sinister," while the European Union's foreign policy chief called it "a revealing illustration of the state of the rule of law in Russia."[10]

In the aftermath of Magnitsky's posthumous trial, a concept that profoundly challenges Western ideas of justice, the Parliamentary Assembly of the Council of Europe (PACE) appointed a special rapporteur to investigate the lawyer's murder. In its subsequent report, PACE concluded that Magnitsky's beating in custody was authorized by Russian officials. "The Kremlin hates these types of reports, just like anything of that sort of multilateral cooperation involving governments: the UN and the Council of Europe," Browder says.

Later in the spring of 2013, the European Parliament recommended that thirty-two Russian officials be sanctioned for their involvement in the Magnitsky case. The recommendation passed without objection. In July 2013, over three years after his death in a Russian prison, a Russian court found Magnitsky guilty of tax evasion.

Browder continued on, telling Magnitsky's story to the world. His aim was to end the impunity of human rights violators not just in Russia, but globally.

BENEFICIARY

The US Treasury published its initial list of eighteen Magnitsky-sanctioned individuals in April 2013.[11] Included were the tax officers in charge of the illegal refunds, the investigator in charge of the Hermitage confiscations, the head of the Butyrka prison, and several judges involved in the fake trials.

The Kremlin reacted the same day by releasing its own sanctions list, which had clearly been prepared in advance.[12] Moscow's list targeted US officials who, according to the Kremlin, had "legalized torture and indefinite detention of prisoners." For example, a retired US general and former commander of the prison at Guantanamo was on the list. The Kremlin also banned US attorneys whom it claimed were involved in the trial of the notorious Russian arms smuggler Viktor Bout, who was sentenced to twenty-five years' imprisonment in the United States.

A year later, in May 2014, the US added twelve more names to the Magnitsky sanctions list.[13] Those included Russian prison officials, tax officials, and the convicted Russian murderer to whom one of the Hermitage companies had been illegally registered.

ooooo

As Magnitsky's name lived on and embarrassed the Putin regime further, a second propaganda piece against Browder was released in November 2014. *Letter M* aired on NTV, the same channel that had shown the first fake documentary. The new film claimed that Bill Browder was an agent of both the CIA and the British foreign intelligence service, MI6, and had conducted a secret mission called Quake in order to "destabilize Russia and Ukraine."[14] The shopworn accusations that Browder had stolen billions from the IMF and was responsible for his business partner's murder were again rehashed. In addition, Browder was now also accused of being behind the death of the Russian oligarch Boris Berezovsky in London in 2013.

To back up these lies, the program presented a wide selection of false evidence. At one point, the film showed a document allegedly printed on CIA letterhead that "proved" Browder was an agent, with the supposed code name of "Solomon." Also, a phony expert, a former French military intelligence agent and a mercenary in Africa, said that he was "100 percent convinced that Browder is a CIA agent and involved in Berezovsky's death."

In order to fight back, in 2015 Browder published a memoir, *Red Notice: A True Story of High Finance, Murder, and One Man's Fight for Justice.* "Red Notice" refers to an alert issued by Interpol when a country asks the police organization to arrest an individual in preparation for extradition.[15] The book was well received and became a bestseller in several countries. Thanks to the book, awareness of Russian government corruption spread internationally.

ooooo

The next serious Russian operation against Browder came directly from Russia's top prosecutor, Yuri Chaika, in December 2015.

Before Chaika's attack against Browder, the well-known Russian opposition activist Alexey Navalny had produced a popular YouTube documentary, under his non-profit Anti-Corruption Foundation, outlining the suspicious connections of Chaika and his two sons to several international luxury properties.[16] The documentary also exposed Chaika as the key official responsible for a variety of illegal corporate raids and takeovers.

Two weeks after the video was released, Browder's phone started ringing constantly. Russian journalists were calling to ask: Had he really done all that? Browder quickly learned that Chaika had written a two-page open letter in the prominent Russian newspaper *Kommersant* in which he claimed that Browder had funded Navalny's documentary. According to Chaika, the documentary was a CIA plot to discredit Russian law enforcement agencies. Chaika also accused Browder of murder and other crimes. "My reaction was that Navalny's film was a fine piece of investigative journalism. I was pretty flattered that they thought I did it, but unfortunately Alexey Navalny gets the full credit," Browder says.

On December 18, 2015, NTV released its third film smearing Browder. Titled "Browder & Co," it followed Chaika's statement that Browder was responsible for Navalny's YouTube documentary. It further stated that the program was produced in cooperation with "Browder's connections to the CIA and MI6." Browder was also accused of attempting to manipulate Gazprom and NTV through ownership of Gazprom shares.

∞∞∞∞

In April 2016, an international consortium of journalists operating under the Organized Crime and Corruption Reporting Project (OCCRP) published a massive investigation of tax havens throughout the world, based on an insider leak. The documents, known as the Panama Papers, revealed information about tax evasion and money laundering in several countries. It also included new details about President Putin's financial arrangements.

The report revealed that Putin's best friend since childhood, Sergei Roldugin, a cellist by profession, had received $2 billion in the form of loans that were subsequently forgiven.[17] "In other words, Roldugin is just a name in which Putin keeps his money, because Putin can't keep it under his own. I think that he's a trustee of Putin, one of many trustees," Browder says. The investigation showed that at least $800,000 from the crime against Hermitage had been paid directly to Roldugin's bank account in Switzerland. The revelation was a breakthrough. "Effectively, Putin was the beneficiary of the crime that led to Magnitsky's murder," Browder shares. "That is the reason why Russia is so interested in the Magnitsky case." It is also likely the reason why Russian police were never interested in tracing the financial fraud in the first place.

But the authorities in other countries have followed the trail of Russian tax money through a maze of banks and shell companies, identifying many of the beneficiaries. In total, law enforcement agencies outside Russia have found and frozen at least $10 million connected to the crimes Magnitsky exposed. Money has been discovered in Switzerland, France, Monaco, and Luxembourg. Some of the money was traced to the account of the wife of Moscow's deputy mayor. Other funds were found in the account of the husband of the head of the Moscow tax office, who was originally in charge of paying the illicit tax refunds to the stolen companies.

The US Department of Justice managed to trace $14 million of the money to New York City.[18] Less than three months after the Moscow tax office transferred the $230 million in illegal tax refunds, several installments landed in a Swiss bank account owned by a company called Prevezon Holdings. Prevezon is owned by Denis Katsyv, a Russian businessman with family links to Russia's top leadership. Katsyv's father, Pyotr Katsyv, is the former minister of transport for Moscow and reportedly one of the wealthiest government officials in Russia. Before the money reached the junior Katsyv's company's bank account, it was laundered through the bank accounts of several shell companies in the British Virgin Islands, Estonia, and Moldova. In 2012, the Swiss police froze $7 million in Katsyv's Swiss bank account.[19] In September 2013, the Department of Justice froze Prevezon's assets connected to Hermitage.[20]

The Katsyv's lawyer is a Russian woman named Natalia Veselnitskaya, who has represented the family for many years.[21]

She has also represented many Russian state-owned companies. Early in her career, she worked in the prosecutor's office in Moscow. Veselnitskaya has close personal ties to the Russian government. She was once married to Alexander Mitusov, the former vice premier and deputy minister of transportation. Mitusov's supervisor was Pyotr Katsyv.[22]

In addition to being represented by Veselnitskaya, Katsyv's company, Prevezon, is represented by the law firm BakerHostetler in the United States.[23] Advised by both Veselnitskaya and BakerHostetler, Katsyv denied the money-laundering charges. The case ended up in a settlement, with Katsyv paying nearly $6 million in fines to the US government.[24]

While advising Katsyv, Veselnitskaya wasn't a household name, and was mostly able to keep her work out of the headlines.

That would change dramatically.

BEHIND THE SCENES

Soon after the OCCRP published the Panama Papers in the spring of 2016, the Kremlin's attacks against Bill Browder intensified.

In April 2016, Russia's Channel One aired a documentary that purported to present evidence of Browder's alleged conspiracy with the CIA and the Russian opposition. According to the "documentary," the CIA had recruited Browder in 1986, and cultivated Alexey Navalny as his agent for a joint project to destroy the Russian regime. The main "evidence" offered in the program was a computer allegedly found in Ukraine, which after decryption supposedly exposed a chain of "instructions" sent by the CIA to Browder, which were then forwarded by Browder to Navalny. However, the fabricated messages were so clumsily put together that, based on the dates marked on them, Browder seemed to send the instructions to Navalny three years after Navalny seemed to acknowledge receiving them.

The film also argued that the only person with the motivation to kill Magnitsky was Browder, backed by the CIA. The program falsely claimed that right before his death, Magnitsky was planning to testify *against* Browder and expose his alleged tax fraud. The evidence for this was a bogus email chain, "hacked from the CIA," which "proved" it was the agency that had orchestrated Magnitsky's death in prison.[25] The film also presented fabricated evidence of Browder's and Magnitsky's alleged tax evasion and claimed they had hired mentally disabled Russians as fake executives of Hermitage companies. Finally, to add drama, the production team traveled to London to film the Hermitage office, declaring themselves victims when Browder's staff called the police.

After the film aired, Channel One staged a ninety-minute studio debate. Most of the guests agreed that Browder was indeed a criminal. One guest, the then deputy chairman of the Russian parliament, compared Browder to intestinal tapeworms. "On both sides of the debate, five people competed with each other," Browder recalls. "One side said that Browder was an asshole, and the other side said that Browder was a real fucking asshole."

Russian state television will frequently run stories about the alleged crimes of opposition figures, such as Pussy Riot or Navalny, shortly before a criminal investigation is opened against them. True to form, right after the Channel One program aired, a new criminal case was opened, investigating Browder's alleged part in Magnitsky's death.

Simultaneously, an old-school defamation campaign was launched against Browder. Enormous billboards depicting him walking a dog with Navalny's face were hung in front of the US embassy in Moscow. Another massive poster was affixed to a wall near Navalny's office. It depicted Browder holding Navalny on the deck of a ship in the same way that Leonardo DiCaprio held Kate Winslet in the iconic scene from *Titanic*.

ooooo

At the end of April 2016, another Russian operation was launched, with the dual aim of destroying Browder's credibility globally and derailing the Magnitsky Act. At the core of the campaign was again a propaganda film, this time aimed at an international audience.

The movie was directed by the Russian filmmaker Andrei Nekrasov and titled *The Magnitsky Act—Behind the Scenes*.[26] Nekrasov had originally pitched the movie as a "freedom of speech project" to his funders in Norway. Browder had initially trusted the filmmaker and consented to be interviewed. But the end result turned out to be completely different from what Nekrasov had described to Browder.

The movie was scheduled to premiere on April 27, 2016, in an exclusive setting in Brussels: the European Parliament. Influential members of parliament were invited to the premiere, which was to include a panel discussion and a cocktail reception afterward. The organizer and host of the screening was Heidi Hautala, the Finnish member of the European Parliament and a close friend of Nekrasov.

Magnitsky's family was not invited.

A week before the scheduled screening, Browder was alerted to the film's content. He learned that Nekrasov presented as facts the same lies that the Kremlin and the criminals involved in Magnitsky's murder had repeated for years, including that Magnitsky had not been beaten in custody; he was not a lawyer; he and Browder had stolen $230 million from Russia; the Hermitage companies were sold legitimately; and that no credible institution had conducted independent investigations of Magnitsky's case. Instead, Nekrasov claimed that he had investigated the case thoroughly himself and had proven that Browder was a con man. He called the whole story about Magnitsky's torture and murder a "perfect hoax."[27] "That was Nekrasov's spin," Browder explains. "He used my voice to legitimize the first hour, and then he says,

'I'm such a master investigator, I found holes in the story, and it's one big hole, and Browder is lying to everybody.' And Nekrasov put a movie together and was about to show it in the European Parliament."

Browder reached out to the film's production company, sent them accurate information, and threatened a defamation suit if they distributed the movie. Sergei Magnitsky's mother sent a letter to the European Parliament stating that the lies about her son in the film could easily be refuted by dozens of original documents.

While the screening did go forward, only a few people showed up. But two individuals who had been named by Magnitsky were there: Pavel Karpov, and Andrey Pavlov. Pavlov is the lawyer for Dmitry Klyuev, the owner of Russia's Universal Savings Bank—which was involved in the stolen $230 million—at the time of the fraud. In April 2021, Kluyev was one of fourteen Russians sanctioned in the United Kingdom under its version of the Magnitsky Act.[28] Six Russian television stations were also present.

However, right before the film was scheduled to start, it was abruptly canceled.

Following the cancellation, the Russian media interviewed several people in the near-empty auditorium. One of them was Natalia Veselnitskaya. The Russian news agency Tass stated that Veselnitskaya was one of the organizers of the premiere.[29] In this capacity, she said that the organizers had received a letter from Browder threatening them with a lawsuit—because, according to Veselnitskaya, the film would have demonstrated "another side of the story," different from "Browder's version"[30] presented to Western audiences. Russia's TV5 even claimed that Veselnitskaya was one of the individuals who gave Nekrasov the "real proofs and records of testimony" that formed the foundation of the movie.[31] Veselnitskaya later posted an update on Facebook, claiming that Browder had "spat on EU values and [that] this will come back on him like a tsunami." Another of her posts revealed that she was traveling with a delegation that included Pavel Karpov.

The Russian media spun a scandal out of the cancellation, reporting that it breached "freedom of speech" and proved the existence of censorship in the West. The international media covered the cancellation, too. Many journalists, without prior knowledge of the Magnitsky case, described a "freedom of speech controversy" over a canceled documentary in the heart of the European Union. Segments of the Norwegian press picked up the narrative of a rich businessman using his connections and wealth to "restrict freedom of speech." "A Norwegian human rights activist said that people liked the story where a bad rich guy lied to everyone, and then this convincing, middle-aged, gray-haired artist exposes the lies," says Browder. "Even though I was trying to stop the defamation of a dead person. To me that is the most shocking part."

After Nekrasov and the Norwegian company which produced the film created a hostile media environment around Browder, many Norwegian politicians were afraid to be associated with him. "Back then I couldn't lobby for the Magnitsky Act in Norway," says Browder. "It's a shame; Norway is one place in which Russian propaganda has worked."

Sergei Magnitsky's widow wrote letters to European television stations that were scheduled to air the movie. As a result, stations in Germany and France canceled their showings, while many others asked for clarifications from the filmmaker. Later, however, when the movie was screened in Washington, DC, and Moscow, Nekrasov went on a media tour, marketing his "investigations" on Sputnik, RT, and other propaganda outlets. He was also interviewed as an expert on the Magnitsky case in the culture section of *Helsingin Sanomat*. There, Nekrasov repeated the same things he had said in the Russian state media: that he was pondering whether "the European Union [was] nowadays North Korea, as there [was] no freedom of speech to present [his] documentary."[32]

UNREGISTERED FOREIGN AGENTS

In Washington, DC, Russia launched an influence operation against Bill Browder and an updated version of the Magnitsky Act, known as The Global Magnitsky Human Rights Accountability Act. The bill had passed the US Senate in December 2015 and was about to go to the House Foreign Affairs Committee. Browder told me that, "For Putin, it was really upsetting that Magnitsky's name was put on a piece of global legislation. It's insulting to Russians that Magnitsky is the symbol of asset freezes, so they came up with a hugely expensive lobbying campaign in Washington."

Nekrasov's movie was part of that campaign, which also included lawyers, lobbyists, and PR firms, who contacted legislators to try and convince them to push back against the proposed law and to erase Magnitsky's name from the bill. The hub used to coordinate the campaign was a Washington-based organization called Human Rights Accountability Global Initiative Foundation (HRAGI), which had been newly registered in February 2016. The goal of the foundation was an exchange: if the Magnitsky legislation was rejected, then the right of American families to adopt Russian children could be restored.

The foundation's website is no longer running, but it can still be found in online archives. HRAGI claimed that its mission was to "strengthen US–Russia relations." It also appeared to collect donations through its site. Later investigations showed that HRAGI was funded by Russian friends of Denis Katsyv and that Natalia Veselnitskaya had helped to oversee its creation.[33]

Browder's team discovered that a man named Rinat Akhmetshin was a lobbyist for HRAGI. According to US officials, Akhmetshin—who holds dual Russian and American citizenship—is a former intelligence officer with the Soviet military. In April 2016, HRAGI paid Akhmetshin $10,000 to lobby against the proposed Magnitsky legislation.[34] One of his lobbying targets was US congressman Dana Rohrabacher, the then chairman of the House Foreign Affairs Subcommittee on Europe, Eurasia, and Emerging Threats, and a well-known supporter of President Putin. In May, Akhmetshin and another lobbyist, a former congressman, met with Rohrabacher. They asked him to delay the Global Magnitsky Act and remove Magnitsky's name from the bill.

The previous month, Rohrabacher had traveled to Moscow, where he met with representatives of the Russian government. At least one of the people he met with was on the Magnitsky sanctions list and a close aide to President Putin.[35] While there, Rohrabacher was given material related to Browder that was marked "confidential." The material had originated with the Russian prosecutor general, Yuri Chaika.

The Daily Beast got hold of the letter given to Rohrabacher, which included the same false accusations that had been presented in Nekrasov's movie and many other Russian programs, as well as in Chaika's open letter, stating that, "Changing attitudes related to Magnitsky in the Congress . . . might pose favorable consequences on the Russian side."[36] Moscow also provided Rohrabacher with a copy of Nekrasov's film.

After his meetings with the Russian government officials and Akhmetshin, Rohrabacher proposed removing Magnitsky's name from the Act—just as he had been advised to do—and pushed for a screening of Nekrasov's movie in Congress, as well as a hearing to question Browder.[37] After all his initiatives were rejected, his staff scheduled a screening elsewhere in Washington, DC.

In mid-June, Nekrasov's movie was screened at the Newseum, a now-defunct news museum not far from Capitol Hill. A handful of congressional aides and two State Department officials were present at the screening. Akhmetshin was there, together with Natalia Veselnitskaya.[38] Radio Free Europe asked Akhmetshin about the funding of the event, which it estimated had cost at least $12,500. Akhmetshin replied that HRAGI would take care of the bill.[39] In fact, the operation had been paid for by Katsyv himself.

Again, Russian officials were activated to smear Browder publicly. Foreign Minister Sergey Lavrov said that "the death of Sergei Magnitsky was all the result of a huge scam by Browder, who is an unscrupulous swindler."[40] Prosecutor General Chaika declared that the film was "a guilty verdict for Browder."[41]

Natalia Veselnitskaya and her client Prevezon also hired lawyers, public affairs specialists, and former journalists for the smear campaign. The paid staff were tasked with spreading disinformation about both Browder and Magnitsky to members of Congress and the US media. One of those hired by Veselnitskaya was Glenn Simpson. Simpson is the founder of Fusion GPS, the company behind the infamous Trump dossier, which supposedly revealed details about the future president's sexual activities in a Russian hotel room.

But US law requires foreign agents and lobbyists promoting the interests of foreign countries to register and identify themselves. Browder discovered that a herd of Russia-connected lobbyists were trying to intervene in the US legislative process, but that none of them had registered. In July 2016, Hermitage filed a complaint against HRAGI, Rinat Akhmetshin, Glenn Simpson, Natalia Veselnitskaya, and six other individuals to the US Department of Justice, accusing them of violating lobbying regulations.[42] "The Russians take advantage, and they find people who are ready to abuse the laws, as we found out in Washington," says Browder.

∞∞∞

While the foreign influence operations against the Magnitsky Act were unfolding on Capitol Hill, the internet trolls were hard at work as well. An online platform called We the People was a project of the Obama administration that allowed American citizens to present their ideas for legislative changes. Many proposals on the platform eventually became law. At one point, a petition was created on the site demanding that Congress repeal the Magnitsky Act. The petition stated that the Act was "adopted as a result of lobbying by two frauds (Browder and Khodorkovsky)" and "it discredits the US legislature." The petition quickly gathered over 200,000 signatures.[43] "It was totally generated from Russia," Browder says. Ultimately, the petition went nowhere.

Finally, in December 2016, the US government passed the *Global Magnitsky Human Rights Accountability Act,* which allowed for the sanctioning of officials engaged in human rights violations anywhere in the world, not just in Russia. Following that, many other countries became interested in passing their own Magnitsky Acts. Estonia was the first to adopt a version of the bill. The following year, Magnitsky Acts were passed in the United Kingdom, Lithuania, and Canada. After the law unanimously passed in Canada, Russia sent yet another Red Notice about Bill Browder to Interpol.

A MASTER MANIPULATOR

More details of the Kremlin's attempts to influence Rohrabacher and derail the Magnitsky Act surfaced during the summer of 2017. The congressman admitted to the news site The Hill that during the previous year he had received "derogatory information" about the Magnitsky Act from the chief prosecutor in Moscow."[44] In the aftermath, one of Rohrabacher's aides, the staff director of the Foreign Affairs Committee, was fired.[45] In 2016, the aide had met with the anti-Magnitsky lobbyists hired by Natalia Veselnitskaya.

On July 7, 2017, major news broke. The *New York Times* reported that Veselnitskaya had met with Donald Trump's presidential campaign the previous summer. The initial reports stated that the meeting was organized after Donald Trump Jr.

was promised "incriminating" material about the Democratic presidential candidate, Hillary Clinton, from Russian sources. It soon emerged that during the meeting at Trump Tower, Veselnitskaya and Akhmetshin, who was also present, had specifically addressed the need to repeal the Magnitsky Act.

At first, Veselnitskaya denied any connection to the Russian government and told the press that she had acted "independently."[46] But when speaking to RT, she gave a very different answer. She accused Browder of masterminding a disinformation campaign as well as manipulating the mass media, and said she had wanted to inform Trump Jr. about the businessman.[47]

ooooo

After Veselnitskaya's high-profile meeting was exposed, Browder was invited to appear before the Senate Judiciary Committee. In testimony given in late July 2017, he described Veselnitskaya's role in the campaign to influence congress to repeal the Magnitsky legislation.[48] Browder named everyone who had participated in the dissemination of false information about him and Magnitsky, adding that, "While they were conducting operations in Washington, DC, at no time did they indicate that they were acting on behalf of Russian government interests, nor did they file disclosures required under the Foreign Agent Registration Act." Immediately after Browder's testimony, Russia issued a Red Notice about him to Interpol for the sixth time. Browder briefly lost his US visa, but it was restored when Interpol identified the alert as politically motivated.

Veselnitskaya later provided written testimony to the judiciary committee as part of its investigation into the meeting at Trump Tower. She wrote that the adoption of the Magnitsky Act was the result of "years of anti-Russian sentiments lobbying and arousing hatred towards Russians and Russia."[49] She also repeated the false claim that Magnitsky's story had never been independently and professionally verified in the United States. Veselnitskaya again attacked Browder, calling him a criminal who had renounced his US citizenship in order to avoid taxes.[50]

Her testimony was notable in that it proved that Veselnitskaya had been investigating Browder and his activities in astonishing detail for years. She was intimately familiar with his public presentations, had gone through all his speeches, and quoted extensively from documents on Browder's website.

The core of Veselnitskaya's statement included the same talking points that the Russian officials connected to the killing of Magnitsky had spread systematically for years. She also added a layer of political commentary to her testimony, stating that, "the passing of Magnitsky Act had undermined all relations" between the US and Russia.[51]

THE ASSIGNMENT

In August 2017, the Senate Judiciary Committee questioned Glenn Simpson about his work with Fusion GPS and his connections with Natalia Veselnitskaya, Rinat Akhmetshin, and others who had lobbied as unregistered agents for the repeal of the Magnitsky Act.

The hearing confirmed two things: that Simpson had been paid by BakerHostetler—the same law firm that had defended Denis Katsyv's Prevezon Holdings in its multimillion-dollar money-laundering trial connected to Magnitsky's investigations—to search for compromising material on Browder; and that Simpson hadn't bothered to research his clients. Simpson claimed to be unaware of Katsyv's background or who his father, Pyotr Katsyv, was. He also told the committee that his company, Fusion GPS, was retained by BakerHostetler, which in turn was working for Veselnitskaya's client Prevezon.

BakerHostetler had paid Simpson to investigate Browder's business practices and activities in Russia, as well as his alleged "history of avoiding taxes."[52] Simpson did that primarily by examining documents provided to him by the law firm and browsing public records. He admitted to having cooperated with several lawyers in the "get Browder" project. Simpson told the committee that he had found evidence of Browder's alleged tax evasion during his time conducting business in Russia. He had asked Browder for more information, but when Browder rejected his request, Simpson started initiating subpoenas in 2014, the goal of which were to compel Browder to speak about his business while under oath in the US. The subpoenas had been difficult to serve, Simpson shared. The final attempt to serve Browder was filmed and put up on YouTube. The clip showed an underling talking aggressively to Browder, following him to his car, and Browder escaping.

Simpson denied that he was working against Browder on behalf of BakerHostetler to undermine the Magnitsky Act per se. But he admitted that the law firm had instructed Fusion GPS to share its research on Browder with Rinat Akhmetshin, who then lobbied against the Act in Congress. Simpson stated that he didn't know that Akhmetshin was registered as a lobbyist with HRAGI. (In December 2017, Special Counsel Robert Mueller began looking into the activities of HRAGI. In an investigation of its finances, Bloomberg News found that Denis Katsyv had donated $150,000 to the foundation and persuaded Russian business associates of his to donate considerable sums as well.)[53] Simpson argued that Fusion GPS couldn't have violated US legislation governing registration requirements for foreign agents because it was hired by an American law firm.

Simpson also shared his assessments of Veselnitskaya. According to him, she wasn't a big political player in the Kremlin, and that "the jury is out" regarding whether she had connections to the Russian government.[54] He said he was stunned to read of her meeting with Donald Trump Jr.[55]

"I THINK WE'RE NOT GOING TO ANSWER THAT ONE"

Later in 2017 it was Rinat Akhmetshin's turn to be questioned by the Senate Judiciary Committee, which wanted clarification about his possible connections to Russian intelligence services as well as his meeting with the Trump team. Akhmetshin denied ever working with Soviet or Russian military intelligence. Instead, he said that his Soviet army unit had supported the intelligence unit and that he had served as a sergeant.[56] In an Associated Press interview the same year, he said that he had served in a Soviet counterintelligence unit, but had never formally been trained as a spy.[57]

Akhmetshin also presented his version of the Trump meeting to the committee. He claimed that Veselnitskaya had invited him to join on short notice, and that they hadn't rehearsed what they were going to say beforehand. He stated that he had simply advised Veselnitskaya to start the conversation with friendly small talk and congratulate the Trump campaign for winning the Republican primaries.

Akhmetshin also said that Veselnitskaya brought her own documents to the meeting, which alleged that a hedge fund run by Bill Browder had committed tax violations and transferred $880 million from Russia. According to Akhmetshin, the hedge fund had also been involved in hiring mentally handicapped people in order to claim tax cuts. He guessed that Veselnitskaya wanted to "expose Browder's role to Trump Jr." The committee asked whether the information in the documents was relevant to HRAGI's work. "No. It's relevant just to show that the person who is behind this Magnitsky law is a con man and a fraudster and criminal. But other than that, no," Akhmetshin answered.

Akhmetshin said that he had also spoken about Russia–US relations during the meeting, which he said could deteriorate based on a lie, referring to the Magnitsky Act. "Don Jr. said: Come back and see us when we win," Akhmetshin told the committee.

The hearing also focused on a dinner attended by Veselnitskaya, Congressman Rohrabacher, and others at the Capitol Hill Club in 2016, as well as a meeting between Akhmetshin and Rohrabacher in Berlin. Akhmetshin claimed that Rohrabacher had asked whether he knew "what's happening with the Prevezon case and Browder." Akhmetshin said that he hadn't asked the congressman to do anything about the Prevezon case "because there's a separation of powers, and the prophet Muhammad couldn't help Prevezon, even if they wanted to. So the suggestion I was ever doing something for Prevezon is absurd and inaccurate."

The meeting in Berlin had been covered by the journalist Michael Weiss in an article for CNN.[58] Without providing evidence, Akhmetshin hinted to the committee that Weiss might have been compensated by Browder for that and other articles, which wasn't true. He cited unspecified "analysis and research" suggesting an "improper relationship" between Browder and Weiss. When asked for clarification, Akhmetshin's lawyer intervened and said "I think we're not going to answer that one."

Akhmetshin also denied having any relationships with Russian officials. He did, however, disclose that in 2016 he had met Prosecutor General Yuri Chaika at Denis Katsyv's birthday party. Akhmetshin described Katsyv as a "nice man."

LEGAL WARFARE

The US Treasury added thirteen more names to the Magnitsky sanctions list in December 2017.[59] One of them was Andrey Pavlov, the lawyer who was one of the suspected architects of the scheme against Hermitage. Another was Artem Chaika, the son of the Russian Prosecutor General.[60]

On Russian television a few days later, Yuri Chaika smeared Browder as the leader of a transnational group that he claimed faced prosecution for tax and other financial crimes committed in Russia and abroad. RT followed up by alleging that Browder was suspected of large-scale money laundering and that he had already been sentenced to ten years in prison in Russia for tax evasion. Both Chaika and Russian Foreign Minister Lavrov gave further interviews that continued to smear Browder.

A few days later, Browder was again sentenced to prison in Russia, in absentia. This time, it was nine years for tax evasion and deliberate bankruptcy.[61] In addition, Russian court documents had surfaced with new allegations: Browder was accused of being connected to the murders of three Russian citizens who had contributed to the tax fraud discovered by Magnitsky.[62]

Browder says that many of the boundaries between exercising freedom of speech and spreading libel have been crossed by several Russian entities and the people who work for them. But he has never been interested in suing those who disseminate defamatory claims about him. Instead, he uses what he considers to be more damaging actions, such as pushing for court cases against the perpetrators benefitting from the crimes Magnitsky exposed, and exposing their money-laundering networks.

ooooo

More twists in the Trump Tower affair occurred in April 2018 when NBC and the *New York Times* revealed that Veselnitskaya's connections to the Kremlin were much closer than she had initially disclosed.

The lawyer's emails, which had been obtained by an organization run by pro-democracy activist Mikhail Khodorkovsky, showed that since 2014 she had been an informant reporting to Yuri Chaika. Veselnitskaya herself admitted that starting in 2013, she had been "actively communicating"[63] with the office of the Russian prosecutor general.

In March 2018, Veselnitskaya was questioned by the US Senate Intelligence Committee. In an interview, she shared that the committee had asked her about the Trump Tower meeting and the so-called Trump dossier.[64]

∞∞∞∞∞

In the summer of 2018, Rinat Akhmetshin filed a civil complaint against Browder, claiming that the businessman had falsely and knowingly told the media that Akhmetshin was a Russian spy and intelligence asset, as well as tweeting that he was a GRU officer. He demanded a minimum of $1 million in damages. In fact, Browder had tweeted news articles which discussed Akhmetshin's connections with Russian intelligence services.

Akhmetshin further claimed that Browder's accusations had caused him significant reputational and economic damage and that he had lost a multimillion-dollar contract because the potential client found him too "radioactive." "No one in Washington seeking assistance on Capitol Hill will hire a lobbyist suspected of being a Russian spy, which is a serious crime against the United States," Akhmetshin wrote in his complaint.[65] He also said he had suffered emotional harm due to Browder's statements.

The District Court in Washington, DC dismissed the case in 2019. Akhmetshin then appealed to the Circuit Court, where the case is still pending. "We're waiting for the outcome," Browder shared in the spring of 2021. "At the end of the day, he's not going to win, it's just a very expensive exercise. It's hard for me to imagine that he's paying for this himself."[66]

∞∞∞∞∞

In August 2020, the Senate Intelligence Committee published a detailed report on Russian active measures and influence operations against the United States. The report was unambiguous in its assessment that at least two participants in the Trump

Tower meeting, Natalia Veselnitskaya and Rinat Akhmetshin, had significant connections to the Russian government, including the country's intelligence services.[67] "I am in legal warfare against Russian foreign services," Browder says. "In order to win them, you have to be more persistent than these people, who are lazy and don't do their job."

AN "INTERESTING PROPOSAL"

As a result of Special Counsel Robert Mueller's investigation into Russian meddling in the presidential election, in July 2018 twelve GRU officers were indicted for allegedly conspiring to hack the networks, computers, and communications of the Democratic National Committee during the election campaign two years earlier.[68]

Three days after the indictment, Vladimir Putin and Donald Trump met for a summit in Helsinki, Finland. They talked through interpreters, without aides present. The summit resulted in an international scandal when Trump, who had earlier described Mueller's Russia investigation as a "Democrat hoax," stated during the press conference after the meeting that he trusted Putin when the Russian leader said that his country hadn't interfered in the 2016 presidential election.

Putin used the press conference, and the attention of the global media, to go on the attack against Bill Browder. First, Putin responded to Mueller's indictment of the twelve Russian intelligence officers by referring to the treaty between the US and Russia concerning the processing of suspected criminals, which dates back to 1999. Putin said that Mueller could have sent an official request to the Russian authorities, who in turn could have interrogated the individuals Mueller had identified. According to Putin, Russia could have also permitted representatives of the United States to be present at the interrogations.

But Putin had a condition: Russia should also be granted

the opportunity to question American officials, including US intelligence officials whom Russia believed to have connections to illegal actions in its territory. The Russian president named Browder as an example. "Browder's business associates earned over $1.5 billion in Russia without ever paying taxes, neither in Russia or the US," Putin declared in the hall of the Finnish Presidential Palace.[69]

Putin claimed that the $1.5 billion had been earned illegally. In addition, he said that Russia had reason to believe that American intelligence officers had guided the transactions. Repeating the accusations Veselnitskaya had shared with Donald Trump Jr., Putin added that a "huge amount of money, $400 million, was sent as a contribution to the campaign of Hillary Clinton." The next day, Russian prosecutors corrected Putin's statement, saying that Browder had donated $400,000 to the Democratic Party, not $400 million as Putin had said.[70] In fact, Browder hadn't donated anything.

President Trump reacted to Putin's proposal to question Americans by calling it "interesting." The White House press secretary said that the president would consider allowing Russian investigators to question the individuals.[71] Ultimately, the US Senate rejected the idea.

Russian prosecutors also published a list of Americans whom they said should be questioned about "connections with the criminal case against Bill Browder."[72] The list included the former US ambassador to Moscow, a Homeland Security official, and former and current State Department officials.[73] One of the officials had helped Browder push the Magnitsky legislation in 2011 and 2012 in his then position as president of the US-based human rights organization Freedom House.[74]

Several news outlets interviewed Browder about Putin's attack. He told Fox News that Putin was "obsessed" with him because he was the one responsible for getting the Magnitsky Act passed, which went after the assets of kleptocrats and crooks and human rights violators, like the Russian president.[75]

But Putin had made one crucial mistake: Browder was not a US citizen, and therefore could not be interrogated by the Russian government based on the *Treaty on Mutual Legal Assistance in Criminal Matters between Russia and the United States.*

BAIT

Rinat Akhmetshin remained in the headlines. In early 2019, BuzzFeed published a report showing that he had received more than $400,000 in cash in his bank account before and after meeting with the Trump campaign team.[76] In addition, he had also been wired large amounts by Denis Katsyv and other wealthy Russians who opposed the Magnitsky Act. Some of the transfers were unexplained, and Akhmetshin hadn't reported all of them to the lobbying register. As the Buzzfeed reporters knocked on Akhmetshin's door looking for interview, he told them to "get the fuck out of here, okay?"

At the same time, Robert Mueller was finalizing his report on Russian meddling in the 2016 presidential election. The media, politicians from both parties, and conspiracy theorists eagerly awaited Mueller's conclusions. Over the course of the investigation, several people connected to Trump or Russia had already been indicted. A few, like Paul Manafort, had been convicted.

But the big question was still open: Had the President of the United States colluded with a foreign government? In March 2019, Mueller delivered his confidential report to the US Department of Justice. Attorney General William Barr produced a four-page summary of the report, which declared that the Trump campaign had not colluded intentionally or knowingly with the Russian government's election-interference operations. But, interference operations had definitely taken place. Mueller had also investigated President Trump's possible obstruction of justice.

According to Barr's summary, "The Special Counsel states that 'while this report does not conclude that the President committed a crime, it also does not exonerate him.'"[77]

Trump supporters and Republicans celebrated, while many Democrats rejected Barr's summary. Trump tweeted out his own view, claiming he had been completely exonerated. The media demanded that the full report be quickly released.

Two days after Barr's summary was published, Rinat Akhmetshin stepped back on stage—even though his name hadn't been mentioned in the summary. He claimed in an interview that the Mueller investigation had resulted in financial setbacks for *him*, as well as making him the victim of groundless personal attacks. "I'm happy and relieved, as the investigation has now come to an end," Akhmetshin said.[78] His statement created the illusion that *all* investigations of him were over, with further hearings unnecessary, and that reports of his possible misconduct sent by bank investigators to Mueller and the Department of Justice were groundless.

Finally, on April 18, 2019, the complete 448-page final report by Special Counsel Mueller was published, still partly redacted. The report described in detail the Russian "active measures," the political warfare carried out by Russian intelligence services against the US election through social media and hacking. It also shed light on emails and other communications sent by Russian diplomats, spies, and cover identities to Trump's team, as well as the campaign's responses to the Russian proposals.

The list of the Kremlin's attempts to push its favored candidate as the president of the world's only superpower was astonishing. For their part, Trump's team was documented to have welcomed all help from Russian entities, without asking questions. However, Mueller didn't find evidence showing that candidate or President Trump or his team had coordinated criminally with the Kremlin or its associates.

The Trump campaign team's secret meeting with Natalia Veselnitskaya and Rinat Akhmetshin in Trump Tower on June 9, 2016 was reconstructed in detail. The meeting had been initiated by an email sent from the Trump family's Russian business partner to Donald Trump Jr. "The Crown prosecutor of Russia . . . offered to provide the Trump campaign with some official documents and information that would incriminate Hillary and her dealings with Russia and would be very useful to your father. This is obviously very high level and sensitive information but is part of Russia and its government's support for Mr. Trump," the email read.[79]

Donald Trump, Jr. responded a few minutes later: "If it's what you say I love it." This reveals that the younger Trump was aware that "high level and sensitive information" was coming from the Russian government to help his father. Trump Jr. was further briefed that the information would be delivered by a lawyer traveling from Moscow.

Fully aware of all that, Trump Jr. invited his inner circle, including his sister Ivanka's husband, Jared Kushner, and campaign manager Paul Manafort, to listen to the "information" from Moscow. But this was something he wanted kept secret, as he forwarded the details about the meeting under the subject line "FW: Russia – Clinton – private and confidential."

The people who organized the meeting on behalf of Veselnitskaya gave Mueller conflicting accounts of their agenda. One of them claimed that the intent was to discuss the Magnitsky legislation, while another claimed Veselnitskaya wanted to provide negative information about Hillary Clinton. The invented story about Clinton appeared to be the bait to get the venal Trump campaign team to open the doors to Trump Tower.

When the meeting actually took place, the main themes proved to be Bill Browder's alleged crimes, and lobbying against the Magnitsky legislation.

IT CANNOT BE RULED OUT

In spite of Akmetshin's testimony to the contrary, the influence operation targeting Trump and his circle had been well-designed and thought out from the beginning.

On June 9, 2016, Natalia Veselnitskaya had invited Akhmetshin to lunch—which was also attended by a Russian translator and two other individuals—where they discussed the agenda for the upcoming meeting with the Trump team. According to the Mueller report, "Veselnitskaya showed Akhmetshin a document alleging financial misconduct by Bill Browder . . . and political donations [from Browder] to the Democratic party." After finishing their lunch, the group headed to Trump Tower on Fifth Avenue. In a conference room in the fifty-eight-story building, they implemented their plan.

Trump's insiders were told the story about Browder and the Magnitsky Act. (In the summer of 2016, the Global Magnitsky Act was still proceeding though the US Congress. At least in theory, it could still be changed, or stopped.) This time, a new element was introduced—that Trump's opponent, Hillary Clinton, had financially benefited from Browder's alleged crimes. The Trump team heard from their Russian visitors that companies connected to Browder had evaded taxes in Russia and the United States and participated in money laundering. The profits had then been donated to Clinton's presidential campaign through Cyprus.

Donald Trump Jr. reminded the visitors that his father was still a private citizen, but he also asked to receive more detailed information about the alleged funneling of money to Clinton. When Veselnitskaya couldn't provide any, Kushner lost his temper and sent an iMessage to Manafort: "waste of time." Kushner also sent a message to his secretaries, asking them to call him, in order to provide him with an excuse to leave the meeting early.

In her Senate testimony, Veselnitskaya stated that the meeting wasn't an attempt to build connections to the Trump campaign. On another occasion, she said the meeting was of a personal nature, and that she wanted to warn Trump Jr., "a friend of my good acquaintance's son," about the "criminal nature of manipulation and interference with the legislative activities of the US Congress," referring to the pending passage of the Global Magnitsky Act. But none of the other participants recalled Veselnitskaya mentioning congress during the meeting.

Mueller's team tried to determine whether candidate Trump had advance knowledge of the meeting or its connections to Russia, but couldn't find evidence of that.

Donald Trump delayed his participation in the Mueller investigation for a year. When he finally testified, he claimed that he didn't have any recollection or record of the matter; nor could he say precisely whether he had been in New York or Trump Tower that day. He said that he could have been there, at least for part of the time. His calendar showed a variety of calls and meetings scheduled for that week, but he didn't know whether the entries were correct, although he didn't have a reason to suspect they weren't.

But one of the witnesses stated that Trump Jr. had told his father about the meeting, leaving the connection to Russia unmentioned. That witness was Trump's former trusted lawyer and "fixer," Michael Cohen, who in 2019 was sentenced to prison for misconduct benefiting Trump's election campaign, which he admitted in court.

ooooo

Mueller also looked into a twist related to the Browder smears.

President Trump had learned in advance that an article about the June 9 meeting was about to be published in the *New York Times*. The then White House press secretary, Hope Hicks, had advised the president to disclose the meeting agenda to the *Times* reporter who was covering the story. Hicks told the Mueller investigators that at first the president had asked her not to give any comment to the press, which she had found odd.

Later the same day, the president asked Hicks what in fact had been discussed in the Trump Tower meeting. Hicks replied that she had been told that it was about "Russian adoption."

"Then just say that," the president directed.

Trump Jr. drafted a press statement, which Hicks wanted to update with a detailed description of the meeting. But the president demanded that the press statement not be filed, as "it said too much." Again, the president urged Hicks to say only that Trump Jr. had had a short meeting "about Russian adoption."

Hicks once more advised Trump Jr. to keep the statement brief. But Trump Jr. didn't approve of the draft she sent him. He wanted to add the word "primarily" to the assertion that the meeting participants discussed Russian adoption because, he texted, "They started with some Hillary thing which was bs and some other nonsense which we shot down fast."

"I think that's right too but boss man worried it invites a lot of questions," Hicks texted Trump Jr. back.

Finally, a brief, edited statement was sent to the *New York Times*, which didn't disclose the names of the participants, or their talking points smearing Browder. Nor was the discussion about trying to influence the Magnitsky Act mentioned.[80]

When answering Mueller, Trump claimed that he didn't remember his team's meeting with Veselnitskaya and the other Russians, or even knowing Veselnitskaya's name. Nor did he have any recollection of whether he had been told during the campaign that Vladimir Putin or the Russian government supported his candidacy or opposed Hillary Clinton. "However, I was aware of some reports indicating that President Putin had made complimentary statements about me," Trump wrote to the investigators.

Trump responded to over thirty questions from Mueller by

replying, "I don't remember," "I don't have a recollection," or that he didn't "have any information." To questions relating to possible obstruction of justice during his presidential transition, he didn't answer at all.

According to Mueller, President Trump's actions on June 9, 2016 and afterward concerning withholding information about the Russian meeting with the campaign could not be seen as obstruction of justice. But Mueller noted, referring to all investigated incidents, that because the evidence was so limited, possible Trump obstruction crimes could not be ruled out either. If they could have been, his report would have said so.

I asked Bill Browder in the summer of 2019 what he thought about the fact that those who had smeared him had ended up in Mueller's high-profile investigation. "I have been aware of Veselnitskaya's and Akhmetshin's attempts to smear me and Magnitsky ever since 2016," he said. "I tried continuously to expose them, but very few people paid any attention. I'm happy that the truth finally prevailed."

MONEY LAUNDERING

In December 2018, a Russian legislator named Konstantin Kosachev proposed in a meeting with President Putin that Russia should start collecting an official list of the most appalling cases of foreign citizens who "spread the most outrageous lies about our country and people."[81] Kosachev believed that this list should be named after Bill Browder.

In early 2019, Natalia Veselnitskaya was indicted in the United States, charged with obstructing justice in the money-laundering case involving her client, Prevezon.[82] When the indictment was announced, the spokesperson for the Russian Ministry of Foreign Affairs demanded an explanation from the US, and described the indictment as "revenge."[83] As of this writing, Veselnitskaya has yet to appear before an American court.

That same year, new reports emerged about the stolen money Magnitsky had uncovered. In Spain, some of it was suspected to have been spent on real estate.[84]

But the bombshell revelation came from Latvia.

The news service Re:Baltica, which specializes in critical journalism focusing on Russia, had investigated Magnitsky-revealed bank transfers in cooperation with the Swedish public service broadcasting company SVT. The investigation revealed that a major financier of the leading pro-Russian party in Latvia had received €270,000 from two of the companies that were part of the Hermitage scheme. "Harmony, which is the favorite party of Latvia's sizable Russian-language minority, gained the most votes in the Latvian parliamentary elections but, as per usual, was left in the opposition because of its perceived pro-Kremlin stance in foreign policy," Re:Baltica reported.[85] In effect, money stolen in Russia and laundered in the West had been used to advance Kremlin-pushed political meddling outside of Russia's borders. Browder filed a criminal complaint about Swedbank's Latvian, Estonian and Swedish units.

Simultaneously, the European Parliament was preparing its own Magnitsky Law. Public debate grew heated over the question of whether the bill should bear Magnitsky's name. Browder testified before the Parliament's human rights committee, saying that it would be immoral and ridiculous for the European Union to drop Magnitsky's name to appease Putin.

The Russian State Investigative Committee quickly attacked Browder in response, now claiming that he had murdered Alexander Perepilichnyy, the Russian whistleblower who had previously leaked insider bank information to Browder and died at the age of forty-four.

The harassment continued as the Russian Interior Ministry opened up yet another investigation against Browder, because he had "as the leader of a criminal community" reported Denis

Katsyv's "alleged" money laundering to the US Department of Justice.[86] The Ministry claimed that Browder had provided falsified information and fabricated evidence about Russian citizens to US officials.

Russia also issued yet another Red Notice about Browder through Interpol. Following this, members of the British Parliament wrote an open letter to the police organization, saying that its credibility was at risk if it didn't start to apply strict methods to counter Russian abuse.[87] Browder visited the British House of Commons to speak about Russia's weaponization of the international justice system.

In May 2019, the Russian embassy in Australia published a meme in which a photo of Browder's face was captioned with the text "REGARDING WILLIAM BROWDER'S CRIMINAL ACTIVITIES."[88] The text under the photo claimed that Browder had stolen over $200 million from the Russian government and committed other crimes forbidden by the United Nations Convention Against Transnational Organized Crime. "By lobbying the Magnitsky Act he tries to escape justice," the Russian embassy tweeted, pinging much of Australia's media.[89] The tweet included a link to a statement published on a website hosted by the Russian Ministry of Foreign Affairs. The embassy wanted to blacken Browder's reputation in Australia, where he had also proposed a national Magnitsky Act.

Browder also lobbied for Magnitsky legislation in France, Sweden, Norway and beyond. For his efforts, in 2019, he was awarded the distinguished American Spirit Award for Citizen Activism.

∞∞∞

In the United States, several names were added to the Magnitsky sanctions list in May 2019. Newly targeted was the Russian State

Investigative Committee's Gennady Karlov, who had attempted to hide the conditions of Magnitsky's arrest, torture, and death. Also added was the head of the Investigative Committee, Elena Trikulya. She too had hidden the abuse against Magnitsky and signed the denial of a petition to launch a criminal investigation of the people who had participated in the crimes against the lawyer.[90]

Following those updates, fifty-five Russian citizens now faced Magnitsky sanctions. According to Browder, forty-two of them had participated in either the financial crimes exposed by Sergei Magnitsky, his illegal arrest, or his murder. "There are still 241 Russian individuals to go," he tweeted.[91]

In the spring of 2019, a private citizen exposed an army of Twitter bots supporting Natalia Veselnitskaya. The bots tweeted English-language versions of messages which all said some variation of "We need more people like the lawyer Natalia Veselnitskaya." Twitter later suspended Veselnitskaya's account.

ANYTHING FOR JUSTICE

Bill Browder's campaign for justice has led to thirty-one countries adopting some form of Magnitsky legislation. In December 2020, the European Union passed its own version of the law, although it wasn't named after Magnitsky. New Zealand, Australia and Taiwan are currently processing their own versions of the Act. "Next, I want to make sure that the law is used," Browder said the in spring of 2021. "Half of the battle is to get the law passed and the second half to get it used. I want to make sure that the law becomes a ubiquitous tool for justice."

Following our first meeting in London, I met Browder on several occasions to document his journey as a target of Vladimir Putin. Two days before one of our discussions, Nikolai Gorokhov, a lawyer investigating the Magnitsky affair in Russia and a representative of Magnitsky's family, was thrown from his fourth-floor balcony. He survived but suffered a fractured skull and memory loss. Before the assassination attempt, he was preparing to share new evidence in a trial in Moscow. He told the press he was afraid for his life but was nevertheless continuing his work.[92]

I asked Browder whether he has ever felt that he was in physical danger: "Sometimes I am, sometimes not. All the deaths of their 'enemies'—poisonings, car crashes, falling off buildings, and suicides—those are the things I'm worried about."

Browder says that for the most part, the disinformation campaigns don't affect him negatively. Instead, he says, he has become more calm and strategic. When he was in the middle of the Nekrasov movie situation in 2016, for example, he was worried that the campaign to get justice for Magnitsky would be destroyed if people started doubting him as a result of the film. "But now that I am over it, I can say the campaigns have been unsuccessful, partly because we're good at fighting them," he says. "None of it really bothers me. It seems like a virtual game. As long as everyone is safe, it's a calm place to be."

Browder says that part of his success against Russian operations lies in his team's resources. His staff is effective; they have good contacts, good sources, and access to intelligence on what the Russians are up to. "So, we can stalk them, preempt them, and attack them," he shares. "We can hire lawyers and do a lot of things that allow us to fight back and cause them great damage. But most people don't have that capacity."

Browder encourages anyone who becomes a target of Russian disinformation to share their experiences with the media and politicians and to file criminal complaints with the police. "The first time you talk about it, people look at you as if you're paranoid, because no one can imagine that this type of evil stuff could go on. But when enough people discuss this for a while, they understand this is a real problem."

He has never thought about stopping his own fight.

"In my case, the reasons for doing this are so big, including the torture and murder of my colleague, that I will do anything for justice."

7.

Special Courses at Moscow State University

IN 2005, WHILE STUDYING JOURNALISM AND international politics at the University of Tampere, I worked as a journalist in Petrozavodsk, Karelia, a region of northwest Russia bordering Finland. I lived in a freezing-cold one-bedroom flat and covered stories for a Finnish-language weekly called *Karjalan Sanomat* (*Karelian News*). It was there that I learned how journalism was completely different in Russia than it was in the West. In the West, journalists were watchdogs, operating with freedom to scrutinize and assess the political decision makers. By contrast, a journalist in Putin's Russia was an obedient megaphone of the establishment, dependent on the ruling elite and subject to its whims. If a Russian reporter delved too deeply and critically into the regime's inner workings, he or she could meet the fate of Anna Politkovskaya, the internationally renowned investigative journalist and author who was assassinated in October 2006 in the elevator of her Moscow apartment.

The same year that Politkovskaya was murdered, I attended Moscow State University, the supposed crown jewel of the Russian education system, as an exchange student. I studied in the faculty of journalism, which was located near the Kremlin. The materials used in the coursework often consisted of Russian state media content, which was unsuitable for an academic education. But I was too polite to criticize the friendly, passionate teacher, who was nearing retirement.

Once, the teacher asked me to analyze a clipping from the state newspaper *Rossiyskaya Gazeta*. The clipping was of a vicious column accusing Finland of "Russophobia": racism and hatred toward Russians. When the teacher asked my opinion on the article, I explained that the content was untrue. She didn't object.

It wasn't until more than ten years later that I found out that the department also offered a course on information warfare, for a small selection of students.

The Russian author and journalist Vladimir Yakovlev used to study journalism at Moscow State University. In 2015, Yakovlev wrote a popular blog post, where he described his experiences being taught "special combat propaganda" techniques. These methods were originally meant for use against enemy soldiers, but are used against civilians as well. "It is an effective weapon, used for the sole purpose of knocking the brains of the enemy out," Yakovlev wrote.[1]

At Moscow State University, "under an atmosphere of secrecy," military officers trained students in the methods of combat propaganda. In my analysis, the ones that are most frequently applied by the troll factories and the Kremlin's international influence agents on social media are those referred to as "rotten herring," "the big lie," and "the 40 to 60 method."[2]

According to Yakovlev, "rotten herring" implies rubbing a nasty smell into a target. This technique involves spreading a false and scandalous accusation against an individual. The goal is to initiate a public debate about the targeted person and have their name and connection with the scandal repeated over and over again.

"The big lie" works similarly. The idea is to come up with a lie so incredible that it is impossible to believe that anyone could actually be lying about it. Yakovlev explains that the lie must be big enough to impart a negative emotional impact on the audience, which in turn influences the way they will react to the targeted person in the future. For example, the conspiracy theory portraying Hillary Clinton as part of a pedophile ring sounds alarmingly like a Russian big lie.

"The 40 to 60 method," commonly known as the 60/40 principle, was the creation of the Nazi propagandist Joseph Goebbels, and is considered one of the golden rules of propaganda. With this technique, the propagandist gains the audience's trust by providing 60 percent information that "aligns with the interests of the enemy" and may be factual. The trust is then abused with the remaining 40 percent of the content, which is falsified.

∞∞∞

Many of the Kremlin's hostile foreign interference techniques are merely updated applications of old-style Soviet practices. In his 1987 book, *Spycatcher*, Peter Wright, a former officer and assistant director of MI5, the British counter-intelligence agency, shares information that was obtained from Soviet defectors in the mid-twentieth century. Wright recounts how in 1958, then KGB leader Aleksandr Shelepin was tasked with modernizing the Soviet Union's security apparatus. The idea was to develop new ways to attack the West, using nonmilitary means. What emerged was the concept of the organized spreading of fabricated information. According to Wright, one of the first KGB-organized international fake news campaigns claimed that there was a breakdown in Chinese-Soviet relations.

Around the same time, several instances of *kompromat*—the use of compromising private information to blackmail individuals into betraying their country—were brought to light. In one case discussed by Wright, the Russians threatened to expose the sexual orientation of a closeted gay British official working with

British and NATO submarine defense projects if he didn't steal confidential documents and hand them over to the Soviet Union.

In a document from the 1960s, the Soviet Estonian KGB instructs its agents on how to dissolve organizations and groups they had framed as "anti-Soviet"—both inside and outside the USSR's borders. Their recommended methods included fueling ideological differences among group members; discrediting the group's mission in the eyes of its participants; highlighting the dissimilarities between the leaders and the rank-and-file; and intensifying the natural competition among members. An integral KGB tool in breaking up communities was to convey material to group members that would induce or enforce the harmful processes from within the organization.

Vladimir Putin is a former KGB agent and FSB spy. As such, he has years of experience in international espionage and meddling operations. He is expert in the skill of character assassination, and has taken the Soviet-era KGB methods to the next level—particularly on social media.

During his time in office, Putin's regime has systematically harnessed both the Russian mass media and international social media as tools to attack foreign entities seen as threats to his interests. The aim of Russian trolls and fake news is to control the opinion climate and people's consciousness throughout the world, just as the state-run television channels try and capture citizens' minds inside Russia. Propaganda outlets like RT and Sputnik attack Putin's critics at home and abroad: trolls, bots, and memes push conspiracies such as accusing Hillary Clinton of being a criminal; supporting US politicians who are seen as favorable to Russian interests, such as Donald Trump; and attacking free elections.

This disinformation network is closely regulated by Putin. As a matter of fact, the Russian president himself often shapes even the most basic messaging about Russia's policies. A person who has participated in numerous summits with Putin shared with me an eyewitness account about how the Russian president controls the country's international communications. Putin once read a statement at a press conference, and while the statement was likely based on a draft produced by assistants, the president had clearly corrected and completed it himself. If anyone thinks that Putin is merely controlled by the machinery of state, this account demonstrates the opposite, showing that he is completely in control of what kind of disinformation emerges from the Kremlin.

8.

The Reporters

NORWEGIAN JOURNALIST THOMAS NILSEN WAS CROSSING from Norway into Russia for work on March 8, 2017 when the Russian FSB guards at the Borisoglebsk border station informed him that he was a threat to the national security of the Russian Federation and denied him entry.

Nilsen is a respected journalist and expert on the Arctic and Russia. He runs the international news service the *Independent Barents Observer* and is one of Norway's leading experts on Russia's nuclear submarines.[1] Nilsen lives in Kirkenes, a quiet harbor town on a rocky peninsula in the northeastern most corner of Norway. He had passed through the same border station countless times without incident, since the days when the border guards still represented the Soviet Union.

Nilsen was traveling that day with a delegation from the Danish parliament's Foreign Affairs Committee, who he was supposed to guide to Murmansk, the world's largest city above the Arctic Circle.

Russia's Murmansk region, on the rugged shores of the Arctic Ocean, is strategically important for the Kremlin. During the Cold War, it was the hot spot for the Soviet Union's nuclear submarines and icebreakers. Today, the naval base in Murmansk hosts Russia's Northern Fleet. The majority of the country's nuclear submarines are based in the area. The Putin regime has high ambitions for the Arctic Ocean, especially its vast oil and gas fields and shipping routes. In Putin's plan to conquer the Arctic, Murmansk is the key location.

Nilsen's experience at Borisoglebsk started out as routine. The FSB immigration officer took his passport, typed his details into the computer, and asked the mandatory question: Where was Nilsen traveling to?

"To Murmansk," he replied.

The FSB officer continued: "What will you do there?"

"Make reports," Nilsen answered.

Typically, a foreign reporter crossing the border to work in northwest Russia is checked by two separate FSB immigration officials. Following protocol, the first official called in his supervisor. But as soon as the supervisor glanced at the computer screen, the routine check was over. He took Nilsen's passport, politely asked him to step out of the queue, and escorted him to the back office. Nilsen guessed that he might be in for the familiar fate of many reporters: he would be forced to answer more questions concerning the purpose of his trip, before being allowed to enter Russia.

In the office, three FSB officers advised Nilsen to take a seat. Then the news was delivered, in Russian: Nilsen would not be allowed to enter the country. The reason given was "state security."

Nilsen asked why he was considered a threat to Russia's national security. The officers claimed not to know. Instead, they encouraged Nilsen to contact the Russian consulate general in Kirkenes for further information.

Nilsen was told that his ban would be in effect for five years. (Only later did he find out that it would be enforced indefinitely.) If he tried entering Russia through any checkpoint, he would be considered a criminal offender.

Still acting politely and professionally, the officials handed Nilsen a document detailing the conditions of his ban. Nilsen was asked to sign the papers, leave the border station, and return to Norway. "Judging by their uniform insignia, the officers were high-ranking," Nilsen remembers.

Nilsen's Danish travel companions were allowed to enter Russia. But Nilsen had to hitchhike two hundred yards back to the Norwegian side of the checkpoint, because walking is prohibited in the border zone. The FSB officials specifically forbade him to hitchhike in a Russian vehicle.

After a five-minute wait, a Norwegian driver on a trip to get gas picked Nilsen up and drove him home to Kirkenes.

∞∞∞∞

Officially declaring someone a national security threat to Russia is a serious accusation. By definition, "state security threats" in Russia include crimes such as engaging in espionage or terrorism. Nilsen had not spied or plotted terror attacks against Russia.

Still, the travel ban wasn't a complete surprise. Before the border incident, Nilsen and his fellow journalists had been the target of multiple hostile operations from Russia. The ban would seriously hinder Nilsen's ability to cover Russia-related news topics going forward. It appeared that his ideals of independent, high-quality reporting had clashed profoundly with the Kremlin's infamous security structures. "The Kremlin views many journalists as a threat to the FSB's understanding of state security," Nilsen says. "Journalism is the cornerstone of all developing societies, thus from the FSB's viewpoint, journalism threatens Russia's national security. Up here in the Arctic, journalism is essential in building good relations across borders. Maybe the FSB doesn't want that."

Nilsen decided to discover why he was considered a security threat to the Russian Federation. In order to find out, and to attempt and reverse the shady travel ban, he saw only one option— to sue the entity that had implemented the ban: the FSB.

ooooo

Norway routinely ranks among the top nations in global indexes measuring democracy and freedom of the press. Stable and safe, the country guarantees excellent working conditions to news platforms, such as Thomas Nilsen and his colleague Atle Staalesen's *Independent Barents Observer*. "Self-censorship is the only thing we never bring with us inside the office. It's not allowed through the door," Nilsen told me at the paper's newsroom in Kirkenes. On the wall hangs a map showing the vast area covered by the *Observer*: the northernmost parts of Norway, Russia, Finland, and Sweden, which form a region called the Barents, and, on top of it, the Arctic Ocean. Between Kirkenes and the North Pole lies over 3000 kilometers of lethally cold sea. Midway from the newsroom to the North Pole is the icy, stunningly beautiful and demilitarized Norwegian archipelago Svalbard.

Nilsen and Staalesen, friends for over twenty years, initially moved to Kirkenes, a harbor town of a few thousand inhabitants, because of its proximity to Russia. Street signs in the town are written in both Norwegian and Russian. However, scratch Kirkenes's tranquil surface, and high-stakes political tension is exposed.

Since the 1960s, Norway has harvested its riches from the oil and gas fields of the country's continental shelf, which flank the mainland and extend to the Barents Sea, adjacent to Kirkenes. The wise use of oil export revenues has been an important factor in creating one of the world's wealthiest and corruption-free countries. Unlike most European nations bordering Russia, Norway enjoys total independence from Russian energy. However, Rosneft, the Russian state-owned oil giant, has long been looking to get its hands on Norway's oil. Because of this, Nilsen says that "Kirkenes is a gold mine for investigative journalists."

That's why in 2002, sitting at Staalesen's kitchen table, the two friends decided to establish their first online news service, which they called the *Barents Observer*.[2] They wanted to publish news about the Arctic, and decided to focus on the region's energy industry, as well as on economic, political, and environmental topics.

Cooperation among citizens is an essential value in the Barents region. Originally, this relationship took shape as a way to support democracy, human rights, and freedom of the press, especially in the former Soviet Union. In 1993, after the Soviet Union fell, the Barents area representatives signed a cooperation treaty in Kirkenes; in the wake of dramatic changes in world politics, the inhabitants wanted to strengthen their ties and secure stability in the area. Nilsen and Staalesen established their website to fulfill that same need. "Russians, Norwegians, Finns, and Swedes live close to each other. But culture-wise, economically, societally, and ethnically, people living on different sides of the Barents countries' borders differ remarkably. We wanted to increase understanding between the people," Staalesen shares.

Nilsen and Staalsen built the *Barents Observer* on the idea of transparency and the free flow of information. All sources were identified in their stories; anonymous sources were avoided to ensure legitimacy and credibility. "By showing our sources, we allowed the readers to assess the articles' credibility and trustworthiness themselves," Nilsen says. "And by being open, we thought the FSB might even learn a thing or two about the Norwegian value of free access to knowledge and information. Maybe we were naive."

The site's expertise in Arctic, and specifically, Russian affairs, the defense industry, security, and nuclear safety were highly appreciated among the journalists in the region. According to Nilsen and Staalesen, none of their investigations could be labeled as "too sensitive" and thus irritating to the Kremlin. Quite the opposite: not once did they disclose Russian state secrets or other data compromising the country's national security.

Over time, the two men developed and grew their news service. In 2005, when diplomatic relations between Russia and other Barents countries were seemingly stable, Staalesen received a job offer from The Norwegian Barents Secretariat, whose mission is to promote and carry out commercial collaborations between Russia and Norway.[3] The secretariat, based in Kirkenes, is owned and led by three northern counties of Norway, Nordland, Troms, and Finnmark. The decision makers behind the secretariat are local politicians and governors. The group receives funding from the Norwegian Ministry of Foreign Affairs. Since 2000, the secretariat has funded thousands of transborder projects, including ones involving the Norwegian state oil company Equinor, formerly known as Statoil, and Rosneft.[4]

After Staalesen accepted the offer, ownership of the *Barents Observer* was transferred to the secretariat. At first, the news service and its new owner worked together seamlessly to further grow the site. In the mid-2000s, there was little tension in Russian–Norwegian relations, and the secretariat felt that the news site helped to advance the connections between the countries in the area. The journalists decided what the *Barents Observer* would cover.

In 2009, Nilsen was appointed editor in chief, and Trude Pettersen joined the team as a reporter. New audiences throughout the Nordics and in Russia found the site. In Russia, the site drew readers especially from Murmansk and Petrozavodsk, near the Finnish border. Many articles were republished and disseminated in Russian media outlets, which back then were less tightly controlled by the Putin regime.

NOT YOUR ORDINARY OIL COMPANY

Nilsen and Staalesen have long covered Rosneft, the Russian oil giant. "History tells us that Rosneft is of utmost importance for the Kremlin," Nilsen shares. He describes the corporation as vital to Russia's activities in the region.

Rosneft is the biggest oil and gas company in Russia, and one of the largest publicly traded oil companies in the world. Many experts agree that Russia may be running out of cheap oil.[5] As a result, it needs to pump oil from colder, deeper, and more remote places. Rosneft is therefore especially interested in expanding into Norway, where oil prospects are promising.

The company has served as a cash cow for Putin's inner circle, the *siloviki*, or security service agents. Rosneft's CEO is Putin's trusted ally, Igor Sechin, who many consider the second most powerful person in Russia.[6] Sechin has served in senior roles in both the Putin and Medvedev administrations, including as deputy prime minister.[7] During his term as deputy prime minister, the FSB reportedly founded Department P, which was put in charge of industrial activities, especially the lucrative oil business.[8] In the same year, 2004, Sechin was promoted to the chair of Rosneft's management board. Two years later, Rosneft received additional muscle from FSB headquarters in Lubyanka, Moscow when the deputy director of the agency's "oil division," Andrey Patrushev Jr., started to work for the company.[9]

In Russia, many FSB officers—like KGB agents in Soviet times—are "seconded" to work in companies, receiving paychecks from both the FSB and the outside business.[10] This system ensures that the companies staffed by FSB officers serve the interests not just of the shareholders, but also of the Putin regime.

Rosneft operates globally, including in Cuba, Canada, the United States, Brazil, Turkmenistan, Georgia, Belarus, Ukraine, Indonesia, and Iraq. To ensure their business dealings, the FSB operatives acting as oil company executives run aggressive influence operations targeting both key decision makers and the public. Once the energy deals are sealed, the *siloviki*-run Rosneft provides a direct channel into foreign countries' internal energy affairs, such as prices and availability.

The *Observer* was the only media source that systematically followed every significant Rosneft-related development in the Arctic.[11] As a result, Russian spies have long had Staalesen and Nilsen on their radar. On several occasions, as the men met their Russian sources in Murmansk, they realized they were being shadowed. "From time to time a man appeared and drank tea by a nearby table. Their point is to make themselves seen by us, and by our sources," Nilsen explains. While the "tea drinkers" never caused much of a hassle, Nilsen and his colleagues nevertheless implemented stricter information security and source protections. Nowadays, they notify their contacts and interviewees that the information they share can be exposed as a result of hacks or communications breaches.

There are other potential factors why Nilsen and Staalsen are in the Kremlin's crosshairs. One might be because their site publishes news in Russian, to Russian audiences. Putin's regime has harnessed most media outlets in Russia as amplifiers of the government's voice, leaving large chunks of the public without access to factual, Russian-language information concerning their political leaders. "In many cases, Russian security services don't care what's written about them in London. They care what's published in Russia. And our news is widely read throughout northwestern Russia" Nilsen says.[12]

When reporting from Russia, Nilsen and his colleagues often raise issues that are blocked by the Kremlin-controlled media. For example, they provide a voice to non-governmental organizations who have run up against the Russian authorities, and interview local human rights activists and opposition politicians, as well as members of the Russian lesbian, gay, bi- and transgender communities. By providing a platform for these groups, the *Observer's* interests profoundly cross those of the FSB.

Another reason why the *Observer* may have gained the attention of the Russian authorities was the paper's role as an opinion leader, with its work often quoted by the international press. In the early days of the Syrian civil war, for example, the *Barents Observer* scooped a secret Russian civilian cargo shipment that had been transported from the Northern Fleet's headquarters in Severomorsk to Syria.[13] "Some of our articles might include sensitive issues, but generally we cover the wide picture, sometimes including military components," Staalesen says. He mentions Russia's big investments in its military in the immediate neighborhood of Norway and Finland. "We cover that. But we haven't dug in too far. Far too little, actually," Staalesen shares.

While this type of coverage may have contributed to the influence campaigns targeted at the *Observer*, it was a Russian diplomat's open offensive against the paper—and specifically, an article that Nilsen had written—that drew the attention of the international community.

THE CONSUL GENERAL

Less than a month after Russia illegally annexed Crimea in March 2014, Nilsen wrote an editorial titled "Barents Cooperation in Putin's Dangerous New Era."[14]

In the editorial, Nilsen analyzed the harm that Russian aggression had caused and would continue to cause the Barents region. The piece listed the Putin regime's recent hostilities against Russian citizen organizations, opposition bloggers, and the media. Nilsen stated that the Kremlin's aggressive tactics would result in an atmosphere that would cause institutions, businesses, state structures, and citizens to lose interest in cooperating with Russia. In addition, Russia's activities could possibly undercut the stable cross-border relations built over twenty plus years in the region. Nilsen mentioned Russia's annexation of Crimea twice in his editorial.

Almost three weeks after Nilsen's editorial was published, in late April 2014, approximately 100 journalists from Sweden, Norway, Russia, and Finland traveled to Kirkenes for a conference.

The Arctic journalism community, whose roots date back to the Soviet era, meets annually to discuss regional developments. Speakers outside the community are invited as well, to provide expertise and insights.

At the conference—the theme of which that year was freedom of speech—a Russian photojournalist shared his experience of being arrested by the police, first in Murmansk and later in Moscow. The Kirkenes police, as well as Norwegian county officials, also delivered presentations. The spirit was positive and constructive.

But the atmosphere changed dramatically when a Russian diplomat in Kirkenes, Consul General Mikhail Noskov, took the stage and delivered his remarks.[15] Noskov attacked the *Barents Observer* mercilessly, specifically focusing on its reporting concerning Russia's annexation of Crimea.[16] Arrogantly, he stated, "We should all know, it was absolutely not an annexation, but a *reunification*." Noskov also claimed that the *Barents Observer's* coverage damaged the bilateral relations between Russia and Norway.[17] He also said that the site could be perceived as representing the views of the Norwegian government.[18] "Because the *Barents Observer* is owned and funded by the Secretariat, a governmental structure, the ownership and funding show in the journalistic content of the paper," the Consul General asserted.

For over half an hour, Noskov captured the attention of the room full of reporters.

Tapani Leisti, a reporter from Yle, was present as the Russian diplomat made his accusations. In an article recounting the event, he wrote that, "According to the Russian consul, a better name for the news site would be 'Russia Observer,' because it writes much less about the other Barents-area countries than about Russia."[19] Leisti added that "Noskov declined to specify his accusations when the audience asked for them."

As soon as Noskov finished, a Russian reporter stood up

and disputed what he had said. Stirring up even more conflict, the consul general characterized the journalists' questions as "provocations, which [he would] not answer."

Then it was the turn of the accused, Thomas Nilsen, to respond. He stressed to the consul the basics of Western standards of freedom of speech and news reporting and clarified the ownership structure of the paper. "I said that the newsroom has the freedom to choose their own topics, and the consul general will never, ever have any control over them," Nilsen recalls. "I also offered him the possibility to be interviewed or write his own opinion piece. He never replied to any of my remarks."

Nilsen and Staalesen later realized that Noskov's denunciation hadn't been cooked up hastily that morning over a cup of coffee. Instead, the wording, the target of the criticism, and the arena had all been carefully chosen. It was evident that the diplomat wasn't operating independently, but was fully supported by his supervisors in the Ministry of Foreign Affairs in Moscow. Most likely, Noskov's bosses had at least read and approved the speech in advance, if not written it themselves.

The presentation triggered an extraordinary chain of events which ultimately led to the end of the original B*arents Observer*.

ooooo

A month later, Thomas Nilsen and Atle Staalesen held their regular meeting with the owners of the *Barents Observer*, the Norwegian Barents Secretariat. The owners are mainly politicians: elected members of the regional county parliament and councils of the three northernmost Norwegian counties. Some engage in economic or business projects with Russian-based companies.

In the meeting, the owners questioned the journalistic independence of the *Observer*, practically repeating the vague accusations of the Russian consul general. The owners demanded that Nilsen and Staalesen guarantee that the site would never write anything jeopardizing the cooperation between Norway and Russia. "Having the owners tell us we shouldn't cover certain topics was alarming," Nilsen remembers.

No decisions were made during the meeting. But as a direct reaction to the Russian consul's false claim that the *Barents Observer* represented the views of the Norwegian government, the owners asked Nilsen, Staalesen, and Pettersen to compile suggestions for reshuffling the paper's organizational structure to give it more independence from the counties' governance. According to the owners, this would strengthen the *Observer's* position as a free and independent news site.

The staff acted as requested and started to brainstorm.

THE *BARENTS OBSERVER* IS DEAD

In August 2014, Rosneft started to explore four oil fields in a joint operation with Norwegian Equinor, then known as Statoil. The operation, named Pingvin (Penguin), was carried out on the Norwegian continental shelf, at a location described by Rosneft as the "most promising and prolific area of the Barents Sea."[20, 21]

At the same time, Nilsen, Pettersen, and Staalesen were busy coming up with new organizational models to keep their owners happy. Among their proposals was anchoring the site formally with the journalistic ethics of the Norwegian media industry, and starting a new foundation or company which would bare sole responsibility for the *Barents Observer's* news reporting.

They presented their ideas to the owners, who accepted them, agreeing to strengthen the journalistic underpinnings and provide more editorial independence to the site. "They wanted to clear all allegations of the *Barents Observer* being financed and thus controlled by the Norwegian state," Nilsen says.

However, just when Nilsen, Pettersen, and Staalesen thought they could go back to focusing on covering the news, their next meeting with the owners, in February 2015, turned everything upside down, as their previously accepted ideas were now rejected. "We realized that this wasn't happening by mistake or a political accident. It was part of a bigger plan to silence the *Barents Observer*," shares Nilsen.

ooooo

In the meantime, the *Observer* continued its publishing mission. In the spring of 2015, it broke another story that gained international interest. This story originated from Svalbard, a peaceful Norwegian archipelago.

Svalbard is home to polar bears, as well as a community of Norwegian arctic researchers and a settlement of about 500 Russian and Ukrainian coal workers. The Russian settlement, called Barentsburg, hosts a Russian consulate, the northernmost diplomatic mission in the world. Svalbard's sovereignty is defined in the 1920 Svalbard Treaty, which states that it belongs to Norway. Since the Kremlin started to militarize the Arctic, it has regularly voiced difficulties accepting the Treaty. "As Russians don't agree with Oslo's understanding of the Svalbard Treaty, Norway's relation with the Russians in Svalbard is probably the most sensitive issue we have in Norway," Staalesen shares.

As part of Russia's recent military expansion into the Arctic, the country has refurbished several Soviet-era bases. One of them is Nagurskoje, which is located near the Franz Josef Land archipelago, approximately 160 miles from the eastern point of Svalbard.[22] The complex houses heavy equipment, aircraft, and advanced anti-aircraft missiles. Regular war drills are organized at the base.

In April 2015, Nilsen noticed that Dmitri Rogozin, who was then Russia's deputy prime minister in charge of the country's defense industry, was traveling to the North Pole. Rogozin is under sanctions by the United States, European Union and Norway for publicly calling for the annexation of Crimea. He has also gained international notoriety as an active social media user. On Twitter, Rogozin has wished for the Japanese to commit ritualistic suicide and threatened Hungary and Romania with bomber jets.[23] Ukraine-related travel bans and sanctions against Russian officials sparked him to comment: "Tanks don't need visas."[24]

Nilsen caught Rogozin sharing the content of his travels on Instagram and Facebook, which revealed that he had stopped in Barentsburg on his way to the North Pole. The sanctions specifically forbid his entry into Norwegian territory. "We picked it up and wrote stories," Nilsen says.[25] "Our stories created international headlines. The Norwegian Ministry of Foreign Affairs learned about the incident from us, as we called them for comment. Rogozin challenged Russia's and Norway's official relationship, knowing his trip was politically sensitive." Norway's Ministry of Foreign Affairs demanded an explanation for Rogozin's trip from the Russian ambassador in Oslo.[26]

Rogozin tweeted links to the *Barents Observer* articles describing his sanctions breach and the Norwegian Foreign Ministry's reaction to it. He commented that they were "just jealous [that] we were swimming at the North Pole" and "after the fight it's too late to wave your fists."[27]

Following that, another high-ranking Russian politician stirred the diplomatic pot further. The first deputy chairman of Russia's State Duma's committee on international affairs, Leonid Kalashnikov, questioned Norway's sovereignty over Svalbard. "For Russia, the Barents Sea and the whole Arctic, this is the only, in fact, access, to two oceans. We should never be held accountable to anyone," Kalashnikov said.[28] Again, the *Barents Observer* reporting on this was picked up by the international media.

After the incident, Norway changed its immigration and aviation laws.[29] Until Rogozin's surprise visit to Svalbard, the names and passports of people entering the archipelago were not checked. But now, anyone entering Svalbard needs to inform immigration officials forty-eight hours before arrival. Russian aircraft landing in Svalbard must provide passenger lists.

∞∞∞

Finally, in the spring of 2015, the Norwegian Barents Secretariat formally ruled that the *Observer* should not follow the Rights and Duties of the Editor. A joint agreement between the Association of Norwegian Editors and the Norwegian Media Business Association, the Rights and Duties of the Editor provides guidelines that establish and defend a paper's "editorial independence from interference by [its] owners."[30] These guidelines are followed by all other Norwegian newsrooms. The unprecedented decision broke all over Norway, and abroad. Many throughout the industry questioned and condemned the ruling. But the massive public shaming didn't move the secretariat to reconsider its decision. The order stayed in place.

As a result, Staalesen and Nilsen, together with Trude Pettersen and photographer Jonas Karlsbakk, published a statement in the *Barents Observer*. They wrote that the secretariat was threatening freedom of speech, violating basic journalistic ethics, and effectively imposing censorship.[31] They informed their readers that from that moment on, the *Barents Observer* should no longer be considered an independent news source.

Following the public statement, the secretariat accused Nilsen of disloyalty, and rebuked him for publishing the statement without speaking to them first.

∞∞∞

Over the summer of 2015, the situation remained fluid, as the politicians on the governing board of the secretariat were focused on the regional elections scheduled for September. Firing a chief editor before the elections would have damaged their campaigns. So they waited until the elections were over.

On September 28, 2015, the secretariat relieved Nilsen from his duties as editor in chief of the *Barents Observer*, effective immediately.[32] In the dismissal letter, Nilsen was accused of acting disloyally and mismanaging his duties. Trude Pettersen was appointed the new editor in chief.

In response, the editorial staff wrote another statement, declaring that the owners were destroying the *Observer's* thirteen-year history of safeguarding freedom of speech and the people's right to information.

Nilsen's sacking sparked renewed protests within the media. The Norwegian Union of Journalists promised to provide free legal assistance for Nilsen if he wished to sue the secretariat, as the firing appeared illegal. The Norwegian Foreign Ministry, the financier of the secretariat, voiced support for an independent *Barents Observer*, hoping that the "owners would work to build a constructive atmosphere."

Then a journalist with NRK, the Norwegian broadcasting corporation, obtained a scoop. A high-profile Norwegian official speaking anonymously, revealed that an FSB officer had specifically asked Norwegian officials to silence the *Barents Observer*. The official told NRK that the FSB had been unsatisfied with "the *Barents Observer's* contributions to the relationship between Russia and Norway."[33] The source further speculated that the FSB had likely voiced similar views to other entities in Norway. When the Russian embassy in Oslo was asked for comment on the suspected FSB meddling, it told NRK that it would be "meaningless to comment on obviously false statements."[34]

One of the county governors of the secretariat told the press that the idea of FSB meddling was "totally unknown and totally surprising." According to him, the *Barents Observer's* reporting about Russia had *never* been mentioned as an underlying reason for the decisions concerning the editorial freedom of the site.

The revelation that the FSB had met with Norwegian officials behind the scenes and asked them to close down the paper, combined with the Russian consul general's attack against the *Barents Observer* the previous year in Kirkenes, raised concerns in Norway. Questions were asked as to whether Russian security officers had applied even greater and more systematic pressure to shut down the *Observer*.

Naturally, any shady contacts between Russian security services and regional or national Norwegian politicians are carefully hidden. The Kremlin's toolbox includes a variety of measures designed to persuade targeted individuals: oppression, harassment, bribery, even extortion. According to the Finnish security service, Supo, the foreign intelligence services cultivate their targets for years, slowly gaining their trust.[35] Therefore, it cannot be ruled out that the FSB managed to cultivate Norwegian politicians, who were then induced to work in the interests of the FSB. The political interests of the Russian consul general, the FSB, and Rosneft—which was hoping at the time for a 20 percent share of the oil field on the Norwegian continental shelf—and the Norwegian Barents Secretariat were aligned: they all claimed to want to "maintain a good relationship between Russia and Norway." And those good bilateral relations were, according to FSB logic, harmed by the independent reporting of the *Barents Observer*. "We only know small parts of a bigger picture," Nilsen states. "It's clear there was more Russian influence on the owners than what has been published. Part of it was the general wish of wanting to be friends with the Russians."

In the end, the plan to fire Nilsen and by doing so scare the rest of the newsroom into producing journalism that served the "Russian and Norwegian relationship" failed miserably, as the entire staff resigned. "It's simple," says Nilsen. "Not one Norwegian journalist would work under those circumstances. No way. After Atle and Trude quit, the *Barents Observer* was dead."

A NEW SITE IS BAPTIZED

Giving up a job with a steady paycheck to start your own company is risky. "We have a long perspective on our work, and we knew it wouldn't be easy to relaunch the paper. But *not* launching a free news site was never an option," Staalesen shares.

With not much more than their laptops, the former staff of the *Barents Observer* rented a new office in the center of Kirkenes. Within forty-eight hours, the *Independent Barents Observer* was up and running. A crowdfunding campaign was launched, which received funds from readers, and later, foundations. Staalesen and Nilsen insisted that the retooled paper operate in accordance with the Rights and Duties of the Editor and accept "no external interference."[36]

The secretariat threatened to file a lawsuit over the name, which they claimed belonged to them. In fact, the name *Barents Observer* had been created by Atle Staalesen. Norway's Ministry of Foreign Affairs intervened, informing the secretariat that they could not use the ministry's funding to sue an independent newspaper.

The legal threat inspired even more support for the new site. Geir Flikke, a leading Norwegian academic and an expert on post-Soviet countries and Arctic relations, started a petition urging the Norwegian Barents Secretariat to stop pressuring the editors, and to let the paper practice free journalism without interference.[37] Forty-five university researchers from Norway, Sweden, and Finland quickly signed the petition.

ooooo

Meanwhile, Nilsen, Pettersen, and Staalesen continued publishing stories on their usual topics. They followed the developments at Rosneft and other Russian oil and energy companies, as well as the joint projects of Statoil and Rosneft in the Arctic and in Norway. In the spring of 2016, they reported an increase in military activity near demilitarized Svalbard: Russian airborne forces were planning to land military instructors and dog teams at Longyearbyen Airport in Svalbard, a possible violation of the Svalbard Treaty.[38] Again, their story broke internationally.

In October 2016, the *Independent Barents Observer* relaunched its Russian-language site after a one-year hiatus.

A month later, Russia issued a secret stop list.

Thomas Nilsen's name was on it.

STOP LIST

The Kremlin has held a grudge against Norway ever since the country joined the European Union's sanctions against Russia. Among other things, the sanctions have hampered Rosneft's drilling plans in Norway. In the opinion of Russian diplomats, Norway does not practice its own foreign policy, but instead just follows the lead of the EU.

On November 28, 2016, a representative from Norway's embassy in Moscow was called into the Russian Foreign Ministry, where he was given a list of people who were forbidden to enter Russia. Norway's Ministry of Foreign Affairs then informed its Russian counterpart that they were not going to contact individuals to tell them that they were on the list, as serving as the courier for the Russian Federation's stop lists wasn't part of the Norwegian foreign ministry's responsibilities.

The appearance of Thomas Nilsen's name on the list was likely Russia's retaliation against the sanctions imposed by the European Union against the "journalist" Dmitry Kiselyov. (The Kremlin believes it is entitled to "sanction" Western journalists because Kiselyov himself was sanctioned.) Since 2013, Kiselyov has led the Russian government's international media agency, Rossiya Segodnya (Russia Today).[39] Rossiya Segodnya's content consists mostly of Russian propaganda masquerading as news. Occasionally, it supplements its content with topical news in an attempt to enhance its image of credibility. According to Jukka Mallinen, the Finnish expert on Russian media, the site is most likely funded or supported by the Kremlin. The writers and editors are very professional, the articles well-done, and the demagogy relatively intelligent, which isn't the case with many pro-Kremlin web operations.

The first targets on the list were two Norwegian members of parliament who were denied visas to Russia. Following this incident, the Russian embassy in Oslo sent an email to several Norwegian media outlets, including the *Independent Barents Observer*, accusing them of disseminating "anti-Russian rhetoric." Right before the email was sent, much of the Norwegian media had reported on escalating Russian intelligence operations in Norway.[40]

Nilsen found out about his ban in March 2017, when the FSB in Borisoglebsk told him he was a threat to national security, and declared him persona non grata in Russia. Two days after he was turned away from the border, the Russian embassy in Oslo published a press release hinting, among other things, that Nilsen would be allowed entry to Russia if Norway dropped the sanctions.[41] The statement didn't detail reasons as to why precisely Nilsen was on the list and a commodity in sanctions blackmail.

ooooo

As soon as news broke of Nilsen's travel ban, the Norwegian Union of Journalists protested the decision to the Russian embassy, while the European Federation of Journalists alerted the European Council's media freedom unit.

Nilsen decided he would leave no stone unturned in his quest to find out why he had been put on the list: "It's my legal right to know. It's difficult, but there is the possibility and having a court in Russia remove my name from the list, due to freedom of speech." Team 29, a well-known group of human rights lawyers in Russia, offered to represent him in court and provide legal assistance in investigating the case.

Nilsen began by sending letters to the Border Service of the FSB, the Russian Ministry of Foreign Affairs, and the FSB border guard unit in Murmansk, requesting information concerning the decision to declare him a threat to national security. Under Russian law, officials are required to answer requests in writing within seven days when addressed with letters priming a court case.

All the agencies responded—shifting the responsibility elsewhere. The FSB in Murmansk said that the case didn't fall under its jurisdiction. The Foreign Ministry as well as the Border Service of the FSB said they hadn't made the decision.

Nilsen and his lawyers then initiated their first court case, against the FSB border guards, due to the fact that the border unit had implemented the travel ban. The case was filed in a regional court near the Norwegian border, but the court dismissed it without even looking into the matter. According to the decision, since no case existed to begin with, it didn't belong to the court.

Eventually, Nilsen and his lawyers managed to get the case heard by the Moscow City Court. "We knew all along that the decision has nothing to do with the border guards," Nilsen says. "The decision was made in Moscow, in the FSB headquarters in Lubyanka."

In November 2017, Nilsen received a summons to appear at a court hearing in Moscow the very next morning at nine thirty. On such short notice, Nilsen's lawyers couldn't possibly prepare adequately. Nilsen was also unable to travel to Moscow in time. In addition, he was still blacklisted. If he tried to cross the border, he would be considered a criminal offender. His lawyers asked the court to postpone the hearing, which it did.

In December 2017, the Moscow City Court proceeded with the case. This time, Nilsen's lawyer was present. The hearing was closed to the public and relatively short. The court agreed with the FSB: Nilsen should not be allowed to enter Russia. However, Nilsen's lawyer wasn't allowed to read the reasoning behind the court's decision because it contained "state secrets." Refusing to provide the full ruling of the court to a lawyer is a violation of Russian law.

Next, Nilsen and his legal team brought the case to the Russian Supreme Court, demanding that the travel ban be rescinded and declared illegal. In May 2018, the Supreme Court sided with the FSB, ruling that the agency didn't have to disclose why Nilsen wasn't allowed into Russia.[42]

Nilsen and his lawyers then complained to the European Court of Human Rights, in Strasbourg. In November 2018, the court informed Nilsen that the case had been accepted for processing. "Now the case is named: *Nilsen v. Russia*—case number 58505/18," Nilsen shares.[43] He believes it will take several years for the case to get to court, as the queue of Russian citizens with cases pending against the Kremlin is long. "Nevertheless, I am waiting for the case to be processed," Nilsen says. "The *Independent Barents Observer* will win and thus continue working for our first priority: free and independent journalism in Norway's and Russia's northern border regions."

Some may consider Nilsen's move to sue the FSB a "provocation." "Suing the FSB is not a provocation," he explains. "It's an attempt to enable the *Independent Barents Observer's* work. I am a reporter and I have rights. Of course, I realize my treatment connects straight to international politics, and I might not stand a chance. But I have the backing of my colleagues, the Norwegian Union of Journalists, and the International Federation of Journalists."

"BLOCK THAT NEWSPAPER TO HELL"

In early 2019, the architects of the Kremlin's information warfare set up a new front against the *Independent Barents Observer*.

The ostensible rationale for the new active measures was an article concerning a gay man from Sweden's indigenous Sami community. The story had originally been published in Sweden, and was republished in January 2019 on the *Observer's* site in English[44] and Russian.[45]

In the article, the Sami man talks about the difficulties he has experienced throughout his life hiding and denying his sexual orientation. But now he wanted to speak openly about his mental health problems—which he had overcome—and how he was able to help Swedish LGBTQ youth with the same issues.

Soon after the publication of the story, the *Observer* received a letter from Roskomnadzor, the Russian communications supervisory body, which is known for censoring online material that criticizes the policies of the Putin regime. According to the letter, the *Observer* had published information which was forbidden by law in the Russian Federation.[46] Roskomnadzor referred to a part of the story in which the Sami man talked about his previous suicidal thoughts, which they said contained an "invitation to commit suicide, information about a suicide attempt, as well as the possible means to carry out a suicide." The *Observer* was given twenty-four hours to remove the Russian-language version of the story, or else the entire site would be blocked in Russia. "For me as the editor it was a completely impossible option to remove the interview, which in my opinion was very good," Nilsen says.

Because Nilsen didn't comply, Roskomnadzor blocked Russian access to the *Independent Barents Observer*.[47] (Today, a reader in Russia needs a VPN connection or Tor network to read the site.) Russian Duma member Vitaly Milonov gave an interview in which he echoed the hate speech so often invoked to discriminate against minorities.[48] "Block this newspaper to hell. It represents degeneracy, and the people behind its ideology have the psyche of a queer," he said. Ultimately, the story turned out to be one of the most popular in the history of the *Independent Barents Observer*—especially the Russian version.

Roskomnadzor's decision drew widespread criticism around Russia and the Nordic countries. Russian opposition politician Alexey Navalny tweeted that Russian taxpayers paid the salaries of Roskomnadzor officers just so that they could keep an eye on Norwegian sites and order them to remove content. "We have a very rich country," Navalny wrote sarcastically.[49] The Sami man featured in the article disclosed publicly that he was left speechless, and then angry, when he heard about Russia's actions. "They claim I encourage people to commit suicide, when in fact it's the contrary. I want to help people," he shared.

With the support of the Russian antidiscrimination and human rights organization ADC Memorial, Nilsen sued Roskomnadzor. He claimed that the agency's interpretation of both the story and Russian law was wrong: it didn't encourage suicide, nor did it give instructions on how to carry one out. "Our main argument was that Roskomnadzor made a wrong judgment vis-à-vis the law," explains Nilsen. A Moscow court heard the case in July 2019, and kept the ban in place. Nilsen appealed, but it was turned down in 2020.[50] Nilsen then appealed to the Russian Supreme Court, where the case is now pending.

Even though Roskomnadzor's official basis for blocking the *Independent Barents Observer* was the law that prohibits suicide promotion, one well-informed Russian source told one of Nilsen's lawyers that "the decision was made at the highest level." The only levels of government above Roskomnadzor are the FSB, and the Russian leadership.

Today, the *Observer* is able to evade the Roskomnadzor ban by publishing a newsletter in Russian and posting stories on social media. In addition, they use mirror servers to distribute their content to Russia. They are also developing new technological solutions, such as audio articles on Spotify, to enable wider dissemination of stories in Russia. The site has also expanded into China, and its international readership is on the rise.

Ultimately, Nilsen is interested in finding out why the Kremlin is afraid—to the point of paranoia—of the free flow of information. "There is no 'foreign aggression' wanting to harm Russia," he says. "Journalism and civil society are factors to help developing states do better. Unfortunately, the FSB doesn't want to develop."

9.

55 Savushkina Street

IN FEBRUARY 2015, I WAS INTERVIEWING Finnish internet users and checking out tips that had been sent to me in response to my article about Russian trolls. Simultaneously, I was preparing for my trip to St. Petersburg, Russia to investigate the Internet Research Agency, aka the infamous "troll factory."

Yle assigned a colleague, an experienced foreign affairs reporter named Mika Mäkeläinen, to travel with me. We were lucky to find an excellent Russian journalist, Irina Tumakova, to work with us as our local stringer.

At the time, the Internet Research Agency was located at 55 Savushkina Street, on the edge of central St. Petersburg. (It has since relocated to Optikov Street). Officially, the agency was registered as a software-development company that also researched public opinion. It recruited new staff online: copywriters, search engine optimizers, content managers, and graphic designers. The employees were paid a monthly salary of $400 to $650, which in St. Petersburg was competitive pay. Many positions at the company involved creating and moderating online content in twelve-hour shifts, including nights. Some jobs required English-language skills.

I asked Irina to call the agency's recruiter and pretend to

be interested in a job as a copywriter. On the phone, she asked for specifics about the kinds of themes she would be expected to write about. The recruiter said that the copywriters produced news, specifically political news, in Russian and English. The content management jobs were similar: writing about politics after being assigned a theme. When Irina asked why the job required mastering the use of search engines, the recruiter promised more details during the interview.

The Russian investigative journalist Alexandra Garmazhapova had already infiltrated the Internet Research Agency in 2013, and written an exclusive exposé for *Novaya Gazeta*.[1] During her job interview, the recruiter had told Garmazhapova that he personally knew many Russian officials, including members of the Duma. He also disclosed that he had participated in the Seliger Forum—a political youth camp organized by the Kremlin-founded fake citizen organization Nashi. Garmazhapova revealed that the workers at the troll factory were encouraged to write nasty things online about the United States and Russian opposition leader Alexander Navalny. Before she resigned, she saved some of her work on a memory stick and included excerpts of it in her article.

00000

In St. Petersburg, we visited the "troll factory" several times. It was located in a four-story office building whose entrance bore no signs or logos. Lights shone from the windows throughout the night. The night shifts enabled the employees to engage in online activities in different time zones. To be able to disrupt and inter-fere in online discussions in the United States, for example, an overnight shift was necessary.

The shift changes at 9:00 AM and 9:00 PM were marked by a steady flow of employees, mainly in their twenties, exiting and entering the building. By the back door, the workers took breaks from trolling on social media to smoke cigarettes. We tried to interview the employees, but no one would agree to talk to us. A few said that they weren't allowed to speak; I later learned that the workers had to sign a strict nondisclosure agreement. Many of them hid their faces or turned away when they noticed us filming them.

One special fake news operation was run from the building's first floor, where workers posted stories to RIA Fan. While the site was represented as being produced in Ukraine, all of its content was created in St. Petersburg. We interviewed the editor-in-chief of RIA Fan, Yevgeny Zubarev, who denied employing trolls or having a budget for social media propaganda.[2] "When our office is accused of having trolls, it's a lie," he told us. "People who believe that are simple. I think this is due to the propaganda warfare." Zubarev said that RIA Fan had been established solely for business purposes; he claimed to have negotiated with advertisers like Sberbank and looked for ways to turn a profit. But the site didn't have ads, a paywall, or subscription deals. One thing Zubarev did acknowledge was that the site published unverified information, "just like all other media outlets."

⁂

Before the trip, I was warned that the troll factory was most likely guarded by the FSB. Ironically, it was the building's security guard who unwittingly confirmed the Russian State's direct involvement. The rare confession occurred on the second day, as Irina and I took photos and filmed outside the main entrance. The guard swaggered outside, complaining about our filming. He threatened to call the police, and then told us, as we captured his words on film, that we needed to leave because the place was an "administrative building."

"Administrative objects" in Russia are protected entities. They were granted special status by a 1998 presidential decree, and include police stations, military units, FSB buildings, and nuclear power plants. By calling the Internet Research Agency office an "administrative building," the guard confirmed that it was a Russian government operation.

ooooo

When we returned home to Finland, Mika and I wrote about our visit to the Internet Research Agency for several Yle platforms and news shows. One online piece was translated into English; it included never-before-seen footage and important details about the troll factory. The articles were shared widely by intelligence and security experts as well as diplomats in many countries. For me, the most important audience was the general public; we received numerous messages from readers who were thankful for our reporting. The stories have since been cited in academic research and security reports.

In response to the articles, the online intimidation against me intensified; Mika Mäkeläinen was targeted as well. Twitter trolls accused us of bribing our interviewees in St. Petersburg. Comments on Facebook swore that our reports were bogus. Our headshots were attached to an image that was a hybrid of a swastika and the NATO logo. We were derided as Russia-hating media prostitutes. Many regular Finnish citizens were influenced to believe the social media vilification. They also seemed compelled to spread the baseless lies about me and Mika and to reject the information we tried to present about the new methods of Russian information warfare. This is where the Kremlin's information propagandists are particularly skillful: they run operations that are unethical, sometimes illegal, violate basic human rights and international justice, but are able to twist the critical and nasty public discussions against their targets. It felt surreal to read accusations about "propaganda spreading" against Mika and I when the proper target for such a critique should have been the Russian troll factory and its strategists. However, the reason special combat propaganda is used against private individuals is because it works.

The campaign against me included noted and influential Finns, too. A parliament official mocked me openly on the Facebook group Russian Troll Army. A former Social Democratic Party member of parliament started a suggestive smear campaign against me. Several Facebook friends of Johan Bäckman also contributed to the social media smearing, including a lawyer who called me a Nazi whore on Bäckman's Facebook wall.

Facebook's Events feature was also harnessed for organized hatemongering against me and Yle. Anonymous operators established an event that invited people to a protest against the "Yle Troll Factory." The organizers set the tone by swearing at me and Mika and threatening to come to Yle's headquarters to demand an explanation for "Yle employees' propaganda spreading" and carry banners exposing the "crimes of Yle bosses and employees." In the end, a handful of protesters showed up in person. Even though the number of protesters were significantly fewer than the number of people who threatened to partake in the protest on Facebook, the operation proved that the social media giant could be successfully and anonymously exploited to create an in-person protest based on Kremlin social media propaganda. Two years later, the Mueller investigation into Russian meddling in the US election revealed that the Internet Research Agency had instigated protests on American soil through the Facebook Events feature: one troll factory-initiated protest opposed the alleged Islamization of Texas, while a counter-protest on the same street rallied to "save Islamic knowledge."[3, 4]

My intimidators also tried an even more psychologically invasive approach to try and scare me. Someone sent me a text message claiming to be my father (who had passed away twenty years earlier.) "My father" texted me that he was alive and .

monitoring me. As my father wasn't a public figure, I realized that whoever the sender was had carefully investigated my personal history and was willing to use the most brutal psychological methods to manipulate me in order to stop my work.

Luckily, I was on my way to meet a friend when I read the message. When I saw my friend, I hugged him hard to stay on my feet.

The police were never able to find any information about the sender.

10.

The Scholar

IN JANUARY 2017, MARTIN KRAGH, AN expert on Russian politics, published an academic paper exposing the Kremlin's propaganda efforts against his home country of Sweden.

Two months later, the then thirty-six-year-old had lost weight, wasn't sleeping well, and was struggling to focus on his work as a researcher at Uppsala University and program leader at the Swedish Institute of International Affairs, the country's most well-known foreign policy research institute. Kragh had become entangled in a media storm fueled by a combination of Russian state media, Swedish neo-Nazis, far-left political activists, YouTube trolls, and Russia-connected actors working in the Swedish media.

It's not that Kragh didn't know how to accept criticism of his work. Throughout his impressive career, his research, books, and presentations had been thoughtfully evaluated and discussed on many occasions. As Kragh puts it, legitimate academic criticism is always welcome. "In the academic world, if you disagree or have better knowledge on the topic, you write your own article. You create new methodology, provide new data, and thus accumulate scientific information. That's the whole purpose of research," he shares.

But Kragh's "critics" never intended to contribute to science. Instead, his name, professional credibility, and ethics were tarnished by the systematic spreading of lies, twisted accusations, and conspiracy theories. And these attacks emerged not only from the anonymity of the internet's darkest corners, but also involved mainstream Swedish journalists.

Sweden is one of the world's leaders in press freedom, human rights protections, and overall citizen well-being. In this type of environment, the campaign against Dr. Kragh was extraordinary. "It's crap, disinformation, lies," he says. "But hypothetically, if my situation with my family or work had been different, and I hadn't received support, I could be lying in a ditch."

FASCISM IN UKRAINE

The article that ignited the hate campaign against Kragh was titled "Russia's Strategy for Influence through Public Diplomacy and Active Measures: The Swedish Case."[1] Coauthored with Sebastian Åsberg, the article was published in January 2017 in the *Journal of Strategic Studies*, a well-respected, peer-reviewed journal that focuses on military and diplomatic issues. The article discussed the Russian-based KGB-style influence operations that were being used against Sweden, focusing on the tools used by Russian security services: forged diplomatic documents, social media propaganda, support of extremist groups, and insertion of the Putin regime's political messaging into the Swedish media. Also exposed were the radical pro-Kremlin organizations active in Sweden and their direct connections to Russian entities. One of the key findings of the article was evidence showing how Russian diplomats and politicians proactively intervened in Sweden's domestic affairs.

The article provided examples of how the Kremlin's fake narratives circulated, not only on Swedish online platforms but in the traditional media as well. One traditional Swedish news organization that was examined in detail was *Aftonbladet*, one of the largest daily newspapers in Scandinavia. Kragh and Åsberg described how *Aftonbladet* published stories in its culture section that mirrored the type of information published in the Russian-controlled state media. For example, in 2014 alone, *Aftonbladet*'s culture section published more than thirty articles about countries of the former Soviet Union in which the main theme was "fascism in Ukraine." In these articles, fascism was repeatedly characterized as Ukraine's emerging political force. Russia's war against Ukraine was referred to simply as a "crisis."

Kragh and Åsberg also presented information showing how the culture section of *Aftonbladet* described the European Union and NATO in ways that closely followed the Kremlin's propaganda lines. They also analyzed how a few of the writers for the section created content for pro-Kremlin social media and publicly spread conspiracy theories. Some of the writers' ties to the well-known Russian anti-Semite, Holocaust denier, and disinformation spreader Israel Shamir were revealed. Shamir is the Russian representative of WikiLeaks, which many in the Western intelligence community consider a front for Russia's SVR and/or GRU.[2]

Typically, the culture sections of most media outlets produce journalism about authors and artists, opera, theater, movies, and other cultural and art-related phenomena. But in the case of Martin Kragh, *Aftonbladet*'s culture section abandoned its cultural mission and turned its focus to politics.

THE NATO QUESTION

Martin Kragh's article created a stir, both domestically and abroad. Many Swedish journalists were inspired by his research, and Kragh became a sought-after interview subject. Established news outlets such as the BBC, the *Guardian*, and the *Huffington Post* published stories based on his article, which quickly became one of the most downloaded on the *Journal of Strategic Studies'* website. Kragh's work was also cited by Michael Fallon, the then British Secretary of State for Defense.

In spite of the international praise and support for his work, the culture section of *Aftonbladet* initiated a public smearing of Dr. Kragh. Under the auspices and direction of its chief cultural editor, Åsa Linderborg, *Aftonbladet* published its first hit piece against Kragh on January 9, 2017, just a few days after the publication of his article. The story described Kragh's findings as "attacks" and "a witch hunt." Kragh's employer, the Swedish Institute of International Affairs, was accused of "Putinism."[3] Other Swedish journalists who had cited Kragh's work professionally were mocked and accused. The article also claimed that Dr. Kragh had labeled one of *Aftonbladet's* writers a "Putin agent," which was untrue. The piece was written in an arrogant and aggressive tone, more typical of vulgar, anonymous blogs than a major Scandinavian news outlet.

A second article was published the following day, which labeled Dr. Kragh's research "part of the information war that aims to cast suspicion on anyone who does not want us to join the war alliance [NATO]."[4] The article insinuated that the secret motivation behind Kragh's research was to push Sweden to join NATO. Turning the discussion to NATO was an attempt to distract from Kragh's original critique of Russian activities. In fact, Dr. Kragh has never stated any policy recommendations concerning Sweden's relations with NATO.

The piece also framed Kragh's research as an attack against freedom of the press, with *Aftonbladet* declaring that it would continue to "write what we want, the way we want, even in a situation in which no one else defends our right to do it." That promise was fulfilled, as between January and June 2017, the paper published more than ten articles repeating false accusations against Dr. Kragh and stirring up a public frenzy against his employers. One article questioned the *Journal of Strategic Studies* because its "editorial staff come from NATO or allied countries, which poses a risk for bias."[5] As "proof," the article listed the home countries of the editors of the publication. Another piece compared Kragh's article to McCarthyism.[6]

In 2017, I met Kragh in Copenhagen at a conference about Russian information warfare. At the time, Swedish journalists were demanding that he explain why he had spread misinformation through his "bad" research. He was visibly shocked.

Yet another writer for *Aftonbladet*, Alexey Sakhnin, who in the spring of 2017 began work for the Russian propaganda channel RT, accused Kragh of spreading conspiracy theories. Later that year, during a massive Russian war drill named Zapad 2017, Sakhnin traveled to Finland to organize a Swedish-Russian "peace protest." Finnish diplomat Hannu Himanen described the protest camp as a Russian operation, which was aimed at influencing public opinion in both Sweden and Finland.[7]

As a Swedish news organization, *Aftonbladet* must follow the country's guidelines for ethical journalism, which require that the media respect the people they report about. According to this self-regulating system, the Swedish media is forbidden to publish negative articles about a person if that person has not been offered a fair opportunity to voice his or her own views. These rules are integral to the press ethics not only in Sweden, but in all Nordic countries. The aim is to prevent the media from unfairly attacking an individual, and to keep information as factual as possible.

However, in its coverage of his article, *Aftonbladet* never asked Kragh for comment. "*Aftonbladet* did ask me once which method I had used when analyzing their content in my research. I replied: text analysis. Other than that, they didn't ask me anything," he recalls.

∞∞∞

As *Aftonbladet's* campaign against him continued, Kragh's research was called an unscientific and antidemocratic "jumble."[8] The paper also brought up the notion of launching a committee to investigate his article. This idea caught on in some corners of the Swedish media.

The media and marketing magazine *Dagens Media*, and *Journalisten*, which describes itself as "Sweden's oldest and largest media newspaper," also joined the fray. *Aftonbladet's* Åsa Linderborg told *Dagens Media* that Kragh's article was "unscientific, and shameless and ugly in its accusations."[9] She also voiced concern that Kragh's findings had been widely quoted in the Swedish and international media. She said she needed to kill the "rumors" somehow and that his article should be retracted. Through these professional papers, read by a large swathe of Sweden's journalists and editors, Linderborg's interpretation of Kragh's "shameless and ugly" research gained a foothold across the country's journalistic community.

ooooo

Kragh and Sebastian Åsberg also became the target of several cyberattacks, the origins of which remain unknown. However, the circumstantial evidence, such as IP addresses, points toward Russia. Åsberg was sent emails similar to the ones which the GRU had used in its attacks against the Democratic Party during the 2016 election. Kragh himself was sent phishing emails. "These cyberattacks surpass my level of technical understanding," says Kragh, "but their purpose is obvious: to deter anyone from publicly supporting me and my coauthor, Sebastian Åsberg. It seems impossible to find out who was behind them, or who ordered them."

ANTI-EUROMAIDAN SWEDEN

Anti-Euromaidan Sweden is the Swedish version of a network of similar groups cultivated internationally on Facebook.[10] In these groups, professional pro-Kremlin propagandists and fake profiles organize psychological operations to advance Russia's social media agenda. The groups serve as de facto hubs for Russian propaganda, offering filth memes about Western leaders, as well as fake news from Russian state-controlled media, and ostensibly "balanced" pro-Kremlin blogs.

"Anti-Euromaidan" refers to the protests organized by Ukrainians against the Kremlin-leaning president Viktor Yanukovych in 2013 and 2014 in Kyiv's Maidan Square. The protests were known as Euromaidan, and obviously, the Swedish Facebook group's name was chosen to mock the movement. Yanukovych responded to the Euromaidan protests with violence. He ordered the special police to repress the crowds who were attempting to restore Ukraine's democracy and turn it away from the Kremlin's sphere of influence. Despite the violence, the protesters didn't give up. In the end, Yanukovych fled to Russia.

Like Russian Troll Army, Anti-Euromaidan Sweden serves as an arena for the mobilization of conspiracy theorists and manipulated regular citizens. At the time of this writing, Anti-Euromaidan Sweden has a little over 1,100 members. The nature of the group is best conveyed by a conversation in which the participants praised one of the most legendary post-factual Russian politicians, Vladimir Zhirinovsky, for "telling the truth." In addition, members post viral videos that depict Ukraine as a Nazi country, and share videos from Ruptly, the video arm of RT.

One visible participant in Swedish pro-Kremlin social media groups has been journalist Maj Wechselmann. Among other activities, Wechselmann regularly provides analyses of Russian and Ukrainian developments for the *Aftonbladet* culture section. She was also connected to a NGO called Swedish Doctors for Human Rights (SWEDHR). The NGO gained notoriety in 2015 when the Russian Ministry of Foreign Affairs approvingly cited its report clearing Bashar al-Assad of accusations concerning his use of chemical weapons against Syrian civilians.[11][12] No one in SWEDHR had any relevant expertise in the field of biological warfare, and several independent UN investigations have since proven that the Russian-backed al-Assad did in fact use chemical weapons, specifically sarin gas, against his own people. Nevertheless, Wechselmann has been able to publish several smear articles against Dr. Kragh in respected Swedish newspapers.[13]

Like Russian Troll Army in Finland, Anti-Euromaidan Sweden has been used as a platform to coordinate smear campaigns against Swedish academicians and journalists. In early 2017, the group urged its members to file complaints about Dr. Kragh to his employer, Uppsala University. This campaign was launched at the same time that Kragh was being relentlessly attacked in *Aftonbladet*. The complaints repeated the same demands that Dr. Kragh and his research about Russian influence operations be investigated for alleged academic misconduct.

In Sweden, when a formal complaint is addressed to a dedicated board alleging scientific or academic misconduct— for example, fraud, plagiarism, or falsifying research data—the board looks into the complaint carefully. Typically, a suspicion of misconduct arises from other members of the academic community, who must present substantiation of the alleged misconduct.

As the complaints are public according to Swedish law, I asked Uppsala University to provide me with those made against Dr. Kragh. Examining them, it was clear they were not written by scholars. Many were mere political opinions; some attacked Kragh personally. None were academic in nature. One complainant sent in the CV of the editor in chief of the *Journal of Strategic Studies* as evidence of the journal's bias. Yet another stated that Kragh's research was not scientific at all; instead, it was the "United States foreign intelligence services' Russophobic plot." "People wrote to the university things such as 'I don't like Martin Kragh,' 'Martin Kragh is an agent of the Pentagon,' 'Martin Kragh is a threat to national security.' In fact, I might very well be a threat to national security, but that's still not scientific misconduct," Kragh jokes.

One of the complainants was Maj Wechselmann. Another was Egor Putilov. Behind this pseudonym hides a Russian immigrant who at the time worked for Sweden's right-wing anti-immigration party, Sweden Democrats, while also operating as a journalist in the Swedish press, using another fake identity. Putilov has used at least five different pseudonyms during his time in Sweden, and has been labeled a security threat by several Swedish security experts.[14] Putilov, in line with Åsa Linderborg, also demanded the retraction of Kragh's article. He also hired a law firm in London to intimidate the *Journal of Strategic Studies*, threatening to take the editors to court. Several months after Kragh's report was published, Uppsala University continued to be flooded with complaints.

Dr. Kragh was eventually cleared of misconduct by Uppsala University. But the damage had already been done, as the news that Kragh was being investigated for suspected academic misconduct spread widely in the Swedish media. In addition to having to deal with the negative publicity, Dr. Kragh was also forced to waste a lot of time and energy trying to clear his name. In the end, none of the journalists who had disseminated the alleged academic misconduct charges against Dr. Kragh followed up with the news of his being cleared.

ATTACKED FROM THE RIGHT
Many Nordic neo-Nazis are deeply influenced by Putin's PR campaigns. They view Putin the way he is depicted by the Kremlin's propaganda machinery: as a master judoka, muscular fisherman, fighter jet pilot, and of course, the war mastermind who enforces "healthy" nationalism by cracking down on Islamic terrorists, first in Chechnya and then in Syria.

In Sweden, as in Finland, the most visible neo-Nazi group is the Nordic Resistance Movement (NRM). These white supremacists promote closing off Sweden and Finland from refugees, fuel hatred against foreigners, and march in the streets chanting antigovernment slogans. They also publish online propaganda to social media, and recruit people, mostly young men, to fight for their cause. The NRM verbally attack anyone they view as an enemy of their model society—which include traditional media journalists who write critically about Russia's policies.

The Swedish chapter of the Nordic Resistance Movement has long maintained connections to Russian extremists. Relations are especially warm with the Russian Imperial Movement, a neo-Nazi group that markets a militant nationalist dictatorship. Its paramilitary branch, Partizan, has participated in Russia's war against Ukraine.

In 2017, a Swedish court sentenced three members of the NRM to prison for violent crimes they had committed in the southern part of the country in late 2016 and early 2017. The neo-Nazis had planted homemade explosives outside the offices of their political opponents, and in refugee shelters. Right before the conspiracy was hatched, two of the plotters had participated in a weeklong paramilitary training camp outside St. Petersburg.[15] Photos of the two men holding Kalashnikovs and wearing military uniforms surfaced on the Russian social media service VKontakte. The organizer of the camp was the Russian Imperial Movement.

In Sweden, several far-right propaganda sites and YouTube content creators have expressed their sympathies toward Putin due to, among other things, anti-Americanism, anti-globalism, and a perception of Russia as the lone bastion of "traditional values" and resister of "uncontrolled migration." Many of these pro-Putin and far-right operators attacked Kragh and Åsberg virtually. One of them was an amorphous YouTube collective named *Granskning Sverige* (Investigation Sweden). In 2017, Swedish investigative journalist Mathias Ståhle infiltrated the group. He discovered that they recruited people directly from Facebook and didn't ask too many questions in the "job interview," conducted via Facebook Messenger.[16]

According to Ståhl's investigation, the responsibility of workers at *Granskning Sverige* is to place hateful telephone calls to Swedish journalists, researchers, and other individuals who have publicly commented on immigration and Russian issues in Sweden. The callers, hiding behind fake names, are further tasked with provoking the target on the phone, for example by accusing the person of lying, spreading fake news, or distorting facts about immigration and crime. The calls are recorded. The workers are then instructed to edit the recording—creatively mixing the original content in a manner that make the targeted people seem as foolish as possible—and upload the video to YouTube and share it on Facebook. If the video goes viral and receives a sufficient number of views on YouTube, the worker is rewarded with the equivalent of about $120 USD. Even though hard evidence of the participation of Russia or Russian operators in *Granskning Sverige's* activities has not been found, its modus operandi is reminiscent of that of other Russian operations in Europe and United States. Russian state-controlled propaganda media organizations, like Sputnik, closely follow the group and link to their trashy YouTube videos.

During the second week of the harassment campaign against Kragh, a Swedish caller introducing himself as "Erik Johansson" started to phone him repeatedly. "Johansson" called Kragh's employer and colleagues, too, accusing them of Russophobia. In addition, he demanded details about Sebastian Åsberg. "Erik Johansson" was later exposed as a fifty-year-old Holocaust denier from southern Sweden, who even tweeted about his project and promised to publish a video. All the calls he made, including those in which Kragh immediately hung up, were recorded and added to an odd YouTube "documentary" titled "Russian Threat, Is It Real or Are We Tricked?"

The *Granskning Sverige* filth video against Kragh and Åsberg was picked up by the English-language edition of Sputnik International, which characterized the Swedish academics' findings as "anti-Russian paranoia across Scandinavia" and viciously targeted Åsberg.[17] The story spun in the Russian propaganda media aggravated the attacks against Kragh and Åsberg, with Kragh receiving death threats from far-right radicals across Europe.

Granskning Sverige's YouTube channel was taken down in the spring of 2018, after the video service was loudly criticized in the Swedish media for allowing hate speech on several of its Swedish-language channels. However, many group members still upload *Granskning Sverige*-branded videos to other YouTube channels, as well as to VKontakte.

ooooo

A month after his article in the *Journal of Strategic Studies* was published, RT also published an article smearing Dr. Kragh.[18] The RT story named Kragh as part of a conspiracy puzzle which included the Bonnier family, a Swedish media family of Jewish origin, and the US State Department. RT also repeated *Aftonbladet*'s false assertion that Kragh was personally responsible for the eradication of free speech in Sweden.

The writer of the RT article was the previously mentioned Israel Shamir, a dual citizen of Russia and Sweden, and editor of the Russian ultranationalist weekly *Zavtra*. (Shamir's son, Johannes Wahlström, is also affiliated with Julian Assange and Wikileaks, as well as being a frequent contributor to *Aftonbladet*.)[19]

Shamir has access to the major Russian media outlets as well as the Russian book publishing industry. In 2015, he partook in an outrageous attack against the respected British journalist Luke Harding. Harding is the author of the internationally acclaimed book *Mafia State*, which describes his years as the Moscow correspondent for the *Guardian*. Harding had to live under constant surveillance and harassment by the FSB.

In 2015, a fake version of *Mafia State*, retitled *Nikto Krome Putina* (*No One but Putin*), was published in Russia with its original content completely gutted.[20] The book was sold in Russian bookshops under Harding's name, but without his consent. The foreword to this edition was written by Israel Shamir. In it, he accuses Harding of "distorting" the *Guardian*'s articles concerning the WikiLeaks cables, "conducting information warfare, and harming Western countries."

Shamir is also personally close to another writer at *Aftonbladet*, the left-wing activist Alexey Sakhnin, who participated in the "peace protest" in Finland, In April 2017, Sakhnin gave a long interview to one of the most notorious pro-Kremlin tabloids in Russia, *Komsomolskaya Pravda*. Sakhnin claimed that Kragh had lobbied for Sweden to join NATO.[21]

Sakhnin also took his anti-Kragh campaign to Vesti, one of Russia's largest television networks. In an interview, Sakhnin claimed that freedom of speech was more secure in Russia than in Sweden, and asserted that Sweden was a totalitarian country, and that he would much rather live in Russia. Earlier, he had moved to Sweden from Russia, claiming to escape political persecution. In 2019, Sakhnin moved back to Russia.

Dissemination of possible defamation in another state's information space and in another language is a much more severe issue than just an ordinary breach of the guidelines for ethical journalism. Martin Kragh has relatives who live in Russia. He travels to the country regularly to work as well as meet his family. Because of the filth stories circling in the Russian state media, sourced to seemingly credible Swedish journalists, Dr. Kragh has been put on the radar of Russian state security authorities. Many others who have been denounced by Russian propaganda outlets have later fallen victim to harassment, intimidation, assault, and, in some cases, murder plots.

THE BAD GUY

Right after *Aftonbladet* began its campaign, Dr. Kragh started hearing the rumors. Someone was spreading lies directly to his colleagues. According to one falsehood, he had been removed from his post at the Swedish Institute of International Affairs. His colleagues asked: "Is it true that you're being fired?"

Dr. Kragh says that the best way to get past the rumors was to get back to work. So he continued giving interviews to the media, teaching students, conducting research, and organizing conferences. His work has been cited by leading news outlets such as the *Financial Times*, the *New York Times*, and the *Economist*. His "scandalous research" has been quoted in more than fifty international reports.

When we met in the fall of 2018, Kragh told me that the attacks against him had calmed down. He said that he was now better prepared for any new hate campaigns that might arise against him. During the most active phase of the disinformation attacks, Kragh had kept a diary. Looking back at it, he was able to see that everything he was alleged to have done were not things that he had actually done. Words that were not his had been attributed to him, citations to his work invented, his motives and honor questioned. Instead of presenting him as an ethical scholar, the trolls had painted him as a politically motivated, dishonest lobbyist for NATO. "Funny thing is, I don't even have a strong opinion about NATO," he told me. "My friends laugh about it. I am, however, unabashedly pro-democracy and pro-rule of law. This is what seems to bother my opponents the most."

Westerners become targets of Russian-fueled disinformation campaigns unwillingly and suddenly, usually without having any prior security training, or expertise in reputation management. Having lived through such a campaign, I asked Dr. Kragh what he would say to people who became targets? "First, you're hit by a feeling of shock," he answered. "It's important to identify that you're in the middle of a shitstorm. You don't have any control over it whatsoever. However, when you throw shit at the wall, some of it will always stick. Therefore, it is impossible to pretend as if these attacks are not happening."

Dr. Kragh emphasizes that the goal of Russian online attacks is to push people into making mistakes they wouldn't make under normal conditions. He admits that he tried to defend himself and push back against some of the journalists who targeted him. But those attempts failed. "To be honest, I said some things which I should have skipped saying, because I was in a bad mood," he shares. "Then my comments were taken out of context, although they were technically true. That was a mistake, as the debate would therefore continue rather than fizzle out." If reporters called today and demanded his comments for their biased articles, Kragh told me he would not answer the phone.

Though we might hope for a more universally efficient response to politically motivated online attacks, Dr. Kragh reminds us that open societies cannot resort to the methods of authoritarian regimes. In a democracy, it is permissible to act, for example, as a paid Russian troll and spread disinformation. "I'm not happy that all this happened," he tells me. "But you grow a thicker skin, an armor. After this experience, it's hopefully a little more difficult to destabilize me." One of the keys to surviving online attacks, according to Kragh, is having both public and private support. In his case, many of Sweden's most well-respected Russian scholars and journalists publicly testified to the quality of his work, which helped restore credibility to his pioneering research.

As a result of his experiences, Dr. Kragh has learned that some journalists have agendas that guide their editorial decisions more than common ethical rules. He wishes that the traditional media would act more carefully before falling into traps set by professional influence agents. When he saw the traditional Swedish media picking up blatant lies, or disseminating highly tendentious claims about him, he realized that the professional propagandists had been able to set the agenda. "They decided I was the bad guy, so they were looking for bad stuff about me."

FAKE ANONYMOUS

The hackers claimed to be from the international group known as Anonymous. However, the real Anonymous is generally politically neutral, and these hackers seemed to be driving a political agenda. The documents they uploaded to their site were annotated with comments in which specific British politicians were picked apart with strong language.[22] In some of the comments, it was claimed that Britain was involved in "waging information warfare against everyone." Some of the material breached privacy laws: private citizen's passport data and home addresses were published.

A significant portion of the documents allegedly belonged to the Institute for Statecraft, a London-based research center that focuses on Russian influence operations and other topical issues, with a specific focus on revealing and countering disinformation spread by Russia. Their project named Integrity Initiative aims at building networks and connections between researchers who focus on Russian disinformation throughout Europe. One of their major funders is the British Foreign Ministry.

The hackers had broken into the institute's computer networks, dug out and possibly edited documents, and then uploaded them to their site. The first batch of documents was uploaded in November 2018, which more following later on. The initial news about the documents—whose authenticity could not be verified—was reported by RT and Sputnik. Troll accounts spread the hack-based stories further on social media.

Martin Kragh contacted me right before Christmas of that year. "The attacks against me have increased significantly in recent weeks," he said. "RT and Sputnik published information hacked from a British think tank. Apparently, I am 'the head of the MI6-run Integrity Initiative's Nordic cluster.'" According to RT and Sputnik, MI6 controlled the Institute for Statecraft. Two conspiracy theories had now become one, with Kragh connected to both.

During one single day, the Russian state media published sixty-two stories about the data breach. Kragh said that meant that the operation was designed in advance. It was likely that RT, Sputnik and others had received word about the hack before it happened. In their stories, the Kremlin's propaganda outlets claimed that the "leaked documents" revealed a variety of scandalous "facts," such as the Integrity Initiative's attempt to install mines around Sevastopol in March 2014 in order to prevent Crimea's "reunification" with Russia.[23] Such an operation never took place. The stories also contemplated the possibility that the Integrity Initiative was tangled up in the assassination attempt on Sergei Skripal, the former Russian intelligence officer and double agent for Britain who was poisoned in 2018.

Several extremist political newspapers in Sweden followed the Kremlin's lead and produced stories based on the hacked documents.

∞∞∞

2019 began with new conspiracy theories being spread by social media influencers against Dr. Kragh. One theory claimed that Kragh had participated in planning an anti-democratic coup. Kragh's web page was also attacked and taken down.

In February, Alexey Sakhnin and Johannes Wahlström published an article in the Russian newspaper *Novaya Gazeta* in which they raked Kragh over the coals.[24] Israel Shamir posted on Facebook that Martin Kragh was the second-biggest enemy of Russia in northern Europe. Kragh estimates that between March 2018 and February 2019, the Russian media published over 600 stories concerning the hack of the Institute for Statecraft. Content-wise, they recycled the same conspiracy theories. The aim of the campaign was to push the stories to local media and information networks.

Also in February, the culture section of *Aftonbladet* struck again. Åsa Linderborg, still the chief of the section at the time (she was reassigned in July 2019), wrote that Martin Kragh was a "democratic problem" and a political enemy who served the interests of foreign states, worked in a secret state security organization in Great Britain, and stigmatized the NATO-critical peace movement under the guise of doing research.[25] "That's why the Swedish media and security police should investigate Kragh," Linderborg urged.

In another story published a few days later, *Aftonbladet* claimed that "according to leaked documents … Kragh is suspected of working for a foreign power, specifically British intelligence,[26] and he sells (false) information about his fellow citizens."[27] Obviously, no evidence to back up these claims was provided. Eventually, Kragh filed a complaint about *Aftonbladet* to Pressens Opinionsnämnd (PO), the Swedish journalism ethics oversight board. In December 2019, PO chastened *Aftonbladet* for claiming that Kragh worked for foreign intelligence services. *Aftonbladet* was required to publish PO's damning decision on its website.[28]

Little by little, the professional Swedish media started to pay more attention to Kragh's treatment. The newspaper *Svenska Dagbladet* and many other prominent papers published stories about the exceptional campaign against him. Many of them finally asked for Martin Kragh's own comments. The stories exposing the campaign against Kragh raised awareness and public discussion. The scope of the Kremlin-instigated filth writing in Sweden came as a surprise to many, even though it had been ongoing for over two years.

ooooo

The hostile influence operations against Dr. Kragh continue to this day. Despite the lies, he continues his work, educating students, holding conferences, and giving expert commentary to the media.

At times, Dr. Kragh fears that the attacks will never stop, and that the death threats will turn into reality. He has a wife and two small children, and they have been forced to take security measures. He has also thought that he might be better off shifting his research focus to other topics. But he believes that if he gives up researching and commenting in his chosen field, the attackers will have won.

Kragh believes that while many people are taken in by the Kremlin's propaganda, there are those who will not fall prey to the lies and slander: "Every target should realize that serious people who understand the phenomenon can tell the difference between truthful allegations and mudslinging."

11.

The Trolls' Impact

AFTER SEVERAL MONTHS OF INTENSE DIGGING, including interviews with internet users, moderators of traditional media comment sections, and security experts, my series of crowdsourced articles detailing the impact of Russian troll operations were published in May 2015 by Yle.[1] The articles were widely read and well-received. Responding to international interest, Yle also published them in English and Russian.

One of the discoveries I made was how many ordinary Finnish citizens were silenced by online attacks from aggressive, anonymous, and fake online profiles. These attacks were orchestrated whenever a user shared negative information or voiced critical opinions concerning the Russian regime. The profiles frequently flooded unsuspecting users with false messages, such as "Putin wants peace and negotiations"; "The Ukrainian president is a warmonger"; "Russia hasn't broken international law by annexing Crimea."

As the snipers of information warfare filled the web with their fabrications, several people told me that they no longer understood what was going on in Ukraine. By sowing confusion, the Russian online warriors had succeeded in depriving these citizens of their right to access factual information—a crucial building block when forming opinions. The most worrisome impact was that after being exposed to propaganda, some people started to share it further in their own networks—without knowing that they had been tricked by a hostile foreign entity.

One piece of good news that came out of my investigation was that many Finns told me of having witnessed operations conducted by anonymous entities and being able to identify them as old-fashioned propaganda techniques delivered through new channels. Those individuals weren't negatively affected by the false information, unlike the other users.

ooooo

One of the sites that my articles exposed as a spreader of the Russian leadership's messaging was MV-Lehti. MV-Lehti is a fake news site that appeared out of nowhere in 2014, and whose original name—in English—is *What the Fuck??!!* MV-Lehti publishes vulgar and scandalous stories disguised as news, as well as applying the Russian combat propaganda "60/40" rule to its narratives. The site accuses Yle and other traditional news outlets of lying and spreading conspiracy theories. MV-Lehti also translates stories from the Russian propaganda network RT into Finnish. The site brags about "telling the stories ignored by the mainstream media," a principal it copied from RT. The majority of the stories are written by pseudonyms and fake identities.

Between 2015 and 2018, under its "news articles," MV-Lehti embedded a comments section provided by a Facebook plugin. The add-on enabled trolls using Facebook to comment directly on MV-Lehti pieces. The comments were full of fake profiles spouting racist hate speech and offering President Putin as the solution to the problems of the Western world. Many individuals and trolls also used the unmoderated comments section to spread their delusional and obnoxious theories on topics including Jews, Muslims, foreigners, the so-called New World Order, and the "globalist elite." (At the time, the site was focusing heavily on exaggerating crimes committed by Muslims and asylum seekers.) On one occasion, I counted more than 100 clearly fake Facebook profiles with bogus names whose task was to immediately comment on a new piece as soon as it was published. In one article, MV-Lehti promised to pay a reward to anyone who provided their "newsroom" with sensitive material about the private lives of journalists.

THE CLOWN OF JOURNALISM

My Russian troll articles had been up for only a few hours when MV-Lehti and its sister sites began dehumanizing me to an extent I had never experience before. Three years later, Helsinki District Court Prosecutor Juha-Mikko Hämäläinen, who would handle the prosecution of my legal case against Johan Bäckman and the others who defamed me, called MV-Lehti's actions an attempt to destroy my life, and to influence my work as a journalist.

In its first slanderous article, MV-Lehti called me a clown of investigative journalism and ridiculed my investigations.[2] I had, they claimed, "accused MV-Lehti of being Russian trolls, because we criticize the Western elite and Illuminati." The site also falsely stated that numerous criminal complaints had been filed against me. Appended to the text of the piece was a meme that depicted my face stamped with a caption in English that read, "JESSIKKA ARO FAKE NEWS JOURNALIST DEBUNKED." Also, my work phone number was published, once again.

As I watched the MV-Lehti attack against me unfold, I noticed the effect it had on its readers on Facebook. One commenter, a former friend of mine, was persuaded to smear me publicly: "This is my old acquaintance. she used to be a no-nonsense person. I dunno what the fuck has happened that she believes in this shit. i thought she was smarter," this person wrote. As I had learned during my troll investigation, I again saw in real time how an individual's opinion could be molded by social media propaganda.

Over the next few months, similar stories attacking me were

published on MV-Lehti and its sister sites, and on conspiracy blogs. The content creators seemed to have received the following instructions concerning me, which they pushed in their articles: that I was "a NATO lobbyist"; that I conjured up Russian trolls from my imagination; that I labeled real citizens as paid trolls; and committed crimes.

Simultaneously, the circle of Finnish pro-Putin fanatics, including Johan Bäckman and other pro-Kremlin extremist bloggers, was again activated. They posted about me constantly, inciting their followers, both real and fake. Bäckman also pushed MV-Lehti stories about me on Facebook and Twitter.

∞∞∞

After enduring several months of this filth campaign, I considered filing a criminal complaint. I believed the false accusations spread on social media against me to be libelous—libel, or defamation, is a crime in Finland. I took screen shoots of the vitriol and showed it to lawyers. Their response was that a criminal complaint could likely go forward in court. One lawyer told me that the activity resembled organized crime, which might provide the legal grounds to hand down a harsher sentence to the perpetrators.

But I was unsure whether to go ahead. Legal battles take years, and I hadn't pursued a career in journalism to end up fighting extremists in court. I was also convinced that if I involved the police, the harassers would likely attack me even harder. So, I decided to continue on with my life as if the hate campaign wasn't happening. I desperately tried to block out what was going on, but the death threats and other online hate followed me from the newsroom into my home.

Finally, in January 2016, after one of the Facebook troll communities spread more privacy-breaching lies about me, and MV-Lehti stalked my holiday travels in Thailand, mocked the color of my lipstick, smeared me as a "NATO bikini troll," and allowed fake profiles on their Facebook plugin comments section to call me a "[n-word] sperm bucket" and fantasize about raping me in a bar bathroom, I filed a criminal complaint.

I told the police that by inciting hate against me online, the trolls had created a genuine threat to my physical security. I had begun to fear walking alone outside.

ooooo

While the police investigated my complaint, a new campaign was launched against me. A professionally produced song was uploaded to the audio-sharing service SoundCloud. The "humorous" song accused me once again of being a propagandist for NATO and the United States, and reiterated the claim that Russian trolls existed only in my imagination. Anonymous trolls tweeted the song to random Twitter users and media organizations in both Finland and Russia, and demanded the song be played on the radio. I reported one of the accounts to Twitter. According to the company's canned response, the account didn't violate its standards, even though I had shown that it was violating at least two of them: it was anonymous, and it was libeling me.

Eventually my employer, Yle, was brought into the song campaign. I was to give an internal presentation about trolls and cyberattacks to the company's staff in a training session. The event was promoted through Yle's intranet site. But someone with access to the company's intranet copy-pasted the announcement, attached its text to a link to the song, and sent the email to my colleagues and supervisors from a fake email address.

At the same time, a music video with English subtitles was posted on YouTube. Titled "Jessikka Aro's Troll Chase," it featured an actress wearing a blond wig and a superhero costume pretending to be chasing Vladimir Putin and nonexistent trolls while waving the flags of the United States and NATO.[3] The video equated "me" with a character named Mary Goodnight from the James Bond film *The Man with the Golden Gun*. My experience as the victim of online harassment was completely belittled, and I was labeled mentally ill. At the end of the video, the actress playing me gets run over by a car.

Several friends informed me that their Facebook news feeds were polluted with a troll group's paid advertisement for the violent music video. The "sponsored" post marketed a link to the song and directed people to a newly established, anonymously administered Facebook site designed to mock and laugh at "NATO troll Jessikka."

Johan Bäckman then contacted me again through Facebook Messenger. Referring to the song and video campaigns, he asked:

> how is it going Mary Goodnight
> it seems you took second place in the infowar ;)

At this point, I was exhausted. I took screen captures of Bäckman's hundred-plus messages to me and gave them to the police. Bäckman, meanwhile, handed the message chain to a Russian fake media outlet called Russia Beyond the Headlines, which quoted them in a bizarre spin article.

∞∞∞

To deal with all of this, I adopted the counterstrategy of publicly speaking about the exceptional measures I was being subjected to. I published information on my social media channels and gave interviews to the media. It was a successful strategy, to a point. As word of my ill treatment spread, I started to receive messages from individuals who had been similarly targeted by Russian trolls. In Finland, the same type of harassment had been aimed at

Saara Jantunen, a researcher at the Finnish Defense Forces and an expert on information warfare, and at Jukka Mallinen, an author and translator. Also smeared were Imbi Paju, an Estonian-born author who specializes on repression in the old Soviet Union, and Sofi Oksanen, a writer and novelist who had written extensively about the Kremlin's information warfare. Heidi Hautala, former Finnish Green Party member of parliament and member of the European Parliament, had also been attacked, because she had raised concerns about the Kremlin's human rights crimes.

At first, I thought that only Finns were being targeted. But then Patrik Oksanen, a respected Swedish journalist, contacted me. He too had written an article about Russian information warfare and instantly become a target of vilification coming from pro-Kremlin fake organizations on Facebook and YouTube. After he was libeled as being a convicted pedophile in the Anti-Euromaidan Sweden Facebook troll group, Oksanen sued the trolls in court and won.

I began to understand that attacking its critics was the Kremlin's strategy. And because that strategy threatened freedom of speech, democracy, and the national security of several countries, it needed to be exposed.

So, I started to plan this book.

12.

The Think-Tanker

AT A SECURITY CONFERENCE IN PRAGUE in 2016, I was introduced to Serbian political analyst Jelena Milić. The two of us gave a presentation about Russian trolls, fake news, and smear campaigns.

The conference organizers put us together because they knew that we shared similar experiences. Like me, Milić had been forced to turn to the police for help after she was made the target of a ruthless pro-Kremlin hate campaign that also penetrated several Serbian media organizations.

To anyone aware of these tactics, Milić's fate was familiar. She has devoted her career to trying to solve the Balkan region's complex ethnic and political conflicts as well as to promoting democracy. In 2018, Politico named Milić as one of the twenty-eight most influential people "who are shaking, shaping and stirring Europe."[1] In addition, she has worked relentlessly to raise awareness among the general public about Russian hostile influence operations in the Balkans.

Before the hate campaign against her started, locals would occasionally approach Milić on the street to pay their respects and ask her views on topical social issues. But as the campaign intensified, she started receiving messages from people who wished to see her raped or dead. During the most difficult period, she needed round the clock police protection. To be able to pick up a bottle of milk, or walk to work in downtown Belgrade, Serbia's capital, Milić had to inform officers of her plans two hours in advance.

She accepted the police protection because some of her most aggressive online attackers were part of extremist movements. Some had been convicted of violent crimes, while others had direct connections to Kremlin-aligned and far-right ultranationalist groups. Even Milić's daughter, who wasn't involved in her mother's work, faced Facebook threats from an extreme-right activist and fanatical Putin supporter with close ties to the Serbian government.

Milić had hoped that Serbian journalists would cover the public smear campaign against her, which had originated with the Russian propaganda outlet Sputnik and the St. Petersburg troll factory. But the reporters didn't pay attention to the Kremlin's media games in the Balkans. Instead, to her disappointment, they wanted to turn her tragedy into entertainment. "The journalists wanted to film my private life with the police officers for a reality show," Milić shares. "I declined."

After living under police protection for a month, Milić called the whole thing off. "The policemen were polite and helpful," she says, "but the operation was under resourced and made my everyday routines even harder." She also filed several criminal complaints with the police about the media, which instead of helping, damaged her reputation. "I'm an example of why 'all publicity is good publicity' is not true anymore. I have to rebuild my reputation again from scratch," Milić explains.

ooooo

Jelena Milić runs a think tank in Belgrade called The Center for Euro-Atlantic Studies (CEAS), which advocates for pro-Western policies in Serbia, and more widely in the Balkans. The organization's mission is to help Serbia gain membership in NATO and the European Union, and to integrate the country into the Western values base.

Serbia's path to forming a stable democracy and justice system has been rocky. The situation is further muddied by the Kremlin having its fingerprints all over the Balkans. In recent years, the Serbian government has taken steps toward autocracy, with generous assistance from the Putin regime. The Kremlin cherishes the myth of Serbia as Russia's loyal ally and "brother."

Russian influence has deep historical roots in Serbia. As an example, one of the first roadside billboards on the way from Belgrade's international airport to the city center celebrates the strong Russo–Serbian energy industry ties. The ad, sponsored by the Russian energy giant Gazprom Neft and its Serbian representative, promises a "partnership for the future." To underline that partnership, the Russian and Serbian flags are pictured flowing beautifully into each other. Many Serbians brag about their government's "good relations" with Russia and take profound pride in Russian investment in their country—when in fact the European Union invests far more in Serbia than Russia does, as Milić reminds me.

In Belgrade, the former capital of the collapsed Yugoslavia, the devastation of the Yugoslav War still shows, a stark reminder of the destructive potential of mass propaganda. As we walk in downtown Belgrade, Milić points out a multi-story building. Its walls are in ruins and the metal bars that once supported the structure are twisted and stick out from the broken concrete. In the 1990s, this was the location of Radio Televizija Srbije (RTS), the Serbian public broadcasting network. When the Serbian regime started to commit war crimes and genocide against civilians, primarily Muslims and Croats, the government-controlled RTS was harnessed to disseminate dehumanizing hate propaganda against both groups, as well as Bosnia and Sarajevo. In 1999,

NATO launched an air campaign against the Serbian government, which was suspected of committing war crimes against Kosovo Albanians. One of the targets was RTS. Sixteen employees of the station were killed in the bombing. In the years since, no one has rebuilt the former RTS headquarters, or other destroyed buildings. "The stated reason is that the reconstruction is too expensive," Milić tells me. Today, the Kremlin exploits the 1999 NATO intervention in its propaganda targeted to the Balkans. "The Kremlin continually demonizes NATO and always fails to mention why NATO intervened. In this way, they influence the local press and rewrite Serbian history," Milić says.

The majority of those who committed war crimes during the Yugoslav Wars are still walking free. Milić assists in trying to bring them to justice before the International Criminal Tribunal for the former Yugoslavia. "One of Serbia's problems is that many who should be investigated for war crimes still hold high positions within the Serbian police, the army, and the government," Milić explains. "Thus, they contribute to the unlawfulness of the country and serve as puppet masters in parts of the media."

Research done by CEAS has revealed the Kremlin's manipulation of Serbian policies concerning the investigation and prosecution of war criminals. Organizing war crime trials is an important requirement of EU membership for Serbia. However, the integration of the Balkans into the European Union and NATO would mean that the ruling circles and war criminals would lose their income from corruption and their control of the security and judiciary systems. Therefore, they heavily protest against integration into the EU, and Serbian membership in NATO.

Since the Kremlin opposes Serbia joining the European Union, it feeds anti-NATO and anti-EU sentiment in the country, as well as trying to obstruct the legal processes against prosecuting war criminals. In contrast, Milić and her think tank promote pro-EU and pro-NATO policies. This puts the Kremlin's interests in the Balkans and Milić's interests in her home country in conflict. That is one of the underlying reasons why Milić has been the victim of a campaign of mental violence.

Yet another reason is that Milić publicly and visibly stood up to a Russian diplomat. In 2013, the then Russian ambassador to Serbia, Alexander Chepurin, gave an interview in which he stated that Russia would "never understand or accept anyone who for thirty pieces of silver would push their country into NATO."[2] He added that the wounds left by the NATO bombings and deaths were still fresh, and not just in Serbia. The reference to thirty pieces of silver comes from the Bible—it's the price for which Judas betrayed Jesus to his murderers.

With this metaphor, the Russian ambassador framed anyone promoting Serbia's alliance with NATO as money-grubbing traitors. Milić posted a response to Chepurin's comments on the CEAS website, highlighting the superficiality, inaccuracy, and offensiveness of his claims.[3] She also gave him a lecture about Serbia's internal development and the benefits of Serbian integration to the West.

The Russian ambassador didn't publicly respond to Milić. Instead, the reaction came from Serbian far-right elements, following the standard Kremlin playbook.

A LIST OF TRAITORS

The first shadowy Russian pro-Putin entity to target Milić was the right-wing group SNP Naši (*Srpski Narodni Pokret*, the Serbian People's Movement). The lobbying group, which promotes pro-Kremlin and anti-EU policies, was founded in 2006, one year after then Russian chief of staff Vladislav Surkov established a similar nationalistic and pro-Putin movement, Naši, in Russia. Naši pretends to be independent, when it is in fact controlled by the Kremlin.

SNP Naši cultivates extremism and Putinism under the guise

of patriotism. Like the Kremlin's Naši, the Serbian Naši attacks human rights activists, academic researchers, and Western-minded politicians. A telltale sign of the group's wide acceptance in Serbia is that its leader, Ivan Ivanović, has been a frequent guest columnist for several of the country's news outlets.

In 2014, SNP Naši published an online list of thirty prominent liberal Serbian public figures, smearing them as traitors. The list included the then Serbian prime minister as well as pro-Western actors, authors, researchers, and journalists. SNP Naši labeled them all as enemies of the Serbian people, with no evidence to back up the allegations.

Jelena Milić's name was on the list.

Because of the lack of evidence behind the accusations, the Serbian state attorney took SNP Naši to court for suspected defamation, calling Milić and the rest of the so-called "traitors" as witnesses. In 2017, Milić appeared in court together with the other people on the list. While she and two other witnesses told the court that they had been intimidated as a result of the public denunciation, the rest of the witnesses answered to the contrary, that they had not been intimidated at all.

The court ended up acquitting SNP Naši on all charges.[4]

ooooo

In February and May of 2016, CEAS published two English-language reports concerning Russian influence in the Balkans. Entitled "Serbia and Russia—Russian Influence on Serbia's Stabilization, Democratization and European Integration," and "Eyes Wide Shut—Strengthening of the Russian Soft Power in Serbia—Goals, Instruments and Effects," the reports carefully examined the complex and warm relationship between the Kremlin and the Serbian regime.[5] Among other interactions, the reports detailed the bilateral meetings of the countries' top politicians in the 2010s, Russia's oil and gas contracts with Serbia, joint war drills between the two countries, and Russia's "gifts" to Serbia: hundreds of millions of dollars' worth of MiG-29 warplanes to "save and modernize" the Serbian air force. "The Serbian government practices an open-door policy to Russian hostile influence," Milić says.

The reports further described the Kremlin's corruption of Serbian politicians and media leaders. Russian attempts to separate Serbia from the West, its efforts to block the country's entrance into the EU and NATO, its support for totalitarian political leaders in Montenegro and Kosovo, and its sympathies toward the far right, were also exposed. Also listed were over 100 pro-Kremlin propaganda sources. One of those was the Serbian branch of Sputnik, which in Serbia has become a relatively popular news source.

In February 2016, Milić and her staff at CEAS organized a publication conference to present the findings of the first report.[6] Russian Sputnik was one of the news outlets to "cover" the event. They mocked the CEAS research and called the jacket Milić wore to the conference "Stalinist."[7] Another Kremlin's mouthpiece, a Serbian online site called Pravda, demanded the conference be canceled.

Simultaneously, fake profiles and extremists opened a full frontal assault against Milić on social media. Fantasies of her death, libelous claims, and detailed depictions of violent attacks started flowing to Milić's social media channels. The hateful content was strikingly similar to what I had received during my troll attacks. It was designed to frighten, intimidate, silence, and demoralize, frequently using sexually violent language. For example, Milić was called "a whore paid by NATO, whose enemies will return and fuck her neoliberal and fascist mother," "a whore who sucks American dicks, who should end up in an abortion clinic," and "a pile of shit, paid by foreigners, and [who] hopefully will spend all that money on medicines." The commenters also shared their hopes that she would "end up dead in a ditch," and that she should "go hang herself" and "drop dead."

In addition to the anonymous online trolls, individuals with direct connections to the Kremlin also attacked Milić. One of them was Nemanja Ristić, a Serbian citizen, pro-Kremlin agitator, right-wing extremist and a founder of the once-prominent media outlet B92. Ristić's close relationship to the Kremlin was revealed by a photo he shared on social media, which showed him standing with Russian military officers and the country's foreign minister, Sergey Lavrov.[8] Ristić has openly stated on his Facebook profile that he works for the FSB.

In March 2016, Ristić sent an email to CEAS accusing Milić of being a paid employee of NATO, whose career would end in a quick trial in which she would receive the harshest possible sentence. In the email, Ristić also labeled NATO a criminal organization that among other things, produced and distributed heroin, and killed civilians. He continued his attack the next month, sharing a fake news piece on Facebook that claimed Milić was addicted to cocaine and alcohol.

In the 1990s, Ristić was a member of a criminal gang, and later served a prison sentence for the murder of a rival gang member.[9] He is also internationally wanted for his suspected participation in the attempted Russian-backed coup d'état in Montenegro in 2016.[10] Montenegrin security officials and the investigative community Bellingcat revealed that the plot was hatched by Russian influence agents and recruits.[11]

Though CEAS filed a criminal complaint about Ristić, Milić hasn't heard anything further about it, despite several inquiries by her legal representative. "My lawyer told me that we have done everything possible to proceed with the case," she says. "But because the justice system is under the command of the executive branch, nothing is happening. The Serbian state doesn't want to put Ristić in jail."

In addition to the public smearing of Milić, CEAS was also targeted by cyberattacks, with multiple DDoS attacks causing its website to crash. As a result, the public was unable to read their reports on Russian influence in Serbia, or any other information published on their site, for several days. The think tank's email addresses were also blocked during the attack.

"THE FACE OF NATO EVIL"

In May 2016, as CEAS released the second part of their Russia research, another wave of public smearing was triggered.[12] This time several mainstream Serbian media outlets got in on the act. The most vicious material was spread by a tabloid called the *Informer*, and Pink, a television station.

The *Informer* claims to be the highest circulating daily in Serbia. In addition to spreading false news, conspiracy theories, and celebrity gossip, the tabloid supports the policies of the Serbian government and its current president, Aleksandar Vučić, as well as those of the Kremlin and right-wing groups.

The *Informer* labeled Jelena Milić a NATO lobbyist, which in the paper's context bore only negative connotations. The tabloid also connected her to conspiracy theories about alleged NATO plots to stage conflicts in Serbia. One article alleged that she had "threatened to beat up a man who opposes NATO." Another story invented a quote Milić had never said, that "Serbs got what they deserved in the NATO bombings." Milić was also depicted as a NATO and Croatian spy; her mission was to spread false news in order to disrupt the Serbian public.

The tabloid also claimed that Milić was paid by and under the control of dubious Western financiers who wanted to destabilize Serbia through her think tank. While CEAS does receive funding from various international sources, such as George Soros's Open Society Foundations,[13] the Rockefeller Brothers Fund, and

NATO's Public Diplomacy Division, the think tank is transparent about where it gets its money from, posting its financial records on its website. The *Informer* used this publicly available information to drum up conspiracies.

The *Informer* also published photos of Milić in which she wore an especially unflattering or angry expression. One picture featured a caption that called her, "The face of NATO evil."[14] The aim of the photos was to create a perception of Milić as mentally unstable. "I always look ugly in the state media of Serbia. They make me look like I'm the mad aunt in the attic," Milić laments.

The *Informer* also played up a fabricated story about a fake Milić. In 2016, anonymous trolls created an imposter account on Facebook, pretending to be Jelena Milić. Fake Jelena posted that she was contemplating the idea of running for president of Serbia in the elections the following year. The post received widespread mockery. The *Informer* picked up the story, with headlines shouting: "Very Funny! Jelena Milić Announces She Will Run for President of Serbia."[15] Following this, angry online users sent threats to Milić, who had played no part in the incident and had never contemplated the idea of running for president.

∞∞∞∞

Pink is a privately owned television station that broadcasts reality shows, soap operas, and salacious celebrity gossip. The channel is owned by a former party comrade of the late Serbian president Slobodan Milošević's wife. Whenever the channel talks politics, it does so through the mouth of the Serbian government.

Pink seems to frequently coproduce content in cooperation with the *Informer*. For example, the tabloid's editor in chief denounced Milić when she was a guest on Pink's morning show, while at the same time the *Informer* created online clickbait stories based on Pink's spin about Milić.

In November 2016, CEAS requested that both the *Informer* and Pink correct their false statements about Milić and her think tank. "In addition to the other fake news, they stated that we received much less funding from the foreign foundations than we actually do," says Milić. "We wanted them to correct that too." According to Serbian law, news outlets must correct untrue statements. If they don't, they can be fined.

A year later, a court ordered the *Informer* to publish a correction to the false claims, enforced by a €1,000 penalty.[16] Pink wasn't fined. While the tabloid published a small column correcting parts of its false statements, it didn't mention that the correction had been ordered by the court. Compared to the damage the *Informer*'s fake news had caused to Milić's personal safety and professional reputation, the correction didn't bring her much justice.

THE BANK LOAN

In July 2016, five months after publishing its first report on Russian influence in Serbia, the CEAS office in Belgrade lost an experienced employee. The woman had answered the office phone, and an unknown caller made a threat. "She got scared and decided to quit her job. It's not easy to recruit or retain people in such a situation," Milić says.

Even finding an attorney who was willing to take on Milić's multiple cases was difficult, as many lawyers were afraid that the mud thrown at Milić would stick to them as well. In addition, before the hate campaign, other residents in the building where the CEAS office is based had been friendly toward the organization. But as the campaign went on, they started to complain to the landlord, asking why he was renting to an organization of such ill repute. The CEAS office mailbox was also destroyed numerous times.

At the same time, trouble was brewing for Milić on the home front. Friends of her daughter had read on a gossip website that

Milić had taken out a bank loan to pay for a breast enlargement to "please her American boyfriend." Milić was shocked. Like many other fake news stories about her, this one included a small element of fact: she had indeed taken out a bank loan, not for cosmetic surgery, but for a series of dental procedures. The story included an interview with an unknown clerk in a bank where Milić did not have an account. In addition, a nonexistent police officer was interviewed who "confirmed" that Milić had had a boob job. Milić quickly realized that only someone with access to her private bank records could have leaked the financial information. "That spooked me as a citizen of Serbia," shares Milić. "I started to worry about the quality of information disseminated to our kids. It's not a pleasant feeling when you realize that so many youngsters read it and ask my daughter, 'What the hell is going on with your mother?'"

AGAINST THE INTERESTS OF SERBIA

Several Serbian politicians also participated in the smearing of Milić. Vojislav Šešelj, the leader of the pro-Putin, far right Serbian Radical Party and a convicted war criminal,[17] called Milić and other Serbian NGO leaders "fascist whores" on Twitter.

But it was Serbia's president, Aleksandar Vučić, who took the bullying to the next level.

Early in 2017, Milić was invited to appear on a Pink talk show to discuss the state of affairs in Serbia with then Prime Minister Vučić. While Milić had been boycotting Pink, she decided to use this opportunity to share her thoughts about the station's ownership and editorial policy.

The live debate became heated. Suddenly, Vučić told Milić on air that, "Everything you do is against the interests of Serbia."[18]

Milić immediately stood up and left the studio in the middle of the program. "The prime minister's statement was an open call for all lunatics to kill me. The prime minister knew that I had given up my police protection, and still he said it publicly," Milić says.

Much of the Serbian media, led by Pink and the *Informer*, attacked Milić for leaving the show, calling her a drama queen. Milić's professional contacts, including members of the international diplomatic community, started to avoid her. "When the media portrays me positively, people on the streets give me friendly looks. But when there are negative articles, people look like they want to beat me up," Milić states.

ooooo

In August 2016, CEAS published a statement saying that they wouldn't invite the Serbian branch of Sputnik, or any other platforms that reprinted Sputnik's fake articles, to an upcoming conference. "I am a nongovernmental organization and I respond to my donors, to the management board, and to my conscience," Milić says.

Sputnik protested, claiming that CEAS was defaming and discriminating against real news outlets. Many influential Serbian journalists criticized Milić's decision and defended the propagandists "freedom of speech." The president of the Independent Journalists' Association of Serbia wrote a post on Facebook criticizing Milić. "They started a huge outcry in the media stating that I can't do this and asking, 'Who am I to decide which are real news outlets and which aren't?' Milić says. "Here, many journalists are concerned about the fake news that interfered with the US elections. But they don't see what's going on in their own country."

FAKE CEAS
In July 2017, Milić learned that someone had set up a fake version of her think tank, deceptively named SEAS (short for Serbian Euro-Atlantic Cooperation.) SEAS copied and imitated the logo

of the real CEAS, and created a new site on Facebook. SEAS hosts sinister social media discussions on Serbia, NATO and other political topics, deceptively reminiscent of CEAS. SEAS was registered in May 2016, at the same time that CEAS was releasing its reports on Russian influence in Serbia.

The fake site's administrators also registered the SEAS Foundation, which describes itself as a "independent socio-neoconservative organization," in contrast to Milić's think tank, which calls itself an "independent socio-liberal think tank organization"[19] SEAS also organized a NATO-themed conference, scheduled suspiciously close to Belgrade NATO week. CEAS has been holding a conference during that time for several years.

The founder and public representative of SEAS is Vencislav Bujić. A resident of Belarus, Bujić is an active social media user in support of Russia; for instance, he has posted photos of himself on friendly terms with a Serbian citizen who fought in the Russian war against Ukraine. Bujić has also engaged in conversations on Facebook with Nemanja Ristić. Several Serbian journalists have mistaken Bujić for a professional expert on NATO and Russia issues, interviewing him as such. In some of his media appearances, he has claimed that CEAS and SEAS are the same organization. Bujić has also approached the funders of Milić's think tank for donations.[20] On July 26, 2017, Bujić posted a photo to social media of himself standing in front of the real CEAS office.

CEAS's legal representative looked for ways to stop the copy-cat organization. However, since they could find no legal measures to counter SEAS under Serbian law, Milić's crew instead chose to investigate and publicly expose their activities.[21]

∞∞∞∞

In January 2018, the US Senate Foreign Relations Committee published a report about Russia's asymmetric attack on democracy in Russia and Europe, which included research done by CEAS.[22] SEAS immediately published social media posts defaming Milić, which set her up as a target for new death threats.

REGIME CHANGE

As of this writing, CEAS has filed criminal complaints against sixteen named individuals and a dozen John Does who have defamed and threatened Jelena Milić.

All in vain.

One of the biggest issues caused by the ongoing smear campaign is the amount of time and energy it takes away from actual research and work. The time Milić spends in defending herself against smears and correcting false information, reading the death and rape threat messages and rebuilding professional connections damaged by defamation, is time away from her think tank's actual work.

The smear campaign has also succeeded in sowing suspicion and dissent between Serbian NGOs and journalists, many of whom are ultimately on the same side: advocating for the rule of law, promoting human rights, and looking for ways to end corruption. As a result, almost no Serbian entities have stepped up and supported Milić's work publicly. Milić describes her think tank as isolated and her own position as that of a sitting duck. By contrast, abroad, her work is well-known. She's a respected expert in her field, and is quoted often in the international. In 2016, her ill treatment was mentioned in a US State Department's report on human rights in Serbia.[23]

Despite the difficult situation, Milić and her think tank continue to produce research and initiatives on the key security issues affecting Serbia and the Balkans, as well as promoting Serbian membership in NATO. Unfortunately, Milić believes that the media attacks against her will continue with impunity, especially if Serbia's general politics shift more toward Russia.

"Key Russian trolls in Serbia are Serbian ministers and members of the Serbian establishment, including the Serbian Orthodox Church and Belgrade University," Milić explains.

Milić's biggest concern is that the Serbian government will lose control and Russia will take over the country. "And if Russia gives direct orders to Serbian leaders, the think tanks and citizen organizations would be the first to be taken down for good," she says. According to Milić, Serbia's biggest problem is that it doesn't have a strong tradition of democracy. "That makes us vulnerable to Russian intelligence operations," she explains. She believes that the only hope is for more independent voices to speak out. "What we're now seeing is not yet mainstream, but it can become mainstream," Milić says. "We need a free, independent media, investigative journalism focused not only on corruption but also on debunking sites that spread Russia disinformation worldwide and telling the Serbian audience about it, as well as proper education and the rule of law."

Milić often contemplates the possibility of physical violence being used against her. When I asked what she would do if her situation worsened, she said, "I don't know. I don't have many resources. But this doesn't only concern me. What bothers me more is the fact that I'm merely one example of the wider trend here in the region."

13.

What the F . . . k??!!

BY 2015, JUST A YEAR AFTER its founding, MV-Lehti had evolved into a full-service hate site, offering an anonymous portal to extremist politicians, renegade activists demanding the closure of Finland's borders to "rapist terrorists," and anti-EU-activists, among other fear mongering elements.

In the autumn of that year, refugees from Syria, Iraq, and Afghanistan arrived in Europe en masse, applying for asylum. As Finnish officials and civil society started to process the sudden increase of asylum seekers, MV-Lehti depicted the refugees as rapists, terrorists, and deadbeats. Its use of inflammatory language—a basic skill in information warfare—was manipulative and cunning, with the site inserting new, dehumanizing words into the Finnish language and then repeating them constantly.

One of the new words was *partalapsi*, or *bearded child* in English. The word alluded to asylum seekers alleged tendency to lie about being underage to immigration officials in order to be eligible for benefits. Another neologism was *matu*, an abbreviation of the word *maahantunkeutuja* (intruders or invaders), to describe the refugees. The word quickly gained popularity on social media. By the summer of 2019, MV-Lehti had published over 430 articles using the word *matu*. According to the site's own statistics, the stories had been clicked over four million times.

As I monitored the articles and comments about refugees on its site, it was easy to identify MV-Lehti's mission: to incite physical conflicts between its readers and the asylum seekers. For example, it published an inflammatory story encouraging readers "to let the dogs out" against Muslims.[1] In some locations, Finnish citizens were mobilized to protest at asylum centers; in several cities, individuals tried to set the centers on fire, using Molotov cocktails and smoke grenades.[2] MV-Lehti championed the idea that Finnish society was in an existential crisis due to Muslim asylum seekers, and that women need to be protected from "rapist" refugees. (An equal opportunity offender, anonymous trolls on the site claimed that Jews had the same genetic makeup as rats.) The site also became the central forum for the racist Finnish anti-immigrant group, Soldiers of Odin. Even though MV-Lehti didn't directly encourage its readers to use violence, it did its best to instill feelings of hatred, disappointment, and suspicion in them.

∞∞∞∞

When it began in 2014, a Finnish citizen named Ilja Janitskin had declared himself the "editor in chief" of MV-Lehti. Janitskin had a history of failed magazine projects, as well as assault and drug convictions. He was also a member of the Bandidos, a motorcycle gang that has been identified as an organized crime entity in Finland.

Janitskin defiantly presented himself as the site's founder and leader. In fact, he did so openly and loudly. This seemed odd, as he was on the run from the police in Finland at the time, living in Barcelona, Spain. However, there was a method behind his boasting: Claiming responsibility for MV-Lehti allowed other contributors to the site to take refuge behind the shield of anonymity Janitskin offered them. I thought that Janitskin's public performance looked like the work of a decoy. As a result, I began to suspect that MV-Lehti and its numerous sister sites were controlled by someone who preferred to lurk in the shadows and allow Janitskin to grab all the attention.

But who?

"WHY DOES YLE HIRE JUNKIES?"

In February 2016, one month after I filed my first criminal complaint with the police, I was nominated for the Finnish Grand Prize for Journalism for my series of articles about Russian trolls. The Prize is the most respected journalism award in Finland.

Not long after my nomination, MV-Lehti hit back hard.

I was enjoying a quiet evening at home in the countryside when I received a text from an unknown number. The sender asked me whether I still liked speed, referring to illegal amphetamines. "I hope you don't buy it with taxpayer money. And, by the way, if your employers didn't know, now they do," the sender added.

As I read the message, my mouth went dry. I quickly realized that my privacy had been forever compromised. I just didn't yet know how. I didn't dare look at social media.

And I didn't have to, as several friends let me know as gently as possible that MV-Lehti had published an article with the headline, "Yle Journalist Jessikka Aro Is a Convicted Drug Offender."[3] To support this assertion, the story presented photos of a twelve-year-old conviction from the district court in my childhood hometown of Hyvinkää. Produced in the infamous "60/40" propaganda style, the article included my private health data from the early 2000s and a photo of a syringe full of liquid. The story had already gone viral, with comments such as, "Fucking crack whore, this is the reason Jessikka is so fucked up and her troll lies so insane."

I immediately called my supervisor at Yle and told him the truth about what had happened. In 2004, when I was twenty-three, I had received a €300 fine for drug use dating back to 2002. Back then I had an illness, which had been diagnosed by a doctor: addiction to amphetamines. Thanks to my loving family, the Hyvinkää city police, and the Finnish drug treatment system, I overcame the sickness and rebuilt my life. It was an experience I had kept private, but of which I am proud and grateful. Now, because of the article, my past was all over the internet, in a falsified form, being used as a weapon against me.

Even though my supervisor at Yle took the news with dignity and professionalism, I couldn't sleep, and spent several hours crying. In the middle of the night, I emailed the MV-Lehti story to the police, asking them to add it to their ongoing criminal investigation.

The next day, my indomitable sister, Pipsa Aro, a private individual who doesn't have anything to do with my work, wrote a Facebook post defending me. The post was widely shared, but as a result, she too ended up in MV-Lehti smear articles and received hate messages from the Soldiers of Odin and other extremist groups.

ooooo

Over the next few days, I watched in horror as MV-Lehti continued its "drug offender" campaign against me, publishing more stories on their site, including an English-language article titled "NATO's Information Expert Jessikka Aro Turned Out to Be a Convicted Drug Dealer."[4] Activists connected to the site also contacted my supervisors and demanded an explanation for why Yle employed junkies. They called for my termination and threatened new revelations against me.

The drug stories quickly spread to MV-Lehti's sister sites, neo-Nazi blogs, and all kinds of counter media outlets, as well as discussion forums, and social media platforms. By the end of the week, my private ordeal from a dozen years earlier had even been discussed in a Finnish tabloid. Though the column was positive, my private information had now been shared—and smeared—to even more people. This was a classic application of the "rotten herring" technique, and it worked just as the officers in the military program of Moscow State University's journalism department had taught: my name was mentioned repeatedly in connection with the scandal, and the resulting stink stuck to me like the smell of rotten fish.

Reading stranger's opinions about my private life was surreal. Yes, I had made mistakes in my youth, but I had paid a heavy price for them, much more than the €300 fine to the Finnish State. About that, MV-Lehti and the anonymous filth sites didn't say anything. I was the only person who knew what my life had been like back then, how much I had suffered from my nightmarish addiction, and how desperately I had wanted to stop it. I had been honest with the police during my hearing and had asked them for help. The filth stories didn't mention any of that, just like they didn't mention that the policewoman who had interrogated me in the Hyvinkää police station about my drug use also took care of me after my hearing. Over the subsequent year and a half, she regularly called me, asked how I was doing, and encouraged me to "keep my head up." Aside from my sister and my mother, I didn't have any safe adult figures in my life watching over me back then. This policewoman did, and for that I'm ever grateful, just as I am to the Finnish drug rehab system, which paid for the cost of my long treatment, over €200 per day.

MV-Lehti didn't share that aspect of my story. Instead, it shouted that I could have horrible diseases connected to drug use, that my brain was possibly damaged, and that I might be delusional and suffering from amphetamine-related psychosis. It lied that I had been in possession of over fifty doses of drugs when I was "arrested" by the police, and that I had lured a severely ill woman to use drugs again. The site used these claims to try and destroy the credibility of the articles I had written, which had been nominated for the most prestigious journalism award in the country.

The support from my superiors at Yle was absolute. My direct supervisor called to check on me, and my top boss called me from his vacation. Eventually, the editors of over twenty Finnish news outlets published a rare joint statement in which they vowed to protect their journalists if they ever became the targets of a smear campaign.[5] Many reporters saw what had been done to me and feared that they could be next.

A few weeks later, in a live televised show, I received the Grand Prize for Journalism.[6] Even though I looked happy, inside I was devastated.

PARTNERS IN CRIME

Determined to find out who was behind the MV-Lehti smear campaign against me, I filed a request for information in Hyvinkää District Court, asking if anyone had asked to receive a record of my conviction. The response was swift: Johan Bäckman. (While my conviction and sentence were public information, the court had made a horrible mistake and also gave Bäckman an attachment that included my health records, which I had shown in court as evidence of my rehab.)

The police then searched Bäckman's devices, which provided hard evidence that he had sent the filth stories about my drug case to Ilja Janitskin. "Ilja, put this to Fincrime, apparently better Google visibility will follow," Bäckman had directed his partner in crime. The stories, written by Johan Bäckman, were then published on MV-Lehti under the pseudonym "Ilja J."—as if the decoy Janitskin had written them.

ooooo

While the police investigated Bäckman and Janitskin, MV-Lehti continued its attacks against me throughout the spring of 2016. By repeating the same stories over and over again as well as cross-linking all its new "Jessikka" stories to the old ones, the site successfully polluted the Google search results for my name. Although I had written hundreds of articles that had been published on the websites of some of Finland's largest media outlets, the propaganda about my drug use now dominated the Google results for "Jessikka Aro." People trying to read the articles for which I had received the Grand Prize were forced to browse several pages of filth stories before finding them. (Someone also updated the Finnish-language Wikipedia article about me with information about my drug case.)[7] While I was aware I could claim the "right to be forgotten," a policy in place in the European Union, and ask Google to remove the filth stories from their search engine, I didn't regard it as the victim's responsibility to send removal requests to social media companies.

∞∞∞

Four months after my initial complaint, the police published a statement encouraging anyone who had been a target of MV-Lehti to file a criminal report. The Helsinki police also announced that they suspected Johan Bäckman of stalking—a 2014 law had made both physical and online stalking a crime in Finland—and Ilja Janitskin of aggravated defamation.[8]

In the summer of 2016, MV-Lehti published confidential documents which showed that the Helsinki police had initiated a takedown request of MV-Lehti because of possible defamation and a wide array of other suspected crimes committed through the site. However, the Helsinki District Court ruled that because MV-Lehti also published stories that didn't break the law, forcing the site to stop publishing would violate its freedom of speech. The traditional press reported the court ruling widely. While the original Finnish server host dropped MV-Lehti, the site soon moved to another host in France.

MV-Lehti then started a campaign against the Helsinki police. When Ilja Janitskin received a summons to appear at the Helsinki police station for a hearing, MV-Lehti published the summons letter, with the fake profiles on the site speculating as to whether I had possibly used drugs with the "mentally ill libtard policemen." MV-Lehti also went after the prosecutor in charge of the case, as well as the head of the investigation, Senior Detective Superintendent Harri Saaristola. Over the years, the site has smeared Saaristola as corrupt, and he has been subject to groundless criminal complaints alleging that he tortured Janitskin. One MV-Lehti story speculated about the murders of both Saaristola and the prosecutor.[9]

In October 2016, the Helsinki District Court arrested Ilja Janitskin in absentia. Wanting to bring him back to Helsinki, the court issued a European arrest warrant and an extradition request, based on the charges of inciting hatred against minorities, aggravated defamation, gambling crimes, and money-laundering.[10]

In revenge, MV-Lehti activists staged an aggressive protest at the Helsinki Court House. The attendees at the rally celebrated Janitskin as a hero of free speech, denounced the judge as a "libtard" (*suvakki* is the Finnish equivalent), and announced that her "background will be investigated."

Someone also filmed the court session, even though the judge had forbidden it. In the video, which was published on MV-Lehti and YouTube, the faces of the judge and Harri Saaristola were recognizable. The extremists later cut Saaristola's photo from a frame of the video and have since used it as a graphic in a number of their smear stories.

The MV-Lehti psychological operations professionals also launched a new concept to describe the police: *poliittinen poliisi*, or *political police*, abbreviated as *polpo*. According to them, the *polpo* was enemy number one of the Finnish people, comparable to the Soviet Union's NKVD, the forerunner to the KGB, because it "persecuted so-called human rights defenders such as Johan Bäckman and Ilja Janitskin." In MV-Lehti's twisted logic, "freedom of speech" was something that could be exploited to defend serial defamation criminals and Russian influence agents.

Unfortunately, many MV-Lehti readers believed and continue to believe in this definition of freedom of speech.

THE MEMBER OF THE PARLIAMENT

In the summer of 2016, I participated in a panel discussion in Helsinki whose theme, suitably, was hate speech as a threat to freedom of speech. The organizer of the panel had marketed the event and published the panelists' names, including mine, on Twitter, as well as in an email invitation sent to members of parliament.

The troll accounts spreading MV-Lehti stories on Twitter, as well as a Finnish member of parliament, a representative of the Finns Party, were instantly activated. The trolls tagged the organizer of the event, while the MP thanked the organizer for the invitation but added that he "preferred listening to unbiased and drug-free media than these heroes. Meaning such media personalities who genuinely support freedom of speech." A national politician was hinting, following the lead of a site suspected of criminal activity, that someone on the panel was using drugs and opposed freedom of speech—both persistent rumors that had been spread about me. Because the event was open to the public, I feared that aggressive stalkers might try and get in. Together with the organizer, my fellow panelists and I prepared for potential disorder.

While taking my seat on the stage, I noticed a familiar face in the crowd, staring at me and smiling menacingly. It was Juha Molari, an MV-Lehti contributor who had been harassing me since my first troll article had been published in September 2014. He had written multiple stories about me for MV-Lehti under his own name, using the usual themes: I was a junkie, mentally ill, a lying criminal. He also smeared a Finnish Defense Forces researcher, as well as a lecturer at Finland's National Defense University who specialized in information warfare.[11]

In plain sight, Molari dug out his video camera and filmed me whenever I spoke during the panel. Even though there were guards in the room, no one could stop him, because to an outsider he looked like a regular person filming the event.

After the panel, another panelist told me that Molari's behavior had also disturbed him. As I walked away from the event, I looked over my shoulder to make sure that Molari wasn't following me home.

The next day, Molari published his videos of the panel in a blog post in which he speculated as to whether I was on drugs during my talk. I immediately filed a criminal complaint against him, and the police investigated him for stalking, aggravated defamation, and spreading privacy-breaching information. In October 2020, Molari was sentenced to five months' probation for persecuting me and defaming the Defense Forces researcher.[12]

After this incident, I decided that I would no longer leave myself open to such hostile activity. I therefore limited my participation in events, even though I was continually being invited to them. The threat discussed on the panel had been insidiously realized—*against me*. Organized hatred had limited my freedom of speech and my ability to live openly in Finland.

∞∞∞

As I exchanged messages with the police, I was always told the same thing: that Finnish legislation didn't enable intervention by means other than the filing of criminal complaints. However, the complaint that I had filed earlier had been used as an excuse to take revenge against me, so I appeared to be in a catch-22. A high-ranking foreign security official told me that in his country, the pro-Kremlin propagandists were placed under strict surveillance. My situation had, according to him, been excessively drawn out, and the actions of the Finnish police ineffective. Even though the criminal investigation was proceeding, and the suspects were subject to legal action, no preventive measures had been implemented, at least to my knowledge. The Finnish police had their hands tied by shortcomings and loopholes in Finnish law. In essence, I was a prisoner of those who were stalking me. My every statement was turned into a scandal in the fake media, with angry readers sending me threatening messages. During the worst times, three new filth pieces were published about me daily.

I told the police and security officials that I was thinking of moving away from Finland.

They listened, but couldn't do anything to help.

THE MOLE

In October 2016, the Finnish police announced that they suspected that someone from inside Yle had assisted Johan Bäckman in stalking me.[13] According to the police, the suspect had provided Bäckman with information about my job assignments and locations.

As the news spread, my colleagues were shocked and wanted to know who the suspect was. I couldn't tell them, because according to the law, the names of suspects are confidential at that stage of an investigation. And because he was a private citizen, the publication of his name would not have been legitimate, based on the guidelines for ethical journalism. I tried instead to direct my colleagues' attention to the more general phenomenon, and to their questions I replied: "Don't ask who, ask where else." It was evident that saboteurs, commonly known as moles, existed not just at Yle, but likely throughout the institutions of Finnish society. One Finnish academic confided to me how Russian spies, under diplomatic cover, had approached him, invited him to lunches, and proposed cooperation. The fake diplomats wanted to start "building a united front opposing European Islamization" and wanted to give lectures at his university. He declined their offers. This revelation caused me to look with renewed suspicion at the content on MV-Lehti as well as the Islamization hysteria spread internationally by global fake news sites.

Most of my time, however, was spent reacting to and trying to assess possible physical threats against me. I was becoming certain that I could find safety only in another country where I wasn't the target of constant filth stories.

ooooo

At the end of October 2016, Ilja Janitskin was caught by the Spanish police and put on trial in Madrid. The court banned him from traveling, but let him out to wait for an extradition trial.

As soon as Janitskin got home to Barcelona, he streamed a live video on Facebook in which he and men he referred to as his "Russian friends" emptied his apartment and destroyed evidence.

Then he disappeared.

The hate campaign against me had been ongoing for two years, and one of the main suspects was now a fugitive. At the same time, the amount of dirt and threats sent to me by MV-Lehti readers was excessive. Anonymous people asked me where I lived, called me a crack whore and a liar, said they were angry about my drug dealing, and accused me of pampering foreign invaders.

I started to look for a way to leave Finland.

I found one, and in February 2017, I made my exit.

14.

The Investigator

THAT DAY, JULY 17, 2014, THE SKY over Eastern Ukraine was filled with hazy clouds.

On top of the haze, a Malaysia Airlines passenger jet glided en route from Amsterdam to Kuala Lumpur, the capital of Malaysia. Flight MH17 carried 15 crew members and 283 passengers, 80 of them children. A majority of the travelers were tourists heading to beach vacations in Southeast Asia. Six AIDS researchers were on their way to a conference in Australia.[1]

In the airspace over Donetsk, air traffic control suddenly lost contact with the Boeing 777. The plane was last sighted thirty miles from the Ukraine–Russia border.

As soon as I saw the first breaking news report, I left early for my night shift at Yle.

Anyone familiar with Russia's warfare in Ukraine had immediate misgivings. Flight MH17 had disappeared flying eastward in the airspace where the Russian military intelligence and Kremlin-directed warlords fought the Ukrainian defense forces with heavy weaponry. Three days before, gangs of Russian-speaking militants had shot down a Ukrainian military cargo plane in the region.

At the Yle news desk, the international wires started flashing with bright red URGENT notifications; according to US intelligence services, the Malaysian plane had been taken down with a missile. Fans of the militants bragged on VKontakte, the Russian counterpart to Facebook, that yet another Ukrainian cargo plane had been downed near Torez. The VKontakte communication was the first sign of the Kremlin-backed militants' involvement in the death of nearly 300 civilians. It seemed that the rebels had downed the passenger jet by accident after confusing it with a Ukrainian military aircraft.

As soon as the international correspondents arrived at the remote Eastern Ukrainian field and started taking photos of the smoking mattress of wreckage, it became evident that none of the passengers on Flight MH17 had survived. Among the blackened, bent splinters of the Boeing, only a couple of undamaged objects stood out: a small, button-eyed teddy bear and a travel guidebook to Bali and Lombok. Holding back tears, I wrote about the crash on Yle's website.

∞∞∞∞

Over 1300 miles northwest of the rebel-held fields, in Leicester, England, the blogger and citizen journalist Eliot Higgins, then thirty-five, learned about the crash. He set out to investigate what exactly had happened to the plane.

Higgins had previously investigated the civil war in Syria and other conflicts in the aftermath of the Arab Spring. He is a self-taught weapons expert, and media profiles describe him as a one-man intelligence service.[2] He conducts his research solely by harvesting publicly available material, i.e., open sources.

Three days before the plane crash, Higgins had launched Bellingcat, a crowd-financed publishing platform for war and conflict bloggers.[3] He wanted to provide a hub for open-source investigators and an educational site for anyone who wanted to learn about open-source research techniques.

As soon as Higgins heard about the disaster, he started to comb through social media. Quickly, he found a video that had been filmed in Eastern Ukraine and published that same day. It showed a missile launcher being transferred via an unidentified country road in an unknown location. The uploader removed the video the same evening, but Higgins managed to save it. He first tried to identify the missile launch system. To locate the transport, he compared the video's visible landmarks with satellite images. In order to verify the location, he asked for assistance from his social media followers. Many wanted to help in the investigation and sent him information. Higgins was able to figure out the direction of the launcher by analyzing the position and direction of the video camera. He verified his findings using Google Earth.

By the evening of July 17, 2014, Bellingcat had published the results of its open-source investigation. The launcher was a Soviet-manufactured Buk, designed to counter missiles and military aircraft, and had been transported southward in Eastern Ukraine from Snizhne, a rebel-held town near the Russian border. Higgins assessed that the launcher—which he located about six to ten miles from the crash site—was involved in the downing of the plane. This is how he started to uncover the first concrete evidence of flight MH17's fate. And Higgins did this all from his own home, before the official international investigation team had managed to physically visit the site and investigate the plane's black boxes.

Led by Higgins, the Bellingcat online community started to put together a puzzle that piece by piece proved the role of the Russian regime in this shocking mass killing. As a result, Eliot Higgins and Bellingcat became the target of systematic and still ongoing defamation by the Kremlin.

FAIR AND JUST

As a former passionate computer gamer and administrative clerk for a company housing asylum seekers, Higgins didn't become an investigator into flight MH17 by chance. Well before he established Bellingcat, he had an unusual routine: every day he browsed videos on as many as 600 YouTube channels, analyzed the most important ones, and published his analyses on his blog, *Brown Moses*, which was popular among conflict experts and journalists.

Over the years, Higgins uncovered YouTube videos exposing atrocities and terrorism in Syria, Egypt, and Libya. He had been the first to reveal to the international community that the regime of Syrian dictator Bashar al-Assad had used chemical weapons against its own people in 2013, acquiring the information from videos uploaded to YouTube by local residents. He also used his skills to assist Human Rights Watch in investigating crimes against humanity.

Higgins originally became a blogger because he couldn't find enough in-depth media coverage of security developments in Libya, Syria, and Egypt. "I was looking at the conflicts and saw all the stuff posted about them on social media. I saw that journalists didn't make use of all the available material. So I thought, I want to start writing about these topics myself. They were interesting and no one else covered them," Higgins told me.

During his time blogging at *Brown Moses*, journalists praised Higgins's expertise and frequently backed up his findings. But hostile feedback also poured in. For example, as he provided proof of the crimes committed by the Syrian regime, the online community supportive of both Assad and Putin attacked him. "I've built myself an audience of people who really hate me. I've had trolls longer than I've had my own children," he shares.

Higgins's experience as a blogger and weapons expert, added to his habit of spending much of his time online, prepared him for the attacks that the Russian government and its propaganda machine had in store for him. RT had already targeted Higgins even before the MH17 investigations. In September 2013, after

Higgins revealed Assad's use of chemical weapons, the London-based RT claimed, contrary to the facts, that Higgins had attributed the chemical attacks to Syrian rebels and opposition forces.[4]

RT is regulated by the Office of Communications (Ofcom), the British communications industry watchdog.[5] In the United Kingdom, Ofcom is the body that licenses commercial television and radio services and maintains the ethical rules of the broadcasters. According to Ofcom, licensed broadcasters must avoid unjust and unfair treatment of individuals or organizations. If a TV program alleges that a named individual has engaged in wrongdoing or incompetence or makes other similar allegations, the individual is entitled to comment and provide their own view.[6]

Higgins filed a complaint, asking the agency to investigate whether RT's coverage of his Syria findings was fair and just. RT responded by filing a counterresponse written by its representative, a multimillion-pound law firm, which supported RT's coverage. In addition, they combed through Higgins's social media channels and used his findings to "prove" Higgins was a "Russophobe."

RT's aggressive response did its job: Ofcom concluded that the outlet's reporting about Higgins had been fair and just.[7] The decision spurred Higgins to dig further. He decided that if he ever became the target of RT's fake news again, his next complaint to Ofcom would be even more detailed.

After Higgins began to expose information about the Russian military's involvement in the crash of flight MH17, he became a regular target of smearing by RT, as well as other Kremlin fake news outlets.

"SATELLITE IMAGES"

For its flight MH17 investigation, Bellingcat published an ongoing series of articles that unearthed Russia's illegitimate and hidden operations leading up to the crash. The community browsed videos, photos, and social media postings in order to further geolocate and expose the missile launcher's path in detail. The materials revealed that the launcher was missing at least one missile.

To hamper the investigation, the Kremlin and its media apparatus pushed innumerable conspiracy theories placing the blame for the crash anywhere except on the warlords it backs and arms in Ukrainian territory. The cultivation of lies and blaming of Ukraine started immediately after the crash. According to the main Russian newspapers and TV stations, the downing of flight MH17 was a "Ukrainian provocation" or even a possible plot to assassinate Putin.[8] The Russian Ministry of Defense presented satellite imagery that Bellingcat quickly debunked as heavily manipulated.[9] The ministry also fed the media falsehoods about the flight path and radar data. On Russian state-owned Channel One, notorious fake news purveyor Mikhail Leontyev broadcast falsified satellite images depicting a photoshop-added Ukrainian fighter jet shooting at flight MH17 from the air.[10] If it had been up to the Russian regime, their theories would have controlled world public opinion.

Official investigations of plane disasters can take years, and verified data usually isn't available before the official investigation results are released. That was the information vacuum that the Kremlin wanted to fill. But Bellingcat's research negated the Kremlin's attempts at obfuscation. Instead, the community's work anchored the debate about flight MH17 to proven evidence and facts, greatly contributing to the international public's understanding of the reasons behind the crash.

A Dutch-led Joint Investigation Team was put in charge of the official criminal investigation into the MH17 disaster.[11] The team was run by the Dutch public prosecution service and the police, and it cooperated with law enforcement in Australia, Belgium, Malaysia, and Ukraine. In September 2014, a few months after the crash, the Joint Investigation Team contacted Higgins and asked him to present Bellingcat's findings to them. Higgins met the team members in London and provided them with the information.

At the same time, Bellingcat continued publishing major reports on the topic. It analyzed the disinformation spread by the Russian Ministry of Defense, as well as the variety of conspiracy theories spread about flight MH17.[12] Bellingcat's groundbreaking open-source research was covered by established media organizations around the world, which helped reshape the public image of the crash away from the Kremlin's narrative.

ooooo

About a year after Bellingcat was founded, I crossed paths with Eliot Higgins for the first time. In that encounter, I witnessed both his and Bellingcat's impact on international journalism.

Around 900 journalists had gathered in Lillehammer, Norway, to learn best practices and the latest trends in investigative journalism. In the venue's main auditorium, Higgins gave a detailed presentation describing Bellingcat's investigation methods. Investigative journalists are a critical and demanding audience. But when Higgins ended his session, a wall of enthusiastic reporters circled him, filming him, snapping his photo, and recording interviews with him with such passion that Higgins was forced to give his comments with his back against the wall. Higgins's know-how in the field of open-source investigations, a skill many journalists lack, had earned him superstar status within the international journalistic community.

But the Kremlin's fake news architects viewed him in a very different way.

EXPOSING THE BS

A new pro-Kremlin propaganda outlet geared to an international audience was launched in September 2014. The site, called Russia Insider, which publishes in English and Russian, claims, just like many other fake news sites, to be a crowdsourced citizen journalism project. It also promises to "expose the BS."[13] Russia Insider asks its readers for donations, sells space to advertisers, and also offers an ad-free membership. In 2018, the site recruited "volunteers" for different roles: writers, video and audio production journalists, manager of their YouTube channel, editors of different sections, and translators. I built a fake identity and offered myself as a volunteer citizen journalist, but never heard back from them.

Russia Insider pieces feature headlines such as "Top Russian Officials: Putin's Superweapons [Which] Are Like Nothing the West Has Ever Seen"; offer praise for former US president Donald Trump; and ask questions such as, "Is There a British Assassination Campaign Targeting Russian Exiles?"[14] [15] The site depicts the United States as a "degeneracy" and runs a section called "The Jewish Question," devoted to demonizing Jews. Several Russia Insider contributors publish using pseudonyms.

Russia Insider also publishes interviews with the Kremlin's top officials, including Leonid Reshetnikov, the director of the Russian Institute of Strategic Studies.[16] (In 2016, Reshetnikov co-authored a piece on the site about the CIA's alleged plan to assassinate Putin.)[17] Normally, citizen journalists or pseudonyms don't have access to such high-level interview subjects. Based on that, and other content on the site, it it is not out of the question that some of Russia Insider's pseudonymous writers either work inside the Russian intelligence services, or receive instructions on what to write from them.

Russia Insider had been in existence for only a couple of months when it started going after Eliot Higgins. The first filth story it published described Higgins as an "Englishman and a life-size dildo" and compared him to the *South Park* animated character Mr. Hankey, a talking piece of feces.[18] Since then, Russia Insider has published nearly a hundred pieces mocking Higgins and Bellingcat. The site has labeled Higgins a NATO and US government lackey, an idiot, a YouTube sleuth, and someone who doesn't understand anything about Russia's Syrian campaign. His personality has been assessed in the online mag as tendentious, insincere, and obsessive. Russia Insider "knows" that Higgins regularly visits NATO headquarters, where he is briefed on "research." Bellingcat's investigations are "wet Buk fantasies" and reinforce US government propaganda. In one of its most disturbing pieces, Russia Insider encouraged its readers to geolocate Higgins's computer and confiscate it.[19] In none of the articles smearing Higgins are the defamatory claims backed by evidence. In regular journalism, the target of criticism is always given the chance to provide his or her views. Russia Insider has never contacted Higgins.

But Sputnik did try to contact him.

Sort of.

READING THE TEA LEAVES

Sputnik's UK branch has also published countless smear stories about Eliot Higgins. One of the most aggressive was triggered when the *Guardian* covered a Bellingcat report concerning artillery shelling from Russia across the border into Debaltseve, Ukraine. Mark Hirst, Sputnik's editor in Edinburgh, emailed Higgins and demanded answers to his conspiratorial accusations masked as questions, asking, among other things, if Higgins had received money from the United States, and how Bellingcat's "citizen journalists" were capable of finding evidence of direct Russian military attacks against the Ukrainian army when NATO and the Western powers were unable to do so.

Higgins was already familiar with Sputnik's methods. "That's what they do: put unconnected statements together and ask me about that. I answered the questions, because they were so stupid, wrong, and ridiculous," he says.

The end result was a conspiracy theory article which

"connected" Higgins to an American organization called National Endowment for Democracy, which Sputnik claimed was a front for the CIA.[20] In fact, NED is a nonprofit organization that supports human rights work and democratic institutions worldwide. Sputnik also tied Higgins to the Ukrainian Maidan protests, which they defined as "a coup."

The next day, Sputnik attacked again. An anonymous piece published in their opinion section claimed that Bellingcat's sources were unreliable and biased, and that the group was advancing the American and NATO political agenda.

In reality, it's Sputnik which uses fake experts as commentators and sources. For example, in an anonymously written, mocking piece, Sputnik quoted an "expert" who represented a bizarre political blog called "Stop Imperialism."[21] The editor of the blog told Sputnik that Bellingcat had been discredited and was known for propagating disinformation. He also accused Higgins of having a history of making false claims, including accusations about Russia. Sputnik has published many similar pieces depicting Higgins as an amateur, biased, working for the governments of Ukraine and the United States, and disseminating false information.

Higgins told me that he doesn't have the time to read Sputnik's content. "A lot of the Sputnik articles concerning me are published in English, but they do them in other languages as well. I'm not sure why. I'm not going to read them or respond to them."

∞∞∞

Sometimes, the Kremlin's propaganda outlets combine resources in their attacks.

In the summer of 2015, a joint operation was organized by Sputnik and an RT show called *In the Now*. (*In the Now* was later separated from RT's brand and organized into a seemingly independent viral propaganda service.) The campaign was launched from *In the Now's* YouTube channel with a video that highlighted anti-Bellingcat accusations originating from an anonymous Russian blogger. In response, Bellingcat tweeted out the video and said that RT was engaging in attacks.

In The Now then contacted Higgins through Twitter and asked to interview him for a "documentary." Higgins jokingly replied that he didn't do interviews with Russian government propaganda channels, as he had plenty of requests from real media outlets. RT's Russian-language Twitter account was then activated, claiming that the "journalist who accuses Moscow of falsifying data on MH17 is afraid to give an interview to RT."[22]

Sputnik continued the operation by publishing an anonymous piece that depicted Bellingcat volunteers as incompetent wannabe investigators and accusing Higgins of writing rude tweets and insulting the *In The Now* host, the American journalist Anissa Naouai. Sputnik presented no evidence to support its claims.

ooooo

RT launched its next big offensive a few months later. This was clear payback for Bellingcat's latest reports, which were again widely quoted and covered worldwide.

The first report that so irritated RT was published by the US think tank the Atlantic Council, with Higgins as one of its authors.[23] It exposed the full scope of Russia's weapons arsenal in Ukraine. Bellingcat also published a report about Russian airstrikes in Syria, as well as a new, conclusive MH17 report, which compiled all its research on the disaster to date.[24]

RT started its weeklong campaign the same morning the Bellingcat MH17 paper went public. In its first piece, the outlet questioned the validity of Bellingcat's information as well as its research methods. The RT video described Higgins as a "thirty-six-year-old laid-off office worker," with no experience in the field nor any higher education.[25] According to RT, Higgins was an amateur, and Bellingcat's work was as reliable as interpreting the patterns of "tea leaves."[26]

RT even sent someone to physically stalk Higgins because they "wanted to find the man behind Bellingcat." In a television spot, a content producer named Nimrod Kamer, introduced as a satirist, traveled by train to Higgins's hometown because he wanted to "experience [Higgins] face-to-face."[27] In a sped-up recording, Kamer is seen roaming the streets hunting for Higgins, and also calling him on the phone "Eliot isn't responding to his phone. I'm going to tweet him again, because he already sent me a few Twitter messages, and he keeps wanting me to email questions," Kamer narrated.

Kamer was then filmed in fast-motion entering an office building and talking with a receptionist. As the receptionist is making a call following Kamer's request, the RT "satirist" takes the phone from her hand and says, "Eliot, sorry—" The person on the other end of the line then hangs up, and Kamer hands the phone back to the receptionist.

At the end of the report, Kamer is seen knocking on the door of an apartment. As the door opens, Kamer sys he is looking for Eliot. The person who opens the door is Higgins's mother. The film then cuts to Kamer asking Higgins not to "hide" from RT. However, Higgins hadn't lived at that address for eight years. "He went to my old house, where my mother lives, and basically asked her where I was," Higgins says. "My mother was very upset by that. Basically he couldn't figure out where I lived, but he made up a strange article claiming 'Higgins is hiding from us.'"

As the report cuts back to the studio, the RT anchor refers to Higgins's coauthored report with the Atlantic Council and claims that the think tank has ties to the US government.

Higgins's account of the story behind Kamer's piece opens a

fascinating window into RT's fabrications. Kamer had contacted Higgins, saying he wanted to interview him. But Kamer failed to mention that he was preparing the piece for RT. Instead, he claimed he was doing the story independently. But Higgins had seen Kamer's material on RT before, so he prepped his answers carefully. Higgins told Kamer that he wasn't available immediately, but promised an interview at a later time. Though they had agreed to an interview, Kamer still traveled to Leicester in order to film a dramatic chase so he could claim that Higgins was "hiding."

Higgins says that he knows many RT staffers. In private, some of them have admitted to admiring his work, and have even attended his lectures in London. But they are afraid of losing their jobs if they're seen speaking with him. "They say, 'Please don't tell anyone, or I'll get in trouble,'" Higgins says. "In RT's worldview, I'm seen as part of a conspiracy against Russia. RT management really believes in this, but cameramen, reporters, and producers are just doing their jobs. I feel bad for them, because they're trapped inside an organization they can't escape from."

Many RT employees start working for the channel directly after their university days, without knowing the real nature of the job. When they want to move on in their careers, they are unable to got employment at regular news networks, due to their association with RT. "People working with RT have told me: 'It's really shitty, but it's a living,'" shares Higgins.

HACKERS

In early 2015, fake security notices started piling up in Higgins's Gmail inbox. According to the messages, an outsider had tried to access his email account, and it was advised he "change [his] password by clicking on the attached link."

Higgins thought the emails were a common scam known as phishing, and assumed that hackers were trying to gain access to his credit card data. He ignored the emails.

Later, Higgins read an article about ThreatConnect,[28] an IT security company that had analyzed the cyber intrusions targeted at the Democratic National Committee as well as at the emails of John Podesta, Hillary Clinton's campaign chairman, right before the 2016 US presidential election.

During the campaign, the DNC's computer network had been infiltrated, and Podesta's personal Gmail account hacked. As Election Day approached, many of his emails were published through WikiLeaks, for the purpose of smearing the Clinton campaign. The hacks were attributed to people connected to Russian intelligence.

Studying the screenshots of the emails used in the DNC and Podesta hacks, Higgins noticed that one of them looked familiar. He searched through his inbox using the wording in the screen capture published in the article, and found seven messages with exactly the same content. A closer look revealed that the emails he had received included the same minor grammatical errors and spelling mistakes as the emails used to penetrate the DNC and Clinton campaign. The links in the emails appeared proper, but led to malware sites.

Higgins also discovered that suspicious emails had also been sent to Aric Toler, a Bellingcat investigator, and the Finnish researcher Veli-Pekka Kivimäki. Kivimäki, a trained coder, had been targeted in March 2015, when attackers tried to gain access to his Gmail account, as well as his computer. As a Bellingcat contributor, Kivimäki was also investigating flight MH17. He therefore considered it likely that hackers wanted to keep track of how much he knew about the crash. Before Kivimäki was targeted, similar malicious emails had been sent to Ukrainian activists, NATO officials, and the official MH17 investigators. The attackers' suspected origin was Russia.

After Higgins realized that his community had been targeted, he and his team decided to send the suspicious emails to two independent cybersecurity companies. The companies verified that the IP addresses, email addresses, and links were the same ones used by the Russian hacker group Fancy Bear in its attacks against the DNC and Podesta—part of the Kremlin's systematic campaign to help elect Donald Trump president of the United States.[29]

The first Fancy Bear spearphishes against Bellingcat had occurred seven months after they launched their MH17 investigation. By July 2016, twenty-seven malicious emails had been sent to members of the Bellingcat team. The majority of them, sixteen, were sent to Higgins. If any of the Bellingcat team members had clicked the links, and changed their passwords at the malicious sites, they could have ended up providing Russian hackers with access to their computers. But they didn't. "We ignored the Fancy Bear emails. We're not idiots who open all emails. It's different if you're a sixty-year-old company employee who opens everything, because you don't know anything about this. But we're aware of this stuff, so it wasn't a problem for us," Higgins says. (Three years after Bellingcat received its first suspicious email, Special Counsel Mueller's investigation on Russia's interference in the US election resulted in indictments stating that Fancy Bear was an operation conducted by GRU, Russia's military intelligence.)[30]

However, the cyber intrusions against Bellingcat weren't finished.

SEX PERVERT

CyberBerkut is an organized alliance of pro-Kremlin hackers known for attacking Ukrainian government websites. The group's name reveals its mission: Berkut was an infamous Ukrainian special police force that the pro-Kremlin president ordered to violently disperse the demonstrators in Maidan Square.

CyberBerkut does the same to pro-democratic, freedom-minded journalists and human rights promoters—in cyberspace. Experts suspect that the group has ties to Russian State security structures. Pro-Kremlin media outlets have eagerly used materials acquired and produced by CyberBerkut as sources. For example, the Russian state-controlled news channel Vesti quoted CyberBerkut's website and published a fabricated organizational chart depicting Aric Toler as a tool of Ukrainian security services, connected to NATO.[31]

Another Bellingcat contributor, a Moscow-based blogger, also became a target of CyberBerkut. He had contributed to many Bellingcat investigations, and his name was on the byline of a detailed open-source investigation into members of the Russian military's special forces unit in Ukraine. In a post, he provided the soldiers' names, roles, and photos, and their connection to a Russian Spetsnaz Brigade.

On February 24, 2016, an outsider accessed the Bellingcat website and posted malicious content which had been intercepted from the contributor's private devices. The attackers published photographs of the blogger hanging from a ceiling, attached to piercings in his back, and wrote that he was a "sex pervert," despite the fact that the activity didn't have anything to do with sex. In addition, his phone number and address, a scan of his passport, the name of his girlfriend, and information concerning his dating and sex life were published on the Bellingcat site.

At first, it was unclear how the criminals had managed to bypass the site's two-step verification process. ThreatConnect analyzed the breach and found that the blogger's old email account had been hacked into, as had his LiveJournal account. From the stolen email account, the attackers found the username and password for his Bellingcat account. They also took over his iCloud account, which hadn't been double secured, and started downloading material. As soon as the blogger learned about the breach, he cut off the attackers' access to his iCloud account.

ThreatConnect concluded that the attackers had either intercepted the blogger's SMS-based two-step authentication or had direct access to the mail servers of the Russian internet services company. In Russia, breaching individuals' privacy is easy if you happen to work for the state security services or are under their protection. According to ThreatConnect's scenarios, Fancy Bear and CyberBerkut might have coordinated their attacks against Bellingcat. It was also possible that they hadn't coordinated the attacks but happened to have the same enemy, i.e. Bellingcat.

The defacing of Bellingcat's website served two purposes: first, through the targeted blogger's accounts, the hackers tried to access information about the group. It was also an attempt to smear the blogger and disgrace him in the eyes of his volunteer colleagues, as well as publicly.

Both attempts failed. As soon as Higgins learned about the illicit content, he removed it. "They were probably looking for emails between [the blogger] and the CIA, and obviously couldn't find anything—as such emails don't exist. Obviously it's not nice to have personal stuff out there, but it wasn't really that bad. Literally, no one gives a shit," Higgins says.

INFORMATION SOLDIER

Next to participate in the campaign against Bellingcat and Higgins was a British citizen named Graham Phillips, a seemingly independent YouTube "journalist." On his blog, Phillips accused Higgins of manipulating videos and photos, but didn't provide any evidence. In a smear story about Higgins, he tried backing up his allegations by encouraging his readers to have a look at the Twitter hashtag #Bellingcrap. I did as Phillips encouraged, and found that the hashtag is used by fake profiles, conspiracy theorists, and the Kremlin's useful idiots, who trash Bellingcat, the UK, democracy, and freedom of speech.

Since 2013, Phillips has traveled extensively in the Russian-occupied Donbas area. Eventually, he was exposed as an FSB asset: a British blogger researched Phillips's activities and collected an impressive number of photos showing Phillips being armed and escorted by soldiers of the "Donetsk People's Republic."[32] The photos showed Phillips saluting the soldiers and smiling happily after receiving a medal from the FSB for his commitment to spreading propaganda. Phillips has also produced content for both RT and the Russian Ministry of Defense publication *Zvezda* (*Star*).[33] In addition, he is listed as one of the contributors to Russia Insider. Phillips has openly bragged about being an "information soldier" in Russia's propaganda war against Ukraine.

In 2014, Ukraine banned Phillips from entering the country because of national security considerations. Two years later, the Ukrainian government issued a warning letter to the UK authorities about Phillips's "disgraceful" activities.[34] But that didn't stop him. In 2018, Ukraine asked the UK police to investigate Phillips' actions, which it described as "terrorist activity."[35]

Phillips is active on social media. He regularly tweeted until November 2018, when Twitter closed down his account. But he really plays to his YouTube audience of over 160,000 subscribers.[36] His viral impact is wide: according to counters, the total number of views of his videos is in the millions. In one video, published in June 2019, Phillips toured Salisbury, England, talking about Sergei Skripal, the Russian double agent who was poisoned in 2018 along with his daughter.[37] In a video spiced up with dramatic music, he described the daughter's appearances in the media as "bizarre and scripted."

Phillips seeks financial support from his audience. Over the years, he has created several crowdfunding campaigns on platforms like JustGiving and Indiegogo. He claims to use the money to fund "objective, independent journalism, an alternative to the standard, mainstream media, and reports from the UK,

Europe, Russia and Donbas." Many of his crowdfunding attempts haven't been very successful: for example, in 2017 he managed to raise only £1,800. Nevertheless, he had enough funding to travel extensively around Russia and Eastern Ukraine. While JustGiving deleted one of Phillips's campaigns and refused to give him the money he had raised, he continues to harvest money through the US-based Indiegogo—without disclosing to potential funders his connections with Russia's security services.[38] Phillips also collects cash through PayPal. Unlike the crowdfunding money, transfers made through PayPal are private. Thus Phillips's profit through the platform isn't visible to outsiders. Anyone can wire him money and thereby unwittingly or intentionally enable his activities.

While investigating the disinformation campaigns targeted at Eliot Higgins, I met a British specialist in social media propaganda. This expert, who wished to remain anonymous, had informed both PayPal and YouTube about Phillips's activities multiple times and encouraged the companies to close down his accounts, without success. "Fake crowdfunded independent journalists are a relatively new phenomenon," the specialist said. "But ultimately they're a scam, fooling people into giving them money."

"AN INSTRUMENT TO DIVERT ATTENTION"

Bellingcat has also been the target of disinformation offensives that have come directly from the Kremlin.

In April 2016, Russian Foreign Ministry spokesperson Maria Zakharova labeled Bellingcat "an instrument to divert attention from investigating the tragedy of the Malaysian Boeing over Ukraine."[39] She stated that the purpose of Bellingcat was to "continue to use all possible 'fakes,' to create quasi-evidence to blame Russia. . . . The aim is once again to give the global community fabricated proof of Russia's aggression." Zakharova's statement was posted on the website of several Russian embassies, including the one in Malaysia. Earlier, similar baseless allegations had been disseminated by the Russian Ministry of Defense.

Eliot Higgins decided to email both ministries, asking for proof of their allegations. "I thought they wouldn't respond, but I decided I'd do it anyway, for a laugh," he says.

They did reply.

On April 14, 2016, the Russian Ministry of Foreign Affairs sent an email which once again questioned Bellingcat's credibility and referred to unspecified instances when its research had supposedly been "called into question even by the Western media."[40] "You can check it by yourself by googling in the 'world wide web', especially since you consider yourself an Internet search professional," read the email, which lacked a signature.[41] The email further accused Bellingcat of cooperating with the Ukrainian authorities. It also chastised Higgins: "You never use information provided by other sides in your research, which is what leads one to suspecting you of bias." The anonymous email failed to provide any concrete examples of Bellingcat's "fakes."

Higgins replied, once more asking for evidence and suggesting that the Foreign Ministry had made libelous claims. He also commented on the accusation of "bias" by stating that Bellingcat had examined all the evidence presented by the Russian Ministry of Defense and had determined that the ministry had lied repeatedly.

Less than a week later, the emailer responded again. This time, he or she wrote representing the Information and Press Department of the Ministry of Foreign Affairs of the Russian Federation. The email's tone was familiar, lecturing Higgins: "Your persistence would find a better use if you did put some effort to performing your self-proclaimed Internet sleuth role."[42] The email also argued that the Ministry of Defense had already provided examples of Bellingcat's falsifications—even though it has never provided any—as well as repeating a lie made by President Putin since 2014: "No one has provided actual proof of Russian Armed

Forces' presence in Ukraine. This is simply impossible because there are no Russian troops there, and there never were."

Finally, the email listed what it claimed were examples of Bellingcat "fakes." Among these were photos of the vehicles that had participated in the transportation of the Buk missile launcher invloved in the downing of flight MH17, photos of the launcher itself, another photo of the missile launch's smoke trail, analysis of the Russian Ministry of Defense's satellite images, and photographs of Russian soldiers.

Bellingcat volunteers analyzed the email's content and determined that the main accusations were plagiarized from old LiveJournal blogs. At least four of the claims were copied directly from a LiveJournal blogger using the pseudonym "albert-lex." Whether "albert-lex" was a paid troll or just a random online writer, the fact is that the Russian Ministry of Foreign Affairs had resorted to stealing the content of an anonymous blogger in an attempt to discredit Bellingcat.

THE ANTI-BELLINGCAT

In July 2016, Bellingcat released a new report which summarized the results from its then two-year investigation into the MH17 crash. The report detailed the Russian brigade's movements, as well as individual soldiers' roles in the convoy that transported the Buk to the Russia-Ukraine border. The report also debunked evidence fabricated by the Kremlin such as flight paths, radar data, and satellite images, as well as public statements by the Kremlin's top politicians and the Russian Ministry of Foreign Affairs.[43]

The forty-two-page report was widely quoted by professional news organizations around the world. In response, Bellingcat became the target of Kremlin-backed fake news sites. Rossiya Segodnya (Russia Today) published a forty-three-page paper titled "Anti-Bellingcat. The Falsification of Open Sources About MH17: Two Years Later."[44] The anonymously written rebuttal declared that it would "reveal opinions and assessments of the really independent experts of space and geospatial information, air defense specialists, journalists and ordinary internet users, united by the desire to expose Bellingcat's falsifications." While the "report" deserves credit for its thoroughness, it misrepresented Bellingcat's findings, denying nearly all of the group's hard evidence and ending with a defiant promise that "the debunking of falsifications provided by the Bellingcat sofa experts and other similar fake groups is not finished."[45]

The international editions of both RT and Sputnik quoted the report, and a follow-up report, which was published several months later.[46] To this day, both reports are cited in RT's articles attacking Bellingcat.

ooooo

Around the same time, approximately thirty Russian-language articles appeared online within a span of about thirty hours. Some of them were published as blog posts on LiveJournal, others on mainstream Russian media. But each conveyed the same talking points. "It was the usual crap. For example, that *Spiegel* Online had to apologize because they used a forensic expert from Bellingcat," Higgins says.

Bellingcat investigated the bizarre cloud of writings and determined that someone had likely sent out a propaganda press release about Eliot Higgins, and that multiple journalists and bloggers had published pieces based on the release. Further research uncovered that the network of sites and bloggers that published the release were connected to the Internet Research Agency, the infamous Russian troll factory. "Some of the LiveJournal bloggers no one had taken notice of," says Higgins. "But now we knew, they belonged to the troll factory network. So all they managed to do was to provide new information." According to Higgins, this particular operation was ineffective because the stories were in Russian, which restricts their target audience. He receives all sorts of eccentric material from "a lot of nutters and crazy people," so thirty troll articles didn't impress him. "If there is pro-Russian commenting in the internet forums, everyone thinks it's a Russian troll anyways. So all the pro-Russian trolls have done is to convince everyone that anyone who is pro-Russian is a paid Russian troll, so that's a 'brilliant' campaign. It's completely counterproductive," Higgins says.

∞∞∞∞

On September 28, 2016, the Dutch-led Joint Investigation Team into flight MH17 held a press conference in the Netherlands. Over the course of two years, the team had examined thousands of parts of the plane's wreckage, tested twenty weapons systems, accessed five billion internet pages, and researched half a million videos and photographs. More than 200 witnesses had been heard, around 150,000 intercepted telephone calls listened in on, with 3,500 intercepted conversations processed in their entirety. Everything was documented in 6,000 official reports. The investigators had sent 60 requests for legal assistance to more than 20 countries and received assistance from many. The team had even detonated a warhead and a missile in a test environment.[47]

The team's preliminary results confirmed Bellingcat's earlier findings.

That same day, RT called Eliot Higgins an "armchair blogger" and put together an edited video which pushed a degrading representation of the Bellingcat leader as a "laid-off admin worker, who made a name for himself by analyzing weapons used in the Syrian conflict," had no background or training in weapons, had "never been to Syria," and "doesn't speak a word of Arabic." The video—which mixed content from Higgins's own presentations with clips from among other things, *Rambo* movies—failed to mention that Higgins was an internationally recognized expert who worked with global human rights organizations.[48] RT also knowingly left out Higgins's work with many universities and think tanks, as well as the countless factual findings of Bellingcat. Basically, RT carefully edited the clip to make Higgins look stupid and unreliable. "So many things in the video are wrong, and it's fake news," Higgins says. "There is no way to watch the video without realizing that it's really poorly and unfairly edited. Using an old quote, which is not about now, this moment, is a way to attack me. To RT it doesn't matter if a hundred experts say you're right: RT will use the one who says you're wrong."

Higgins decided to again complain about RT to Ofcom. He was hopeful that this time, his complaint would succeed.

"I WILL MEET YOU WITH A GUN"

In addition to being attacked in the media, Higgins's work has also made him a physical target. For example, conference organizers have had to frequently hire armed guards when he speaks. This happened in Latvia, which borders Russia and where the awareness of Russian-originating threats is higher than in many other countries. "Certain governments are careful about the security and have decided, based on their assessments, that we need more than just a hotel room—we need protection," Higgins shares. "So when we go to a restaurant, the guards sit at different tables, watching the room at different angles. Then the staff is looking at them, looking at us, wondering who we are and why we're getting this kind of treatment. It's good, it's like having a taxi service with guns."

There have also been instances when the police have had to intervene on his behalf. In September 2016, Higgins attended the Joint Investigation Team's press conference in the Netherlands, and gave a lecture at a local university afterward. Before the lecture, a Twitter user publicly threatened Higgins, saying that, "I will meet you with a gun." When Higgins arrived at the university, he discovered that two police officers had been sent to protect him. The police had monitored his Twitter feed and reacted to the threat.

Higgins has also had to contact the police himself on occasion. A Twitter activist once created a series of websites using Higgins's name and published harassing material, including Higgins' home address. "There's a certain line, where they attack you and you slag people off, and you expect to get some shit online, that's just life," Higgins says. "But when people start posting your address and photos of your house online, that crosses the line."

Higgins contacted the websites' hosts and got the sites taken down. But when the stalker found a new web host, Higgins went to the police, and announced to his social media followers that the harasser was being investigated. Following this the stalker, as well as several aggressive Twitter troll accounts, disappeared. Higgins had to help the police investigate the case. "The thing is, the police didn't have a clue," he says. "They asked me how to conduct the investigation, and I gave them tons of information. The person was sloppy and his website was badly done, so you could see his IP address. Six months later, the police asked, had I heard anything else from him? I said no, they said okay, case closed. I was like, fucking hell!"

Higgins figures that someone would have to be incredibly stupid to do something truly threatening to him, as he is well connected with journalists and law enforcement, who follow his endeavors closely: "If someone starts giving me shit in a major way, it's not just journalists making notes, it's policy makers, government people, and military intelligence. Military intelligence and government intelligence are very interested in what I do, even though they won't say it directly. People who know people tell me they're big fans and they love Bellingcat. They're very interested whenever I start getting shit."

DEEP STATE

In February 2017, a fake news site named SouthFront joined in the smearing of Higgins. SouthFront produces multilingual stories and videos specifically about the Russian military's actions in Syria. The stories are allegedly crowdsourced citizen journalism, but many of the details are so specific that they must originate with officials and soldiers working for the Russian Federation. In a 2016 article I wrote about cyber warfare,[49] I observed that the site looks suspiciously like a Russian military intelligence information operation; after the article came out, I became a SouthFront target myself.[50] One anonymous citizen activist, worried about Russian information warfare, told me he had infiltrated SouthFront as a content producer. He sent them professional and factual pieces for publication, but the editors revised his articles to feature a pro-Kremlin slant.

SouthFront ran an anonymous "opinion piece" in which it called Bellingcat "an instrument of a hybrid war against Russia" and a "manifestation of the Hydra-headed intelligence 'deep state.'"[51] According to the theory drummed up by Russian trolls, the deep state—a secret shadow government, possibly tied to the military-industrial complex—governs outside of democratic institutions in the United States. The theory became increasingly popular during the 2016 presidential election, especially among Trump supporters. After the election, the concept was pushed by Trump's former chief strategist Steve Bannon and his fake news site *Breitbart News*, among others, as well as by President Trump himself. One of the most active deep state advocates has long been Alex Jones, of *Infowars* fame.

At the same time that SouthFront published its piece connecting Higgins with the deep state, Russia's Foreign Ministry launched a new international operation: an official website on which it claimed to identify "fake news" published around the world.[52] According to the ministry, the website was launched as a counterreaction to the European Union's East StratCom Task Force's site "EU vs. Disinformation," which exposes Russian propaganda operating in the European Union.[53] But the Russian site's specialty is labeling articles by professional journalists as fake news; for example, articles from the British newspaper the *Guardian*. False articles from SouthFront, MV-Lehti, or RT are never included. The Twitter account of the Russian embassy in the UK pinged Higgins to inform him of the new Russian fake news site. "They copied me on the tweet, which I thought was very funny. And rubbish," Higgins says.

ooooo

In January 2018, Ofcom came to a decision concerning Higgins's second complaint against RT. In what was a surprise to many experts, the UK broadcasting regulator again ruled that RT's reporting was fair and just.

To Higgins, Ofcom's decision was obviously disappointing, though the complaint did result in some positive developments. "I have noticed RT reaching out to me more frequently and asking my response to claims about my work," he says. "And the complaint seems to have discouraged them from writing about me. So at least my complaint had some impact."

Soon thereafter, Ofcom was finally forced to take RT disinformation more seriously. After Russian military intelligence agents, whom Bellingcat helped to identify, poisoned the former Russian military intelligence officer Sergei Skripal and his daughter in Salisbury, England in early 2018, RT's "reporting" about the matter was such that Ofcom opened multiple investigations into the clear bias of their news and current affairs programs for possible breaches of the UK broadcasting code.

In December 2018, Ofcom concluded that seven RT

programs had broken the impartiality regulation. In July 2019, Ofcome fined RT £200,000 ($270,000) for "serious failures to comply with our broadcasting rules."[54] RT appealed the fine, but the ruling was upheld by the British High Court in March 2020.[55] RT appealed a second time, to the Court of Appeals, which again ruled against the network in October 2021.[56]

"YOU LIE EVEN IN SUCH SMALL DETAILS"

In May 2018, President Putin continued to try to muddy the waters about who the guilty party was in the downing of flight MH17. The Kremlin leader's platform on this occasion was the St. Petersburg International Economic Forum, an annual Russian business event attended by high-profile politicians and CEOs of global companies. The influential forum provides a perfect opportunity to stage information operations.

Putin was onstage with French president Emmanuel Macron, the Japanese prime minister, the Chinese vice president, and the IMF Managing Director. The previous day, the Joint Investigation Team had released an update on its work, positively mentioning Bellingcat's previous investigations.[57] Putin attacked the international investigators. "If there is no comprehensive investigation, it will certainly be very difficult for us to accept the conclusions of the investigating commission which works without us," he said.[58] Apparently, in Putin's view, the conclusions of the Joint Investigation Team would only be acceptable if it included participants from the Russian authorities who were responsible for the crash in the first place.

The panel's moderator, Bloomberg News editor in chief John Micklethwait, asked Putin: "Are you saying that it was not a Russian army missile?"

Putin answered: "It was not, certainly. Certainly not."[59]

A month later, in June 2018, Dmitry Polyanskiy, Russia's

ambassador to the UN, continued the familiar accusations, claiming on Twitter that Bellingcat used "fakes."[60] When Bellingcat asked for evidence of his charges, Polyanskiy tweeted a photo of the Buk launcher used in Bellingcat's research and stated, contrary to the facts, that "the direction of sunshade of one car can't be opposite from the direction of sunshade of another....It's against the laws of physics. This photo is a FAKE. You lie even in such small details. How can anyone trust you?"[61]

Bellingcat investigator Aric Toler responded and showed the ambassabor how he was wrong. But the ambassador wouldn't accept that. On July 17, 2018, the fourth anniversary of flight MH17 being shot down, Polyanskiy wrote a letter to the UN Security Council demanding a thorough and objective international investigation—even though one had been underway for four years. He called Bellingcat "pseudo investigators ... known for their fake news."[62] The following month, The *Washington Post* published an article about Bellingcat's work and the Russian harassment targeted at the group.[63]

Polyanskiy's revenge was immediate. He wrote a letter to the editor in chief of the *Post*, which he also published on Russia's UN mission site.[64] In the letter, he stated that he was "very much disappointed by this publication which clearly does not meet the standards of an unbiased journalist report." He also portrayed Russia as a victim and claimed that its government systematically supported the attempt to find the guilty parties behind the downing of the plane. He also took the opportunity to mock both Bellingcat and the Dutch investigators.

Simultaneously, it was revealed that WikiLeaks had leaked internal chats that showed that an account with the pseudonym "wikileaks" had claimed that the financing for Bellingcat was coming in part from Britain's Ministry of Defense. The same false and unverified claim was quickly spread as fact on RT and Sputnik, from whence it was further wildly spun. The shadiest sites claimed that Bellingcat was financed by British foreign intelligence, as well as by Swedish researcher Martin Kragh—and by me!

"STUPID STUFF"

In early 2019, the foreign affairs committees of the three Baltic states, Estonia, Latvia, and Lithuania, jointly nominated Bellingcat for the Pulitzer Prize.[65] Actions like this make it obvious that Russia has not been able to cause the negative impact against Bellingcat it has hoped for. "Well, RT can show a bad video about me," shares Higgins. "But to me, if you watch Russia Today, you're totally lost. Their fancy videos don't influence anyone who has influence in any interaction with me in any serious way. The people I meet don't care about RT stuff or haven't heard of it. If they have, they're on my side." Higgins actually considers every attack from the Kremlin a confirmation that Bellingcat's work is accurate. It is also difficult for Russia to undermine Bellingcat's credibility because the community only uses information that is publicly accessible and well-sourced.

People sometimes ask Higgins why he writes "so much" about Russia. It's because the Kremlin keeps lying. "If they didn't lie, we wouldn't have anything to write about," he says. "There's this idea of Russia as a master propagandist—they're not. They lie, and they don't have media in the West that critically examine it. The media should have been doing this for years, but many journalists say, 'It's so complicated, we can't really look into it, therefore the truth is in the middle, here's two sides of the story.' Two sides of the story only work if both sides are truthful."

Instead of being distracted by what he calls "stupid stuff from Russia," Higgins prefers to focus on his justice and accountability work with the International Criminal Court, which he assists in the use of social media evidence, a complex issue that is currently unregulated by international standards. Higgins wants to help create guidelines, so that war criminals and other criminals can be held accountable.

He also continues to teach law enforcement, citizen groups, and other organizations how to use social media investigations effectively. Newcomers to the field might be worried about becoming the target of Russian-organized smear campaigns. How would Higgins, as a superstar of open-source investigations, advise someone interested in investigating Russia? "Do it," he says. "Just beware that if you become too well-known and too popular, they will try to undermine and attack your work. So, if you have skeletons in your closet—like if you murdered someone or were a drug dealer—you probably don't want to come along." Higgins promises to help anyone who becomes the target of state-sponsored operations. "Propagandists see this as an information war. I never want to be a part of a propaganda war, but if they want me to become a part of it, hell, I will make sure I fight it," he says.

In 2021, Higgins published *We Are Bellingcat: An Intelligence Agency for the People*. The book discusses his personal story as the founder of Bellingcat, as well as going behind the scenes of many of the community's high-profile investigations.

For its part, the Bellingcat community continues to publish high-profile investigations into Russian military secrets, which are often quoted by the international media.

THE INDICTMENT

In June 2019, the Joint Investigation Team held a press conference in which they announced that four individuals would be prosecuted for their participation in the downing of flight MH17.[66] The four were Igor Girkin (Strelkov), Sergey Dubinsky, Oleg Pulatov, and Leonid Kharchenko.[67] Girkin is a former FSB colonel, while Dubinsky was a military intelligence officer with the Donetsk People's Republic. Pulatov is a former lieutenant colonel in the Russian Armed Forces. The Joint Investigative Team confirmed Bellingcat's previous statement that all four had been following orders from Russia.

The indicted individuals were allegedly responsible for transporting the missile launch system from Russia to Ukraine. All four were charged with the murder of the 298 people onboard flight MH17. All four have denied their involvement in the crash. The trial began in June 2020 in the Netherlands. As of this writing, the defendants have yet to appear in court.[68]

15.

The Trial

IN MAY 2016, I WROTE AN English-language report for the
Wilfried Martens Centre for European Studies, a Brussels-based
think tank. In "The Cyberspace War: Propaganda and Trolling
As Warfare Tools," I described how the Kremlin had broadened
its arsenal of illegitimate social media influence methods outside
of its own borders, and how the use of social media trolls was a
security threat to many countries, which needed to be countered
with stricter legislation.[1] I also explained how the Kremlin was
attempting to meddle in the democratic selection of the leader of
the world's only superpower. My report was widely praised and
quoted. In November of that year, Donald Trump, the trolls' choice,
was elected as the forty-fifth president of the United States.

In 2017, the US Department of Justice appointed Robert
Mueller to investigate Russian interference in the previous
year's presidential election. The investigation revealed that the
Internet Research Agency had bought Facebook ads portraying
Democratic candidate Hillary Clinton as a criminal and a liar. The
troll factory also organized groups on Facebook to spread hatred
against foreigners and Muslims. The online agitators managed to
attract a significant American audience, who were clueless to the
fact that they were following and sharing material from Russian
trolls, and not grassroots-generated content.

I read the news about the investigation with a feeling of dismay, as the troll operations against the US election were so similar to what had been targeted against Ukraine, Finland—and myself.

∞∞∞∞∞

The greatest enablers of the Kremlin's cyberoperations are the social media companies such as Facebook, Twitter, YouTube, and Google. In my writings and professional dealings, I have tried to encourage these companies to take a more robust stance against the hostile actors exploiting their services, while at the same time encouraging legislators throughout the world to pass laws regulating their conduct.

In the fall of 2017, Google approached me after I had delivered a presentation at a journalism conference in Washington, DC. The company's PR manager had heard my remarks and wanted more details about the organized pro-Kremlin and extremist campaigns on their platforms, which include YouTube.

I was surprised that they weren't already intimately familiar with the issue. The topic was—and continues to be—hot, especially within the security and intelligence communities. Even back then a vast number of in-depth articles had been written on the subject. Several major advertisers had already pulled their Google campaigns because their brands had been tarnished by YouTube's filth channels.

But as soon as I got over my surprise, as well as my frustration that Google forbade me to record our discussions for my book, I decided to provide them with information, in the spirit of voluntary citizen activism. What I disclosed shocked them, and they lamented how difficult it was to build algorithms capable of erasing fake news from their search results.

Later on, another Google representative approached me

after one of my presentations in Europe and told me that the company had taken note of the trolls' search engine optimization, and that there had been "internal discussions" about the topic. But he explained that the situation hadn't been addressed because "journalists would call it censorship." I told the representative that in that case he didn't understand what censorship and freedom of speech meant. We eventually agreed that I would send him a list of hate sites that had been suspected of spreading criminal material, so that Google could remove them from its search engine results. I sent the list, but the content of the sites still appeared at the top of Google's search results for many years after my complaints.

My meetings with Twitter and Facebook were equally frustrating. Both promised to act if I wanted to personally "escalate" and provide them with more information about the accounts and communities that were harassing me. Given that I was drowning in filth spread on platforms provided by these companies and needed the constant assistance of the police and the Finnish justice system just to try and live a normal life, I concluded that offering my assistance would have been a waste of my time and resources. Besides, I had already filed user reports about the harassment, as the companies required. If they had followed their own guidelines, the problem would have already been handled. I felt that individual users of Facebook, Twitter, YouTube, or Google should not be forced to meet face-to-face with the representatives of the companies in order to have suspected criminal accounts that spread toxic propaganda removed.

At a conference, I asked an eloquent Facebook representative what specific actions the company had taken to protect users from state-sponsored, illegal, digital campaigns. She explained that Facebook protected vulnerable communities and removed fake profiles and fake news from its platform. Since her statement, the site has been used to fuel the genocide of the Rohingya Muslim minority in Myanmar, among other crimes, so Facebook still has a lot of work to do when it comes to protecting vulnerable communities.

"ILJA, I LOVE YOU!"

It was July 2018. A crowd of people were packed by the door to room 510 of the Helsinki District Court. The number of observers allowed in the courtroom was limited, and those standing outside wanted to secure their seats.

In addition to being in demand by traditional journalists, those seats were also desired by a few dozen MV-Lehti activists and pro-Kremlin hate-tubers. According to their conspiracy theories, this was to be a show trial, the aim of which was to make Finland part of NATO.

When the guards opened the doors, a hassle broke out as people fought for the seats. Only a fraction of the audience managed to squeeze into the room, while the rest were left outside in the hallway. The MV-Lehti activists took many of the seats meant for journalists. Someone who didn't get a seat yelled, "ILJA, I LOVE YOU!"

In the courtroom, there were three defendants.

Johan Bäckman was on trial for aggravated defamation, stalking, and encouragement to commit aggravated defamation, all against me. The prosecutor, Juha-Mikko Hämäläinen, called the campaign "information influencing" with the intent of interfering with my work as a journalist. Bäckman had tried everything he could to avoid the trial. On multiple occasions, he had voiced his supposed desire to "settle" with me. He had even told me through his lawyer that if I agreed to settle, we could resolve other matters in addition to the ones within the district court's jurisdiction. Bäckman had made his final settlement offer on the Friday before the trial. I flatly rejected it, repulsed when thinking of the number of important cases which the Russian influence agents in Finland and abroad had obliterated with money. I saw Bäckman's settlement offers as pressure, as well as a way to try and buy my silence.

The second defendant was Ilja Janitskin. After an escape from justice and a lengthy legal process, he had finally been caught in Andorra and extradited to Finland for trial. He was charged with aggravated defamation against me. The third defendant was a middle-aged woman from northern Finland who was suspected of temporarily running MV-Lehti while Janitskin was in custody. The woman, who used, among others, the nickname T2 at MV-Lehti, was charged with aggravated defamation against me. There were other victims as well; I was the first of many plaintiffs.

I had traveled back to Finland specifically to participate in the trial. I sat in the front row with my lawyers and my mother. As a security measure, I was isolated from the defendants and onlookers by a wall. I was allowed to move around the courtroom only when escorted by the police, through the same hallway in which inmates were transported to the courtroom.

A large portion of the audience had been encouraged to disturb the court's proceedings. Several weeks before the trial began, after Janitskin had arrived in Finland as a remanded prisoner, his successor at MV-Lehti spoke on a YouTube show about having met with Janitskin in prison. He claimed that Janitskin had encouraged his followers to protest the trial. In addition, MV-Lehti activists were advised to film me in the courtroom and then post every "lie" I said in court to social media. It was also openly speculated on YouTube as to which door I would use to enter the courtroom; according to the MV-Lehti community, it would be the *pelkääjän ovi*—the expression which refers to the side door leading to the courtroom, which is used by witnesses who need protection.

ooooo

When a YouTube user is approved to monetize a channel—meaning that the user can conduct business, such as advertising—they can also activate a feature called Super Chat. The feature enables people watching on a livestream to buy visibility for their individual chat comments. Super Chat, available on YouTube since 2017, was copied from porn sites, where the people watching are able to make paid suggestions to the individuals performing on the livestream.[2]

The MV-Lehti community used Super Chat to collect money from its followers, saying, for instance, that the funds would be used "to support Ilja." Sometimes they managed to collect hundreds of euros during a single show. I had mentioned the exploitive use of Super Chat to the Finnish police in the spring of 2018 because there was no legislation in Finland that regulated the feature's use. It was thus an open question whether money collected through Super Chat was legal. The police thanked me for the tip.

Before the trial, the MV-Lehti YouTube channel had aired an admiring interview of Johan Bäckman, and then exploited Super Chat to agitate against me. One of the viewers in the comments section threatened to show up at the courthouse and "accidentally Jessikka will trip down the stairs."

ooooo

The trial lasted for four days. The amount of police material presented was massive, even though it included only a fraction of the filth stories that MV-Lehti and Johan Bäckman had produced about me.

During the investigation, the police had also uncovered several interesting financial transactions. For example, Janitskin's right hand woman from northern Finland had been paid tens of thousands of euros through PayPal. She claimed that the payments were "loans" from Janitskin, even thought there was no loan agreement. She had also received payments in cryptocurrency—Bitcoin, favored by Russian hackers—worth of tens of thousands of euros. She told the police that they were given to her by a "private philanthropist who wanted to support MV-Lehti."

Johan Bäckman responded to the charges of aggravated defamation and stalking by saying that his actions were "regular political debate." Ilja Janitskin, accused of publishing twenty-seven smear pieces about me on MV-Lehti, claimed that he wasn't responsible for the site's content. (I counted the stories with my lawyers, and at that time MV-Lehti had published 220 pieces about me, 170 of them during Janitskin's period as "editor-in-chief.") The defense lawyers said that the majority of the charges should be dismissed and that my demands for damages, which totaled over €130,000, were too large.

For four days I listened from behind the security wall as the defendants spun their claims about me. At the same time, the MV-Lehti activists mocked my testimony, and smeared my witnesses. While my supervisor at the time, then Yle editor in chief Atte Jääskeläinen, testified how the hate campaign had affected my ability to work as a reporter, it was hinted on a livestream aired from the courtroom entrance that I had had an inappropriate relationship with Jääskeläinen, and that we had probably used drugs together.

In addition to me and my witnesses, the chairman of the district court was also made the target of vulgar name calling and racist hate articles. The journalists who covered the sessions were also harassed, with protesters outside the courtroom yelling at them and calling them names. One journalist was pushed against a wall in an attempt to block his access to the courtroom, while another received an elbow to the ribs during a scuffle. Many of the reporters covering the trial were attacked on social media. On one occasion, the police reacted to MV-Lehti activists fantasizing on their YouTube channel about killing a journalist during the trial by interrogating them, and then shutting down their channel. Before Johan Bäckman and his accomplice Ilja Janitskin started their campaign to stir up hate, such open, violent, and broad hostility against journalists was unheard of in Finland. Now, methodical, systematic attacks against journalists and civic society had become the new normal.

CONVICTION

In October 2018, the Helsinki District Court pronounced the defendants guilty of all charges. The court said that the defendants' actions were premeditated and that Janitskin's motivation was revenge.

Bäckman received a one-year conditional prison term, a stricter sentence than the prosecutor had requested. Janitskin was sentenced to an unconditional term of one year and ten months. His verdict included convictions for illicit gambling and fundraising, breaches of confidentiality, incitement against minorities, and copyright infringement.[3]

The third defendant received a three-month conditional prison term.

All three defendants were jointly ordered to pay me damages of over €80,000. They all appealed their convictions.

In the Russian state media, the verdict was covered as proof of the rotten state of the Finnish justice system.[4] The troll factory's fake news service RIA Fan demanded lighter sentences for Bäckman and Janitskin from the appeals court. According to the news agency RIA Novosti, the worst stalker in Finland was in fact me.

16.

The Insider

ON MARCH 5, 2014, ANCHOR LIZ WAHL was on air at the RT America studio in Washington, DC, presenting the news. Suddenly, she ignored the prewritten script running on the teleprompter. "I cannot be part of a network funded by the Russian government that whitewashes the actions of Putin," Wahl told her viewers. "I'm proud to be an American and believe in disseminating the truth. And that is why, after this newscast, I'm resigning."[1]

As she walked away from the anchor desk, the Russian director called Wahl into his office and demanded an explanation. She repeated what she had just said on air, then left the RT newsroom for the final time.

Wahl's on-air resignation became worldwide breaking news. "As I walked out of the station, my phone started to blow up. The news literally spread around the world so quickly. I never could have imagined that," Wahl shares.

The traditional media bombarded her with so many interview requests that she didn't have time to answer them all. For several days, Wahl appeared on CNN, MSNBC, and other media outlets, recounting her experience working for RT. Later, she testified about Russian information warfare before the US Congress.

RT's management didn't bother to address Wahl's criticism. Instead, it questioned her mental health, tangled her in odd conspiracies, and influenced a network of influential pro-Kremlin YouTubers and internet trolls to go on the attack.

∞∞∞

Liz Wahl is an experienced journalist and a talented television professional. She was born to a military family at the US naval base at Subic Bay, in the western part of the Philippines, close to the capital of Manila. Her grandparents had experienced first-hand the Soviet Union's aggression. In 1956, they sought refuge in the United States after citizens in their home country of Hungary were attacked by Soviet-backed security forces for resisting the communist regime.

At the time of her resignation, Wahl had worked at RT for two and a half years. While there, she had witnessed how the Russian news directors at the network's Washington bureau continually and unethically interfered with the editorial process. In particular, as Russia's military operations in Ukraine intensified, the network's higher-ups made Wahl and her colleagues' attempts to produce fact-based journalism impossible.

Shortly before Wahl resigned, a report she had done on Ukraine had been sabotaged. She had recorded an interview with a US congressman, asking for his views on the Russian soldiers invading Ukraine, after it had become apparent they had entered the Crimean Peninsula illegally. But the final, aired story did not include Wahl's interview, as the Russian news directors had asked the editors to cut it. According to the general narrative disseminated by the Kremlin and broadcast on RT, no Russian military operations were taking place in Ukraine. "Before the war in Ukraine, it was never quite like that. You were allowed to ask questions from the interviewees. But at this point, you weren't allowed to do that. With RT, you had to denigrate and downplay Ukraine," Wahl explains.

The RT supervisors also urged Wahl to report about Ukraine's "new neo-Nazi government," although no such government existed. The channel also pushed conspiracy theories stating that the United States, European Union, and the CIA had meddled and interfered in Ukraine.

Wahl considered her employer's reporting disturbing and unethical. She was especially troubled by how openly RT blackened her own homeland, underscoring the flaws of American society.

∞∞∞

Originally it was RT who approached Wahl to work as a journalist in its Washington office.

In 2011, Wahl was employed at a small news station in the Northern Mariana Islands, a US dependency in the Pacific Ocean. RT's news director had seen a report Wahl had done about the nuclear power plant disaster in Fukushima and wanted to recruit her. The channel had recently rebranded itself, abandoning its original name, Russia Today, and started marketing itself as a legitimate news outlet. Only several years later would the full scope of RT's mission as the Kremlin's international "information weapon" be analyzed in-depth in the West.[2]

During her employment negotiations, RT was sold to Wahl as an "international news station focusing on stories that the mainstream media ignores." The news director equated RT America with Al Jazeera English, the network that covered the Arabic world. Wahl had her doubts. She asked about the journalistic independence of RT. "The bosses answered that the idea of RT's lack of journalistic independence was a 'Cold War mentality' and laughed," she says. "They said that such ideas were part of the image of Russia that they were trying to get away from. And that's why they had the international channel."

But the network's de facto mission was revealed by its Russian editor in chief, Margarita Simonyan. In a 2012 interview that discussed, among other topics, Russia's information war with the West, Simonyan stated that, "when Russia is at war, we are, of course, on the side of Russia."[3]

While weighing the job offer, Wahl checked the content produced by RT. In 2011 it wasn't yet a 24/7 propaganda factory. "RT did cover stories that were 100 percent truthful and legitimate—but those stories would always focus on problems in Europe and in the US, and never in Russia," Wahl says.

Despite her misgivings, she accepted the offer.

ooooo

At first, the processes at RT seemed no different than those at other news outlets. Wahl conducted interviews, produced news packages, and presented live newscasts. She would gather information, sometimes travel to cover stories, make video reports and book studio guests and interviewees for future shows. The working routines at the channel seemed familiar.

But the choices of news topics, viewpoints and the interview subjects were under the strict control of the Russian directors. "On the surface, it seemed like you had a lot of freedom," says Wahl. "But along the way, you learned that you only had freedom when you criticized the US, the West, or the European Union. When the story was about Russia or Russia's allies, it was not so free."

The directors were pleased whenever Wahl pitched story ideas about troubles in the United States. Protests against the US government were always a hot topic. However, the stories were often taken out of their original context and blown out of proportion.

In the beginning of Wahl's RT journey, one special area of interest for the network was the Occupy Wall Street movement. The citizen initiative against financial inequality and in support of human rights launched a series of street rallies worldwide. In the United States, people gathered in Manhattan's Wall Street area, demanding that the power of the banks be reduced and that other societal problems be addressed.

The movement was an important and legitimate news topic that required media coverage. However, RT's coverage was magnified and slanted. Wahl saw how the network used people's worries about the US government's handling of the 2008 financial crisis and its decision to bail out the banks to prove that the whole of American democracy was in ruins. RT reporters were enthusiastically sent to film police officers patrolling the streets in full combat gear. "The Occupy Wall Street coverage was obsessive," Wahl recalls. The channel employed multiple reporters to live-report the protest in cities throughout the United States.

With its disproportionate coverage, the network wanted to create the impression that the mainstream media wasn't genuinely interested in the protesters' frustrations, and that RT was the only media source people could rely on. "RT doesn't have to invent the problems, because they already exist. RT amplifies them. RT is really good at playing up the real problems of people who are upset with the government or feel they're not getting a fair stake in society," Wahl shares.

Even as the street rallies tailed off over time, and other news outlets moved on, RT continued to interview the few remaining activists. According to the network, the "corporate media," as RT characterizes American news outlets, including the ones funded with public money, had abandoned the protestors. "It got to the point where the employees said this is it, we're beating a dead horse here," Wahl says. "But the news director was very adamant about continuing the coverage."

ooooo

Another important story that revealed RTs attempt at political influencing was that of US Army soldier Chelsea Manning, then known as Bradley Manning.

In 2010, Manning was suspected of disclosing US military secrets to Julian Assange's WikiLeaks. The material Manning handed over included a video showing American soldiers in a military helicopter, fatally shooting employees of the Reuters news agency. Also included were several hundred thousand diplomatic cables, which bore confidential information. The material created an international scandal, and criticism of US military and diplomatic activities.

RT assigned Wahl to report on Manning's trial. However, the point of view of how the story should be reported came from the news producers. "According to RT, Manning was a little guy blowing the whistle on the mighty US government, who alone stood up and fought for freedom of speech," Wahl says. "For that, the US government wanted to shut him up."

Manning was charged and later convicted of multiple crimes,[4] including violations of the Espionage Act of 1917, which prohibits activities such as interfering with military operations, supporting the enemy during war, and resisting orders.[5] For RT, Manning's convictions were more proof of how "freedom of speech is suffocated in the US," says Wahl.

Edward Snowden, the NSA contractor who similarly exposed confidential US intelligence information to the global press, also received favorable treatment from RT, because he, too, made the American military and security agencies look bad.

For RT, the Manning and Snowden revelations were golden. They made the network's information warfare efforts easy, as the channel didn't have to invent negative news about US security structures—Manning and Snowden provided the basic information. All RT needed to do was endlessly repeat, boost, and amplify that information to the world.

THE PERFECT JOURNALIST

Liz Wahl didn't go to work every morning thinking that she was a cog in an international propaganda machine. She didn't feel that her supervisors forced her to say or do anything. But a form of self-censorship was gradually planted in her mind and the minds of the rest of the staff by the management at RT. In a particular danger zone were young journalists, who didn't possess previous experience at regular newsrooms with common journalistic practices in place to ensure factual reporting. "If you didn't know how to provide context and how to check that your sources were sound or weren't familiar with fact checking, RT would mold you into the perfect journalist," Wahl says. The management appreciated those employees who were obedient and expressed hostility toward the US government. "A perfect journalist would quote RT's guests carefully and was willing to push the envelope when it came to publishing half-truths and conspiracies whenever they made the US, NATO, or EU look bad," Wahl shares.

An employee with the desired mentality often quickly moved up the corporate ladder.

Conversely, when a staff member wasn't perceived as moldable, and questioned the supervisors too often, his or her career would get stuck. "If a journalist didn't automatically self-censor, the supervisors would step in and give bad feedback. Or one of the higher-ups would edit your script, take away lines, change them, or make it more suggestive," Wahl says.

As a result, the dominant mindset in the newsroom, was, as Wahl describes it, "anti-establishment thinking." She witnessed many coworkers, even American citizens, becoming swept up in the conspiracy theories waged inside the walls of RT: "You feel like you're fighting the powers that are controlling the world."

The Russian supervisors didn't disclose from where or from whom they received their directions. Instead, the atmosphere was secretive and mysterious. Frequently, the Russian directors would create a rundown of the next day's planned topics and then cancel some without explanation. "There were no pressing or obvious reasons. Unless if someone from higher up forbid the coverage of some specific topics," Wahl shares.

Even though the majority of RT's reporting staff were American citizens with American backgrounds, the most "difficult" stories were assigned to the Russian journalists. "For example, the stories that showed the US in a bad light were given to Russian journalists," Wahl says. "They would deliver, whereas the American anchors and reporters would feel resistant."

"BAGS PUT OVER OURS HEADS"

One important job responsibility for Wahl was booking studio guests. Conspiracy theorists, extremists, and individuals voicing frustration and criticism toward the West were always warmly welcomed. "RT will find those voices and give them airtime, to voice their anger and disillusionment with the US government, system, and status quo," Wahl explains.

Sometimes the producers chose the guests; other times, the reporters were tasked with finding a commentator with an "alternative" point of view. "Healthy skepticism is part of democracy. But the more furious the guest was, the more likely his comments were used as sound bites," Wahl says.

Often, it was the channel's regular guests who were the most belligerent in interviews. During Wahl's tenure, the most popular political commentators included the British member of the European Parliament—and later leader of the Brexit Party—and relentless critic of the EU Nigel Farage, *Infowars* social media conspiracy theorist Alex Jones, and action movie actor and producer Steven Seagal.

In March 2012, during the Obama presidency, Wahl interviewed Alex Jones live. The topic was Executive Order 13603, which addressed "national defense resource policies and programs under the Defense Production Act of 1950."[6] RT was biased in presenting critics of the order, many of whom characterized it as a government power grab. When Wahl asked Jones whether Americans should be alarmed by the executive order, he replied, "Americans should be extremely alarmed."[7] He then contemplated the idea of the president's potential to "secretly kill Americans and have bags put over our heads and have us thrown into black vans to disappear forever."

Wahl was also assigned to interview Steven Seagal. The action film star, who has no education or expertise in foreign policy, declared Vladimir Putin a strong leader. "I can't tell you the excitement that the news producer had over Seagal. He was one of the most ridiculous people I was told to interview. But at RT, he was considered a VIP guest." Later, Seagal was granted Russian citizenship.[8] President Putin personally handed him his Russian passport in a public ceremony, which was proudly broadcast on RT. Seagal has continued advocating for Putin ever since.

Some RT interviews are so stiff and formal that they seem like preplanned performances, raising questions as to whether the guests—and reporters—were given instructions in advance.

That's not the case, according to Wahl.

"These people don't need to be trained," she says. "You'll find citizens of the United States who are willing to say things that make the US look very bad. In turn, they are in line with the Kremlin's narrative. And on RT, there are guests with varying degrees of sanity."

Wahl interviewed Nigel Farage on several occasions. At the time, he was not as widely known a Euro-skeptic as he is today. But at RT, he was viewed as the renegade of the European Parliament, providing "another viewpoint" and passionately bashing the EU. Later he became the face of Brexit. Coincidence or not, Brexit was vehemently pushed by the Kremlin's social media troll farms and by RT. "Seeing the way things have played out, I have to come to understand why Farage was a preferred guest on RT," shares Wahl. "He didn't get that much airtime in the Western media, but for us he was a VIP."

During the 2012 presidential election, RT drummed up its favorite candidate, Ron Paul, a Republican congressman from Texas. By reporting on Paul, the network covered a candidate who had allegedly been "silenced" by the mainstream media. As Wahl familiarized herself with Paul's policies, she realized that RT was obsessed with the congressman because by speaking out against US intervention in the international arena, he voiced the most critical opinions toward Western foreign policy. This in turn benefited the Kremlin, which was already planning its invasion of Ukraine.

∞∞∞∞

RT's employment recruitment policy was as revealing as its choice of guests. Journalists who stood little chance of finding work in the traditional, highly competitive field of journalism in the US became stars at RT. For example, the American social media celebrity Abby Martin, a former RT host, originally gained public attention by promoting New World Order conspiracies, accusing the powerful elite of silencing the masses through the "corporate media" and claiming that 9/11 was an "inside job." At RT, Martin was awarded her own regular show, *Breaking the Set*, which aired from 2012 to 2015.

The management at RT also didn't find it ethically questionable if a journalist covered stories about her own father's business. That was the case with the daughter of Russia's former ambassador to the UN, who worked at RT and covered her father without restriction, simultaneously pushing Russian political narratives.

VIRAL MANIPULATION

One constant aspect of RT's coverage is so-called media criticism.

To be clear, media criticism at RT isn't the kind of sophisticated, scholarly, or carefully argued analysis of news standards and other elements of modern journalism which is discussed in most newsrooms' internal feedback sessions. Instead, it is a monotonous, repetitive bashing of the traditional media, which, in reality, RT itself systematically engages in: namely, obscuring the truth, spreading propaganda, and falsifying news. For example, during Wahl's time there, RT continually labeled the Western media as "corporate media," which merely sought profit, with RT as the only viable alternative from which to get real news. "As RT wasn't tied to the demand of generating profits, and the truth was its main goal, RT was the only media source that had the freedom to tell the truth. That is one way of saying how RT is superior to the Western media," Wahl says of the how the network portrayed itself.

RT's internal discussions about its audience relationship are revealing. Wahl recounts that the staff was never told what the ratings were, and they were never analyzed. At regular news stations, the producers follow the ratings, and they're discussed with the staff. To Wahl, it appeared that the viewer numbers weren't important at RT. Instead, the network's social media presence was highlighted, as all its television segments were uploaded to YouTube. Success was measured by how frequently the audience shared and spread RT content further on social media. "The number one interest was to get the message out and build up a lot of internet traffic. YouTube views were a big thing," Wahl says. RT America has well over one million followers on Facebook, and even though many of them are likely paid trolls, the network also has genuine fans all over the globe, who trust the channel enough to recommend its content to their social media networks—unaware of how strictly that content is censored and directed politically.

Just like other Russian disinformation and troll sites, RT knows how to attract social media viewers: sex and violence, cute animals, fear, hatred, and anything else that manipulates viewers' emotions. To attract more young male viewers, for example, it has used porn stars as news commentators. Nonpolitical clickbait stories serve as decoys to lure unsuspecting viewers to the channel's political content. When a viewer clicks on one video, YouTube's algorithms recommend an endless flow of similar videos. RT likely pays for visibility on YouTube. Not many viewers would think that the content has been funded with Russian government money and produced by a channel that serves Russian national security in the information space.

And that's the whole point.

"STAGED PSY-OP"

As time went by, Wahl became increasingly uncomfortable with her employer's mission of portraying the United States in a negative light. According to universally accepted journalistic ideals, the media should operate as a watchdog, and question the government. "But it was apparent that RT wasn't on a virtuous mission to hold the US government accountable. It was bashing our military, our leaders, and our way of life," Wahl says.

Wahl also became alarmed at RT's coverage of world events, in particular the crisis in Syria. Her colleagues filed false stories claiming that the Syrian rebels had used chemical weapons against Syrian civilians, leading to casualties of women and children. In fact, it was the Russian-backed Assad regime that had staged the chemical attacks against the population. Wahl found RT's coverage on Syria horrific: "There were videos of dead children, and here you have an RT interviewee saying it was a false flag Western media conspiracy. It's disturbing. If a chemical attack happens, the least the media can do is to try and find out who is responsible."

As Russia's invasion of Ukraine intensified, RT further distorted reality while presenting itself as the ultimate truth-telling outlet. Wahl felt disgusted by the network. It was time for her to leave. She gave her final live broadcast, told the audience that the channel spread propaganda and whitewashed Putin's policies, and resigned. "You can't stop the machine altogether, but at least you can try to spread the word. I wanted to do my part to set the record straight," Wahl shares.

After her resignation, Wahl received supportive messages from several of her former colleagues, many of whom shared her concerns about the nature of the channel. As word of the RT anchor's resignation spread around the world, strangers sent messages thanking her for her courageous act.

But when her now former supervisors at RT saw that the video of her resignation was spreading like wildfire online and started to receive requests for comment from traditional media outlets, they launched countermeasures. Two days after Wahl quit, RT published an online statement that condemned her behavior as unprofessional. "When a journalist disagrees with the editorial position of his or her organization, the usual course of action is to address those grievances with the editor, and, if they cannot be resolved, to quit like a professional," the statement read.[9] "But when someone makes a big public show of a personal decision, it is nothing more than a self-promotional stunt." RT also portrayed Wahl's resignation as a "staged psy-op."[10] The choice of words speculated that Wahl had carried out a preplanned military psychological operation.

Even Margarita Simonyan, editor in chief of the international RT, got involved in the smear campaign, publicly portraying the channel as a victim of the traditional Western media. According to Simonyan, the "lynching and lambasting" that RT had received from the major news organizations in the wake of Wahl's resignation was "all typical of a media war," in which RT "stands alone (!) face-to-face with thousands and tens of thousands of Western news outlets."[11] Simonyan would later gain international fame herself when she provided RT as an open platform to the two Russian military intelligence agents suspected of poisoning Sergei Skripal and his daughter.[12]

Another attack came three days after Wahl's resignation. Paul Joseph Watson, a protégé of Alex Jones and a promoter of far right and pro-Kremlin ideologies, released a video to his vast YouTube audience titled "The Truth about RT Host Liz Wahl's Resignation."[13] In the video, Watson called Wahl's action a cynical stunt that reeked of hypocrisy, using the exact same arguments as RT. Many of his viewers sent Wahl hate messages.

ooooo

As part of its campaign against Wahl, RT also aired several television pieces which accused her of being a neocon. In one segment, it was speculated as to whether Wahl's resignation was a premeditated ambush organized by a "group of neocon think tanks." During the segment, a person dubbed by RT as a "media critic" stated that, "[t]he battle waged against RT is in fact a proxy battle for neocons, who are pushing a certain foreign policy agenda."[14] Wahl's former colleague Abby Martin used one of her shows to frame Wahl as a "neocon." Wahl shares that neocon is a propaganda buzzword that RT uses it to smear anyone who criticizes the Russian regime's policies: "Since it's so ridiculous, there's not much meaning behind it. It's just a slur they use. I'm not sure whether the trolls even know what it means. I never thought I was a neocon, and still don't think I am. But apparently, I was a neocon."

Wahl's tweets were also embedded in RT's online stories, attached to mocking and hateful comments. Some of the agitated feedback she received was anti-Semitic; she was called a "Jew puppet," as well as a CIA plant who served the Western power elite. For a while, Wahl tried to ignore the slurs on social media. But as RT intensified its fake news campaign and the messages turned more aggressive, she started to find the situation disturbing.

Wahl's Wikipedia page was also poisoned, as anonymous contributors quoted one of the network's stories. "It smeared my character, hinted I suffered from depression and that I wasn't mentally stable," she says. Wahl wrote to Wikipedia and told them that the article was untrue. The false information stayed up on the site for at least a month before it was corrected, which was way too long, considering how many people searched for information about Wahl during the spring of 2014 and found the Wikipedia piece. "The damage was already done," says Wahl. "In this kind of world, where information is so up-to-the-minute, people want to check the credibility of the source from Wikipedia."

FIGHTING THE GOOD FIGHT

By calling out the network that employed her live on air, Wahl did what she felt was right. She wanted to raise the issue of the conflict in Ukraine, and the Russian media's role in covering it. But then RT turned the spotlight on her in order to destroy her integrity as a journalist. And because she still wanted to do what was right, she was drawn into a conflict waged in cyberspace. "I think the campaign was effective. It called into question who I was as a person, and shifted the story away from Russian propaganda, how it works, and what the Kremlin is doing in Ukraine," Wahl says.

Sometimes, she regrets having spoken out: "It has ruined my life and taken a toll on my personal life. I'm not sure whether the fight was worth it."

Since Wahl resigned from RT, she has traveled the world, educating the general public as well as experts in Russian influence operations and cyber warfare. She is a highly respected contributor at conferences, and provides her insight to multiple initiatives that aim at countering the Kremlin's information aggression against the West.

On April 15, 2015, Wahl testified before the US Congress about Russia's weaponization of information. During a hearing before the House Committee on Foreign Affairs, Wahl described how RT was being mobilized as an online propaganda tool. "Why RT works is because it provides a place where people can feed off of each other's biases. It's like a community, almost like a cult, formed online. The people feel that they're part of an enlightened cult fighting the establishment," she testified. Wahl also urged congress to counteract the Kremlin's efforts to mislead the public: "The best weapon against this rapidly expanding propaganda campaign is the truth. We just need to fight for it."[15]

The same day Wahl testified, RT's In the Now posted a report that called the house committee hearing a "Russia bashers' get-together" and mocked the US government's plans to fund countermeasures against Russian propaganda. Like all other RT pieces, the video was also uploaded to YouTube, where it received well over 100,000 views. The comments section of the video was polluted with hundreds of insults against Wahl.

By September 2018, the video had been up for over three years. I reported it to YouTube. To date, I have not received a response from the company. One would assume that the US-based YouTube would be interested in the fact that a foreign government systematically uses its products and services for political harassment.

ooooo

Alex Jones then joined the attack against Wahl in a manner that looked like it could have been orchestrated by RT.

On his show, the Kremlin-loving, anti-American extremist

excerpted the video clip of Wahl's congressional testimony and spoke over it, commenting sarcastically on Wahl's speech and laughing at it maliciously. He also repeated RT's accusations that Wahl's resignation was "staged." Jones also claimed that Wahl was using "White House narratives" during her testimony, and described the hearing as a "sick meeting." Jones's colleague chimed in, saying that Wahl was a "government agent," an accusation perfectly aligned with the popular Russian propaganda line smearing Russia experts as CIA agents.

Jones also invented quotes from Wahl, claiming that she had characterized all "people who challenge the establishment" as a cult, which Wahl never said. Jones also started yelling while reading out loud quotes from Wahl's testimony, calling them "a total joke."

Jones did all this knowing that his viewers would never fact check his false statements about Wahl.

While Jones' *Infowars* YouTube channel has since been deleted, the video was up for years, and was copied to other channels, even though the video violated YouTube's own regulations and clearly accused Wahl—potentially illegally and at the risk of harming her career—of being a government agent. Google search results for "Liz Wahl" show that this smear continues to make the rounds across the internet.

∞∞∞∞∞

Liz Wahl periodically reminds herself of what she stands for, so that she won't get distracted by the smears. "If you become intimidated and the propagandists see that their operations work, they continue their efforts," she says. "But as long as the targets speak out and people keep calling it out, the harassment loses effectiveness. The same works with propaganda."

After leaving RT, Wahl went on to work for Newsy, a

Washington-based social media news outlet. There, she produced mini-documentaries about Russian hybrid warfare, influence operations, and online conspiracy theories. She often provides her insight on Russia issues as a commentator for CNN and other media outlets. In addition, she hosts international conferences and was a congressional candidate from Texas in 2020. It seems that the operation against her has backfired, as the perpetrators didn't succeed in harassing her into silence.

Wahl shares that exchanging supportive messages with people who appreciate her efforts has helped her overcome the pressure exerted on her by a foreign state: "It's encouraging to get inspirational messages from people in Ukraine and in the Baltic states who are very worried about Russian influence. The messages make you feel like you're fighting the good fight."

ooooo

In 2017, the U.S. Department of Justice demanded that RT register as a foreign agent. In the spring of 2018, the channel was taken off the air in the Washington, DC area.[16]

Despite these actions, RT still continues full force in the United States. Its shows are still broadcast, uploaded to YouTube and shared on Facebook, Twitter and LinkedIn.

17.

The Return

FOLLOWING THE ADVICE OF MY EMPLOYER, Yle, and encouraged by the Helsinki District Court's verdict against Johan Bäckman and Ilja Janitskin, I began to plan for my return to Finland in late 2018.

While living abroad, I had monitored the political atmosphere back in my home country, and was dismayed to see that Bäckman and Janitskin were now enjoying the public support of a major political party, the far-right, anti-refugee Finns Party. The party had criticized my trial verdict, comparing the monetary damages the court had awarded me to the amounts awarded in cases involving child sexual abusers.[1] "Seven years of child sexual exploitation. Damages 10,000 euros. Causing ill feelings to an Yle journalist. Damages 80,000 euros. Because the criminal damages are the price tag that the society places for the breached justice, it can be stated that our society's values are fucked," the then chairman of the Finns Party posted on Facebook. The party's 2018 presidential candidate shared a tweet saying that I would receive "35,000 euros based on the suffering caused by the violation" and asked: "When do we get a government that takes child molestation this seriously?"

In addition, a journalist from *Suomen Uutiset*, the taxpayer-funded magazine of the Finns Party, interviewed Janitskin in prison in the spring of 2018.[2] Janitskin shared that his biggest crime was that he "received too many readers," and that he was in jail "because MV-Lehti wrote NATO- and EU-critical articles." The story was published right before my trial, likely as an attempt to try to influence the proceedings. Many of the online comments on the interview asserted that Janitskin was innocent and should be released from prison. Other readers made racist comments about Muslim "child rapists" and "bad" migrants. The intensity of the comments revealed how MV-Lehti had managed to build a cult of personality around Janitskin, fueling hatred and prejudice in the process. This played directly into the Finns Party's desire to create support for its policies cracking down on refugees and immigration.

MY LOCATION REVEALED

In December 2018, I was invited to a conference in Finland, where I would appear with two Finnish Members of the European Parliament (MEP) to talk about threats to freedom of the press. The audience was to be made up mostly of high school kids.

Several online activists supporting Johan Bäckman and Ilja Janitskin planned to attend the seminar. Tiina Keskimäki, a PR person for MV-Lehti,[3] had already registered as a participant. Keskimäki can best be described as a social media influencer, whose specialty was writing complaints about the police and other officials who were investigating Janitskin's suspected crimes. Keskimäki had previously filed a groundless criminal complaint against me, as well as publishing over 100 posts in which she labeled me a criminal, a drug user, a liar, an employee of US special services, or something else similarly shady.

Fortunately, the organizer of the conference decided that individuals affiliated with MV-Lehti would not be allowed to attend. There was also strict security in place due to the presence of the MEPS. Ultimately, it turned out that the danger was not inside the conference, but outside.

On the morning of December 7, 2018, I headed toward Helsinki's Europe Hall, looking forward to an inspiring discussion. As I stepped into the street, Tiina Keskimäki walked toward me and glared. That afternoon, she posted on VKontakte that she had seen "Jessikka Aro in Ruoholahti," a neighborhood in Helsinki, revealing my physical location to her readers. This left me exposed to preplanned threats as well as impulsive harassment.

I reported this new potential threat to the police. Effectively, I was now in the same situation as before my escape from Finland.

COMMON FACTORS

By January 2019, I was back living in Finland, and working again at Yle. I familiarized myself with my new duties and colleagues.

Despite this new beginning, the character assassinations against me continued as if my trial and the subsequent convictions had never happened. By the end of the month, at least thirteen new filth pieces had been published about me on MV-Lehti since the trial. The total number of MV-Lehti stories against me had now reached 230.[4] The new stories mainly repeated the same old themes: that I was a liar, delusional, drug-dependent, against freedom of speech, a stalker, and an information soldier recruited by foreign security services. The readers of the stories and the fake profiles discussed topics including whether I needed money for speed; that I had snorted my book's crowdfunding finances "up my nose"; that my book project was fake; that I had "offered [my] ass" in the hopes of receiving dope; and that I carried the intravenous drug users' disease, hepatitis C. One reader discussed "fucking [me]" and mused about the possibility of selling me into prostitution. Another profile thought that I should be hit in the back of the head with a baseball bat so hard that my head would come off. Based on click counters, the new stories received over 250,000 views.

It seemed to me that many of the comments on the MV-Lehti stories were libelous and thus illegal under Finnish law. But in the

MV-Lehti universe, where reality was turned upside down, *I* was the criminal.

ooooo

As 2018 turned into 2019, Ilja Janitskin once again claimed to be running MV-Lehti. In a video interview published on the site, he also declared his intention to run for the Finnish Parliament.[5] Janitskin was joined in his electoral aspirations by several other MV-Lehti activists, including far-right supporters and several convicted criminals.

In addition to their candidacies for the Finnish Parliament and their criminal backgrounds, these individuals had another common bond: Johan Bäckman. Some had posed in photos and videos with him, while others had their candidacies promoted by Bäckman. One had traveled with him to Russian-occupied territory in Eastern Ukraine.

Yet another common thread connected all these people.

Me.

One of the activists had produced degrading "speed whore" videos about me, while two others had physically followed me to a presentation at the University of Oulu in order to stream my presentation directly to MV-Lehti. Another had published numerous stories denouncing me as a NATO troll and worse on his YouTube channels and his website. One activist had, before my trial, threatened to assault me on the stairs of the Helsinki District Court; as a result of this threat, she ended up in a police hearing.

THE AWARD

In early 2019, I received a message from the United States embassy in Helsinki, asking whether I would accept the International Women of Courage Award, granted by the US Department of State. The award is given annually to ten women "from around the globe who have demonstrated exceptional courage and leadership in advocating for peace, justice, human rights, gender equality, and women's empowerment, often at great personal risk and sacrifice."[6] The work I had done since 2014 on Russian trolls—the articles I had written, my social media activism, this book, and the court cases I had initiated—had merited my receiving the award.

I enthusiastically answered, "Yes!"

I was sent an official invitation, signed by then US Secretary of State Mike Pompeo. At the ceremony in Washington, DC, Pompeo would give a speech, and First Lady Melania Trump would present me and the nine other women with our awards.

I was sent a personal schedule for the two-week trip to the United States. While there, I would give lectures and meet journalism organizations and students. I was especially excited to meet the other award-winning women. I also valued the opportunity to introduce my troll investigations to an American audience, especially at a time when the country was still waiting to learn the results of the Mueller investigation.

∞∞∞

In February, a cartoonish picture depicting me as a drug addict injecting myself with a needle began to make the rounds on social media.

While my online friends encouraged me to ignore the photo and continue my work, a stranger named "Angus Gallagher" wrote on my Facebook wall that "this girl is not a journalist but a NATO troll, who is paid to run a disinformation campaign against Finland. Integrity Initiative is the master that pulls the strings of this puppet." "Angus" claimed that I was actively engaged in undermining Finnish democracy.

When I refuted Gallagher's claims online, he went on an even more convoluted rampage, writing on my Facebook wall that the Atlantic Council paid me "through the Helsinki cluster." My actions, Gallagher wrote, were part of a state-sponsored disinformation campaign. And, he added, the Finnish people should thank him (Gallagher) for this information.

A friend later discovered that Gallagher was an author for the English-language version of Sputnik. In 2016 and 2017, he had written at least thirty-eight pieces for the site. In his writings, he asserted that only Russia would survive a zombie apocalypse, mocked people who drew attention to the Kremlin's disinformation campaigns, and warned about "Europe's women branded whores and liars" as well as EU and NATO "cyber trolls."[7]

In 2017, the BBC had interviewed Sputnik's UK editor, who said that Gallagher was a volunteer who published pieces on the site that purportedly "reflect[ed] the views of a good chunk of the audience."[8] Also interviewed was a university professor, who considered Gallagher's content "paranoid," typical of Sputnik's commentators.

ooooo

A month before the cartoon picture of me appeared online, Facebook announced that it had removed "coordinated inauthentic behavior," as it refers to trolls and their content on its platform.[9] A total of 364 pages and profiles active in the Baltic countries, Central Asia, the Caucasus, and Western and Eastern Europe were removed, all of which had been operating out of Russia.

The seemingly independent Facebook sites and profiles had provided content about weather, travel, sports, business, and politics. A portion disseminated anti-NATO views, promoted local protest movements, and addressed corruption. The fake sites and accounts had managed to gain a large following: over 790,000 users followed at least one of the sites. The sites also bought advertising, spending a total of $135,000. The first ad had been bought back in 2013. In addition, they had tried to organize over 200 events in the real world.

According to Facebook's cybersecurity manager, the deleted accounts and sites were all connected to Sputnik employees in Moscow.[10]

Facebook also removed another 107 Russian-run Facebook sites, accounts, and groups, as well as 41 Instagram accounts that had posed as Ukrainian and spread content about "health conditions in schools." Facebook stated that the activity resembled what it had uncovered before the US midterm elections in 2018.

CHANNELING RUSSIA'S INFOWAR

MV-Lehti has published numerous stories in Finnish that have been sourced from RT.com. They also livestream RT's international, often English-language videos on topical news events. The site is especially eager in its use of clips from the video service Ruptly, which is part of the RT media group.[11]

Ruptly is based in Berlin, in an attempt to hide its Russian origins. The German news portal T-Online investigated the "video agency" and discovered that Ruptly's subsidiary companies, Redfish and Maffick, spread viral disinformation without disclosing their ties to the Russian government.[12]

The RT and Ruptly content on MV-Lehti deals with topics which favor the point of view of the Kremlin. Europe, for example is portrayed as unstable, rocked by ongoing waves of civic unrest. Among the supposed causes of European instability are corrupt leaders and asylum seekers. During Ilja Janitskin's reign, asylum seekers were frequently presented as enemies of the Finnish way of life. In 2018, researchers at Tampere University counted "anti-immigrant views" in half of MV-Lehti's stories.[13] According to the researchers, the contributors to the site had "strong hopes" that their actions would influence Finnish societal debates and public policy. However, the authors didn't feel that they were spreading

Russian propaganda, but rather were challenging "the biased journalism which was perceived as pro-Western and pro-NATO." After Janitskin passed away in early 2020 and Janus Putkonen started to run the site while residing in Russian-occupied Eastern Ukraine, the majority of the racist material was replaced with conspiracy theories about the coronavirus as well as agitating for vaccine-hesitancy—the latest hot topics in the Russian state media.[14]

RT isn't the only Russian state-sponsored outlet whose content is cross-posted on MV-Lehti. In April 2015, Sputnik started publishing online propaganda articles in Finnish. However, almost no Finn read them, so it stopped after less than a year. But on MV-Lehti, Sputnik found new life. Like RT and Ruptly, MV-Lehti's translated Sputnik stories frequently fueled reader's emotions using anti-immigrant rhetoric by claiming, for example, that "white Swedish men aren't wanted as police officers due to immigrant quotas." Other stories described the "threats Russia faces on its borders" and talked about "small children raped by ISIS." MV-Lehti has published hundreds of pieces sourced from either RT, Sputnik, or Ruptly.

While MV-Lehti has long overstated the threat of jihadist terrorism and smears all asylum seekers as Islamic extremists, rapists, illegal immigrants, and violent criminals, it portrays Vladimir Putin as a strong leader and problem solver who takes care of the terrorists. MV-Lehti also frequently praises certain other public figures such as Nigel Farage, Alex Jones, French far-right and Russia-indebted politician Marine Le Pen, and Hungarian prime minister Viktor Orbán. When he was president, Donald Trump was king of the site, which mocked the "libtards" after he won.

"DOES ANYONE STILL READ IT?"
Throughout the spring of 2019, I met Finns who had read about

the hate campaign against me. Many were genuinely surprised when I told them that MV-Lehti was still fully operational. Some of them laughed and asked, "Does anyone still read it?"

To answer the question about who was reading MV-Lehti, I decided to investigate the site using the metrics service Alexa and other analytics tools. Alexa measures site traffic and gathers user information, and while its results are not 100 percent accurate, by providing meta information, it would give me a basic idea of the makeup of the MV-Lehti audience.

I discovered that the site that linked the most to MV-Lehti—beyond MV-Lehti itself—was *Suomen Uutiset*, the online magazine of the Finns Party. The analytics further revealed that Finns Party supporters were a major segment of MV-Lehti readers. I had previously noted that the trolls spread MV-Lehti links in a forum used by Finns Party supporters. In one thread, which was over sixteen pages long, the anonymous commenters shared the notion that I was a convicted criminal. (Interestingly, many of the users on the Finns Party forum deny the existence of Russian trolls.)

In response to those question whether MV-Lehti had any readers, I cited the 2018 *Digital News Report* from the Reuters Institute at the University of Oxford, which stated that 4 percent of Finns had read MV-Lehti the previous week.[15] In addition, Alexa's list of the most popular search terms that brought traffic to MV-Lehti included my name.

SHITSTORM

Eight days before I was supposed to travel to the United States to receive the International Women of Courage Award, the US embassy in Helsinki informed me that the award would not be given to me, and that I would not be traveling to the United States.

After all the careful preparations and paperwork, I didn't

understand the sudden cancellation, which I did not receive in writing. I had already postponed my previously scheduled speaking engagements and training events to be able to travel to the United States.

My lawyer and I submitted a formal request for information to the US Secretary of State, asking *who* specifically had canceled my award, and *why*.

At the awards ceremony on March 7, 2019, Secretary of State Mike Pompeo thanked the ten ladies who were present for their efforts. Someone else had been selected to fill my spot on short notice.

Simultaneously, *Foreign Policy* published an online story about my troll work and the crimes I had experienced.[16] The article included a scoop: American diplomatic sources said that my award had been rescinded because of a tweet in which I had criticized President Trump. The magazine reported that the diplomats hadn't appreciated the cancellation and that internally the decision had created a "shitstorm."

In the article, a State Department spokesperson referred to me as a "candidate," inferring that I had never been approved as a recipient of the award in the first place. He also said that it had been "a regrettable error" and blamed "a lack of coordination in communications with candidates and our embassies."[17]

The story caused a small-scale scandal in the US. The ranking member of the Senate Foreign Relations Committee in charge of overseeing the State Department, Robert Menendez, tweeted out the *Foreign Policy* story and wrote: "The United States presents this award to women who, like Jessikka, stand up to dictators and risk their lives for fundamental freedoms including of the press. We should treat journalists better than Russia does."[18]

Many international media outlets covered the story as well, and I was asked to give live interviews on American television. But I didn't consider it appropriate to do interviews, as I didn't want to become involved in American internal political tensions concerning the Trump administration and speculate about the matter in the US media.

∞∞∞

On March 8, 2019, I watched on Yle's morning news show as Robert Palladino, the spokesperson for the State Department, stated during a press conference that I had never actually been given the award. "We incorrectly notified this individual that she'd been selected as a finalist. This was an error. This was a mistake," he said.

The assembled reporters grilled Palladino, but he repeated his story. Inspired by his statements, the trolls and far-right activists laughed at me on social media. One of the people who had been convicted of defamation against me wrote an article on MV-Lehti, calling me a NATO mannequin who was left without a human rights award after bashing Trump.[19] She also said that I had wept during my trial. Another MV-Lehti story accused me of having invented the Russian trolls, and once again, brought up my drug fine from 2004.

Russian-held Eastern Ukraine woke up, too. Janus Putkonen mocked the rescinding of the award and called me a professional liar and an information soldier serving the Western agenda. He further posted on Facebook that I had been hurt by my "masters."

The next in line to attack me over the award was the troll factory in St. Petersburg. The factory's fake news site, RIA Fan, published a piece that said I had "made a name for myself" with "high-profile investigations," which it claimed had been described as tendentious and selective interpretations of the facts, and a flagrant use of Western propaganda clichés, all for personal gain.[20] They went on to say that I had declared Russia as my number one enemy, long before the US establishment launched the witch hunt against alleged Russian interference in the 2016 presidential election. The author of the article quoted Robert Palladino, and also invented a quote I had never said, according to which I had accused top US diplomats of political censorship.

Alexander Malkevich, a Russian citizen who works on many projects for the Kremlin, was interviewed for the article. Malkevich used to be editor in chief of USA Really, another fake news site of the Russian troll factory.[21] USA Really[22] is targeted at Americans, and its content resembles that of an English-language MV-Lehti, with fearmongering about "rapist illegal immigrants." Malkevich was arrested when entering the US and interrogated by the FBI because he had not registered himself properly as a foreign agent.[23] In April 2021, he was sanctioned as part of the US Treasury Department's actions against entities and individuals who had attempted to influence the 2020 presidential election at the direction of the Russian government.[24]

In the article, Malkevich stated that I deserved some sort of consolation prize for not receiving the award from the State Department. He later sent me a private message, saying that he wanted to meet in person, where he would hand me an award for my loyalty as a defender of freedom of speech, on behalf of all the professional journalists in Russia.

I declined his "invitation."

The award cancellation was covered in many other Russian media outlets. It was a hot topic because it offered the opportunity to smear me and the United States at the same time.

∞∞∞

On the same day that Palladino made his remarks, the chairman of the House Foreign Affairs Committee published a statement, setting the record straight. Democratic congressman Eliot L. Engel wrote on the committee's website that he found the withdrawal of the award "shameful," and that he was troubled by the information that it was a result of my criticism of President Trump. "One of the hallmarks of America is our First Amendment right to freedom of speech, and it's one of the core democratic principles the State Department promotes abroad. That the Department would rescind Aro's award for the exercise of this right is truly shameful," Engel stated.[25]

Yes, I had written about Trump on Twitter and responded to some of his tweets, in which he had mocked the "rigged and corrupt media" as "THE ENEMY OF THE PEOPLE!" to his tens of millions of followers. I had also tweeted out critical news reports, which listed all of Trump's attacks against the Mueller investigation. But no one knew for certain if this was the actual reason my award had been rescinded, and my lawyer's request for information was never answered by anyone in the Trump administration.

ooooo

Later, I watched on YouTube as Melania Trump handed out glass statuettes during a distinguished ceremony to women from around the world who had promoted and fought for human rights.[26]

I celebrated those women, annoyed that I wasn't there to exchange ideas with them.

NEW WTF

I was surprised to say the least when I found out that my situation with the Women of Courage Award was responsible for the launching of an investigation by Senator Robert Menendez. Menendez's investigation focused on the public statements of the State Department's spokesperson, Robert Palladino. The Democratic staff of the Senate Foreign Relations Committee had obtained the relevant documents and compared them to the communications by the State Department. They came to the same conclusion as I had: yes, I had really received the award, and no, Palladino's statements to the contrary were not true.

The evidence showed that I had been asked for my social media account information, which I had sent to Washington. As event organizers frequently attach speakers' social media handles to their programs and websites, I assumed no nefarious intent in this request. But in this case, the request was considered "particularly troubling," especially given "President Trump's frequent, well-documented, and corrosive attacks on the media."[27]

In March 2019, Menendez released a forty-page report detailing his findings, which was accompanied by a letter, which he sent to the inspector general of the State Department. Menendez asked the IG to further investigate why my award had been rescinded. The letter was signed by seven other senators in addition to Menendez. In September 2020, the IG released the results of his investigation, which confirmed that my award had been rescinded because of my tweets criticizing President Trump. According to a press release from the office of Senator Menendez, "The Inspector General confirmed that State Department officials decided that Ms. Aro, a renowned campaigner against Kremlin propaganda, was 'not suitable' for the award after they discovered she had criticized President Trump for labeling journalists as 'enemies of the people.'"[28]

CONSOLATION PRIZE

I was working at a conference in Switzerland in early 2019 when I started to receive bizarre messages on Twitter at around 11:00 PM. I quickly discovered that a former Finns Party candidate had shared a screenshot of an MV-Lehti story. "Now the foil hatting and guessing about Jessikka Aro's hustles has come to an end," the story yelled. It went on to claim that I belonged to a Western troll factory. That story, and another posted soon after, had over 40,000 readers.[29, 30]

As with the case of Swedish researcher Martin Kragh, material for the stories claimed to have been hacked from the British think tank, Institute for Statecraft, allegedly by the hacker group Anonymous. In Britain, the hack was investigated by the National Crime Agency, and was reportedly the first hack-and-leak operation targeted against the UK.[31]

The Institute for Statecraft suspected that the hack was conducted by Russian military intelligence. Kragh had revealed how the hacked documents had first been circulated on RT and Sputnik. From there, they slowly streamed to local, multilingual fake news sites. In Finland, these sites included MV-Lehti. On social media, the stories were spread by Janus Putkonen, Ilja Janitskin and his network, and the Finns Party, among others. As MV-Lehti shared the stories on VKontakte, their readers hoped I would end up in jail and called me a "speed whore" and an "old cunt with a loose pussy," among other obscene insults. The trolls then attempted to break the trust between me and my employer by emailing the stories to my supervisors at Yle.

When two Finnish journalists separately asked me to comment about the claims against me, I again remembered why anonymous troll publications exist: so that their theories can enjoy the wider dissemination of the traditional media.

"CRIMINAL COUP ATTEMPT"

In April 2019, I was speaking about trolls, fake news, and harassment against journalists in Washington, DC, at a conference organized by Reporters Without Borders (RSF) and the *Washington Post*.[32] RSF had just published its annual Press Freedom Index. In the index measuring press freedom throughout the world, Finland had risen to number two. One factor in the country's enviable new position were the convictions that had been handed down in my trial. The United States had dropped, owing to President Trump's hostile remarks about the media, to 48th place. Russia was 149.

During the conference, Special Counsel Mueller's final report was published.[33] I noted, with pleasure, that a full twenty pages were dedicated to the troll factory's operations against the 2016 US presidential election. According to the report, the factory had targeted—well before the election—operations at the so-called purple states, with the goal of turning undecided voters into Trump supporters. Trump was the Kremlin's favored candidate, whom Putin himself had described as "unquestionably talented."[34]

First, Russian spies had mapped out the opinion climate among voters—without having registered as foreign agents. Then, fake profiles posing as US citizens founded fake news pages and lured real American citizens to them. In these virtual communities, directed from St. Petersburg, trolls shared memes and materials that aimed at dehumanizing the Democratic candidate, Hillary Clinton, as well as Muslims and Mexicans. People were agitated into hating foreigners, just as they had been on Finnish social media and MV-Lehti.

The Mueller Report further described the interference of Russian military intelligence hackers and WikiLeaks in helping Trump and working against the Democratic Party and Clinton.

Johan Bäckman—who had represented the Russian Institute for Strategic Studies in Moscow (which in 2017 had been exposed as having designed the trolling and cyber operation aimed at pushing Trump as president)—was instantly on social media mocking the Mueller investigation and claiming it was a "criminal coup attempt."[35]

ANOTHER VISIT TO SILICON VALLEY

I continued my travels throughout the world in 2019, educating audiences about Russian online trolls. Along with two other European journalists, I appeared before the British Parliament's

Foreign Affairs Committee to talk about the urgent threats to freedom of the press as part of Parliament's project to initiate new legislation and measures to counter those threats.[36]

In May, the citizen organization Avaaz invited me, along with three other victims of social media bullying, to Silicon Valley to take part in a remarkable campaign. Together, we visited the headquarters of Facebook, Twitter, and Google/YouTube and told the companies' executives how their services were being systematically exploited. I personally handed the company representatives user reports about hate speech and crimes committed against me which had not been responded to appropriately. I demanded that they take action to counter the ongoing crimes and propaganda targeted at private citizens, listing several people who had faced systematic harassment on their platforms—many of whom were discussed in this book.

The other individuals who met the social media companies with me were Tun Khin, a member of the Burmese Rohingya minority, and American citizens Ethan Lindenberger and Lenny Pozner. Tun Khin recounted how social media had been abused to wage genocide against the Rohingya, while Lindenberger described how it was used to fuel anti-vaccination campaigns.

Lenny Pozner had been forced to move multiple times as a result of social media harassment. His son Noah was murdered in the Sandy Hook school shooting in 2012, but the social media trolls claimed that Noah didn't exist and that Pozner himself was a "crisis actor." (These theories have also been spread by Alex Jones.) Because of the threats, Pozner had to participate in the meetings by phone.

I had hoped that our visit would spark the social media companies to take concrete measures. While Twitter did remove the account of a Burmese genocide-waging general, and some anti-vaccination accounts were also taken down, on social media, Kremlin stooges and hate writers still violate real citizens' rights with impunity to this day.

WET WORK

During the summer of 2019, my identity was stolen at least three times. First, my name was used by someone ordering "penis enlargement pills" from a foreign online shop. The Finnish Post actually shipped the pills to me, even though they had been ordered to the wrong address.

On another occasion, I received a phone call from child protection services in another part of Finland, asking for additional information about the report I had filed. I couldn't provide any additional information because I hadn't filed a report.

The third identity theft was pure Russian psychological violence. A British organization, which according to MV-Lehti had paid me a salary for waging information warfare, was sent postcards signed with my name from Helsinki. In the text written on the cards, I was described as "the best independent defense contractor money can buy." Additionally, a former Finnish secretary of state was said to be my "former fuck buddy," and I was also said to "fantasize about wet work Langley style." "Wet work" is Russian mafia and intelligence services slang, referring to assassination. The cards also directly referred to my workplace, Yle.

I showed the cards to Russia experts. They agreed with me that the handwriting revealed that the writer was a Russian native. The police never found the sender.

∞∞∞

In July 2019, while working on this book, I received a message from the US House of Representatives. The House Foreign Affairs Committee's Subcommittee on Europe, Energy, The Environment and Cyber wanted me to appear as a witness in a public hearing about the Kremlin's disinformation attacks in Europe. The subcommittee wanted to specifically hear recommendations on what the United States could do to defend against Russian information warfare.

I submitted my written testimony and on July 16 gave oral testimony along with three other experts.[37] The hearing was streamed live on YouTube. I shared the results of my troll investigations and stressed that no one had the whole picture of the Kremlin's operations against Western citizens, or their impact. I suggested several measures, including international cooperation among Western police organizations and intelligence services, and a commitment to investigate and reveal the troll operations to the general public while they were happening—instead of years later, when they had already impacted citizens' minds and behavior. "Maybe it's time that we start addressing the Kremlin's troll farms and digital disinformation as what they really are: crime factories and digital crimes," I said. "These criminals don't want your money; they want to control your thoughts."

I told the committee that the Kremlin was also interfering in the United States between elections, and that when people are fed disinformation, it's difficult for them to make choices about who they should vote for or what kind of policies they should support. Kathleen Hall Jamieson found out in her research that the Russian troll and cyberattacks had had a significant impact on the results of the 2016 presidential election.[38] According to Jamieson, by building polarization and spreading targeted messages, the cyber campaign influenced as many as 80,000 votes in three different states, which was just enough to swing the election to Trump.

At the end of the hearing, Congressman Jim Costa replied to my suggestion about conducting research into influence operations by saying that maybe legislative changes could be used to address that.

The following week, Special Counsel Robert Mueller testified before Congress. He warned about the same phenomenon that I had: "It wasn't a single attempt," Mueller said of Russia's election interference. "They're doing it as we sit here."[39]

After my testimony, I received a lot of supportive feedback from within Finland as well as abroad. At the same time, a pro-Kremlin YouTuber posted a four-hour video in which he denounced me, as well as the members of Congress, and other experts. Commenters on the video claimed that I had been under the influence of "speed" while testifying.

Despite the ongoing information war against me, I was proud that my investigations into Russian trolls, done in cooperation with many Finnish citizens, had made its way all the way to the US Congress.

∞∞∞

At the time of the writing of this book, I still didn't have a child, which I had dreamed of when the crimes against me started back in 2014. But I am honored to have gotten to know the individuals presented in this book, and to have been able to tell their inspiring stories. Many of them sacrificed themselves on behalf of human rights and freedom. They have become like family to me.

Notes

1.Escape

1. VTA.,"Jessikka Aron Trollijahti," YouTube video, 4:10, February 26, 2016, https://www.youtube.com/watch?v=igOa1EXKzTI.

2. Harris, Lasana T., and Susan T. Fiske, "Dehumanizing the Lowest of the Low: Neuroimaging Responses to Extreme Out-Groups," *Psychological Science* 17, no. 10 (October 2006): 847–53, https://doi.org/10.1111/j.1467-9280.2006.01793.x.

3. Aro, Jessikka, "Putinin Entinen Neuvonantaja Yle Uutisille: Venäjä Informaatiosotii Suomessa—'Haluaa Näyttää, Kuka on Pomo.," *Yle Uutiset,* September 19, 2014, https://yle.fi/uutiset/3-7480089.

4. Гармажапова, Александра, "Где Живут Тролли. И Кто Их Кормит," *Novaja Gazeta,* September 9, 2013, https://www.novayagazeta.ru/articles/2013/09/07/56253-gde-zhivuttrolli-i-kto-ih-kormit?print=true.

5. Seddon, Max, "Documents Show How Russia's Troll Army Hit America," *BuzzFeed News,* June 2, 2014, https://www.buzzfeednews.com/article/maxseddon/documents-show-how-russias-troll-army-hit-america.

6. Aro, Jessikka, "Kyberturva-Asiantuntija Limnéll: 'Suomi on Hybridisodankäynnin Kohteena—Tätä EI Pidä Hyssytellä,'" *Yle Uutiset,* September 18, 2014, https://yle.fi/uutiset/3-7371020.

7. Bäckman, Johan, Johan Bäckmanin blogi, n.d., https://kohudosentti.blogspot.com.

8. Bäckman, Johan. "Johan Bäckman Official," YouTube video, November 22, 2008, https://www.youtube.com/channel/UCqMol3k-DIlbbUBV94We5rQ.

9. Stormark, Kjetil, *The Spokesman—a Documentary from Aldrimer. no.* YouTube video, 34:00, April 17, 2016, https://www.youtube.com/watch?v=vEbPZxlk8o8&ab_channel=KjetilStormark.

10. "Information Warfare," *LevadaCenter,* January 25, 2016, https://www.levada.ru/en/2014/11/12/information-warfare/.

11. Laakso, Antti, "Kohudosentti Ja Demaripoliitikko Edustavat Itä-Ukrainan Kapinallisia Suomessa," *Yle Uutiset,* July 25, 2014, https://yle.fi/uutiset/3-7376165.

12. Juujärvi, Tiina, "Pieksämäeltä Sotilaaksi Itä-Ukrainaan—Petri Viljakainen ODOTTAA Rintamalle Pääsyä Donetskin Liepeillä," *Helsingin Sanomat*, July 31, 2015, https://www.hs.fi/ulkomaat/art-2000002842087.html.

13. "Бекман Эркки Йохан," Myrotvorets.center, July 15, 2015, https://psb4ukr.org/criminal/bekman-erkki-jokhan/.

14. Sajari, Petri, Anssi Miettinen, Esa Mäkinen, Suvi Vihavainen, Jussi Konttinen, and Laura Saarikoski, "Bäckman on Tehtaillut Yli 90 Valitusta Ja Rikosilmoitusta," *Helsingin Sanomat*, February 12, 2012, https://www.hs.fi/sunnuntai/art-2000002596812.html.

15. Private Interview, personal, n.d.

2. The Diplomat

1. "Republic of Belarus - Presidential Election," *OSCE*, March 19, 2006, https://www.osce.org/files/f/documents/4/c/19395.pdf.

2. "В Парламенте Грузии Предлагают Провести Экспертизу Аудиозаписи, Представленной в Программе 'Однако,'" *naviny.by*, June 15, 2016, https://naviny.online/en/node/81086.

3. БАРТАШЯВИЧЮС, Валдас, "Вильнюсские Дипломаты Попали в Западню Москвы," *ИноСМИ.Ru*, November 16, 2015, https://inosmi.ru/world/20060424/226990.html.

4. "Суда Не Будет, Однако," gazeta.ru, April 25, 2006, https://www.gazeta.ru/2006/04/25/oa_197425.shtml.

5. https://www.belaruspartisan.org/politic/102283/ RL note: This page does not exist

6. "Putin: Soviet Collapse a 'Genuine Tragedy'," NBCNews.com. NBCUniversal News Group, April 25, 2005, https://www.nbcnews.com/id/wbna7632057.

7. Lepomäki Elina, *Vapauden Voitto*, Helsingissä: Kustannusosakeyhtiö Otava, 2018.

8. Tracevskis, Rokas M, "Secret Agent's Death Is under Re-Investigation," *The Free Library*, January 13, 2010, https://www.thefreelibrary.com/Secret+Agent%27s+death+is+under+re-investigation.-a0217184755.

9. "Jukka Mallinen Valta Puhuu Rahan Äänellä," netn.fi, n.d., https://netn.fi/sites/www.netn.fi/files/netn102-18.pdf.

10. "President Presented Letters of Credence to Lithuania's Ambassador to Hungary," President of the Republic of Lithuania, n.d., http://www.adamkus.lt/en/activities/press_releases/president_presented_letters_of_credence_to_lithuanias_ambassador_to_hungary.html.

11. "Two Lithuanian Ambassadors Removed from Office after Phone Tapping Scandal," *Baltic News Network—News from Latvia, Lithuania, Estonia*, August 29, 2013, https://bnn-news.com/lithuanian-ambassadors-removed-office-phone-tapping-scandal-102193.

12. Мокрушин, Валерий, "Скандал Вокруг 'Восточного Партнерства': Опубликованы Переговоры Дипломатов Об Армянах," www.nakanune.ru, August 5, 2013, https://www.nakanune.ru/articles/17989/.

13. "Скандал Вокруг 'Восточного Партнерства': Опубликованы Переговоры Дипломатов Об Армянах," *LiveJournal*, August 5, 2013, https://iolantaz.livejournal.com/420974.html.

14. Landry, David, "YouTube-Gate? Ambassador Scandal Repercussions in Lithuania," *Budapest Business Journal*, August 20, 2013, https://bbj.hu/budapest/culture/history/youtube-gate-ambassador-scandal-repercussions-in-lithuania.

15. ibid.

16. "L. Linkevičius Siūlymą Dėl Ambasadorių Pateiks Penktadienį," *Kauno diena*, August 21, 2013, https://kauno.diena.lt/naujienos/lietuva/politika/llinkevicius-siulyma-del-ambasadoriu-pateiks-penktadieni-410233.

17. "Dalia Grybauskaitė Considers Provocation Publication of Lithuanian Diplomat's Conversation about Nagorno-Karabakh," *armenpress.am*, August 5, 2013, https://armenpress.am/eng/news/728302/dalia-grybauskaitC497-considers-provocation-publication-of-lithuanian-diplomatE28099s-conversationabout.html.

18. "Lithuanian Foreign Minister Decides to Recall Ambassadors from Hungary and Azerbaijan but Keep Them in Diplomatic Corps," *15min*, August 23, 2013, https://www.15min.lt/en/article/politics/lithuanian-foreign-minister-decides-to-recall-ambassadors-from-hungary-and-azerbaijan-but-keep-them-in-diplomatic-corps-526-363404.

19. "Lietuvos Ambasadorius Azerbaidžane Prašo Atšaukti Jį Iš Pareigų," *DELFI*, August 6, 2013, https://www.delfi.lt/news/daily/lithuania/lietuvos-ambasadorius-azerbaidzane-praso-atsaukti-ji-is-pareigu.d?id=61995743.

20. "Felavatták Hedvig És Jagelló Szobrát Budapesten," *BDK*, October 31, 2013, https://bdk.hu/2013/10/hedvig-es-jagello-szobrot-avattak-budapesten-4/.

21. "National Security Threat Assessment," *MEPOFORUM.SK*, 2013, http://mepoforum.sk/wp-content/uploads/2017/04/Threat-Assessment-Lithuania-2013.pdf.

22. "Mirė Lietuvos Diplomatas Renatas Juška," *15min*, September 4, 2019, https://www-15min-lt.translate.goog/naujiena/aktualu/lietuva/mire-lietuvos-diplomatas-renatas-juska-56-1197614?_x_tr_sl=lt&_x_tr_tl=en&_x_tr_hl=en-US&_x_tr_pto=nui%2Cop%2Csc.

3. Psyops

1. Topelius, Karoliina, Facebook, n.d., https://www.facebook.com/notes/karoliina-topelius/ylen-toiminta-perustuslain-henkil%C3%B6tietolain-ja-rikoslain-suhteen-ven%C3%A4j%C3%A4%C3%A4n-liitty/1015272973523049?fref=nf&refid=12.

2. "Infosoturi Janus Vaihtoi Kiväärin Kirjaimiin," *Loviisan Sanomat*, February 24, 2015.

3. Toivonen, Janne, "Suomalainen 'Infosoturi' Janus Putkonen Nousi Ukrainan Kapinallismedian Johtohahmoksi," *Yle Uutiset*, November 1, 2015, https://yle.fi/uutiset/3-8416989.

4. DONi News Agency (@Dninews), Twitter, https://twitter.com/dninews?lang=enhttp%3A%2F%2Fkhpg.org%2Fen%2F1508187981.

5. MarkoSE, "Janus Putkonen Ja Doni News—Disinformaatiota JA Harhaanjohtamista," *Vartiopaikalla Blogspot*, October 16, 2016, https://vartiopaikalla.blogspot.com/2017/10/janus-putkonen-ja-doni-news.html.

6. "EgorovaLeaks: Filtering and Control of Foreign Journalists in DPR," *Inform Napalm*, August 9, 2016, https://informnapalm.org/en/foreign-journalists-in-dpr/.

7. Verkkomedia JanusPutkonen, *"Suomalaissotilaan Haastattelu Donbassin Etulinjan Tukikohdassa - DONi News,"* YouTube video, 11:46, March 31, 2016, https://www.youtube.com/watch?v=Y2Apsq5GUys.

8. Losh, Jack, "Inside Rebel-Held Ukraine's Palaces of Propaganda," *VICE*, March 28, 2016, https://www.vice.com/en/article/neyqa8/inside-rebel-held-ukraines-palaces-of-propaganda.

9. Leinonen, Nina, "Massiivinen Tietovuoto Donetskissa - Todistaa Yhteydet Venäjään," *Iltalehti*, August 7, 2016, https://www.iltalehti.fi/ulkomaat/a/2016080722024403.

10. Aro, Jessikka, and Antti Kuronen, "Itä-Ukrainassa Venäjän Puolesta Taistelleet Suomalaiset Kehuskelevat Kokemuksillaan—Muualla Euroopassa Vierastaistelijoita on Tuomittu Rikoksista," *Yle Uutiset*, November 26, 2021, https://yle.fi/uutiset/3-12153718.

11. Johan Bächman Official, "Zaharchenko Lahjoittaa Janus Putkoselle Ladatun Makarov-Pistoolin," YouTube video, September 2, 2016, https://www.youtube.com/watch?v=y5t6W7cfGHE&ab_channel=JohanB%C3%A4ckmanOfficial.

12. "Venäjän Trolliarmeija," Facebook, https://www.facebook.com/groups/389891377829035.

4. The Volunteer

1. "Informnapalm International Intelligence Community," *InformNapalm.org*, April 4, 2017, https://informnapalm.org/en/.

2. "Conflict in Ukraine's Donbas: A Visual Explainer," *Crisis Group*, September 21, 2021, https://www.crisisgroup.org/content/conflict-ukraines-donbas-visual-explainer.

3. USA for UNHCR: The UN Refugee Agency, "Ukraine Refugee Crisis: Aid, Statistics and News," *UNRefugees.org*, https://www.unrefugees.org/emergencies/ukraine/#:~:text=More%20than%20three%20years%20of,sought%20asylum%20in%20neighboring%20countries.

4. "Donbas In Flames," *Prometheus*, 2017, https://prometheus.ngo/wp-content/uploads/2017/04/Donbas_v_Ogni_ENG_web_1-4.pdf.

5. Weaponry of the Russian Federation in the War against Ukraine, *InformNapalm* 2018.

6. Osipova, Natalia V., "How the Buk Missile System Works," *New York Times*, July 21, 2014, https://www.nytimes.com/video/world/europe/100000003010629/how-the-buk-missile-system-works.html?searchResultPosition=1.

7. "Buk-M2E Air Defence Missile System," *Army Technology*, November 17, 2021, https://www.army-technology.com/projects/buk-m2e-air-defence-missile-system/.

8. Kharkova , Marina, trans., "A Nest of Electronic Warfare Forces of Russian Federation in Luhansk Tax Administration Office Building," *InformNapalm. org*, December 24, 2015, https://informnapalm.org/en/nest-electronic-warfare-forces-russian-federation-luhansk-tax-administration-office-building/.

9. Dobrovolska, Christina, ed., "Russian R-378B Jamming Station Identified in Donbas," Translated by Mc Joy, *InformNapalm.org*, October 9, 2016, https://informnapalm.org/en/russian-r-878b-donbas/.

10. Klymenko, Oleksandr, trans., "The Newest Electronic Warfare Systems 'Borisoglebsk-2' Are Noticed at the Border and in the Ato Zone," *InformNapalm. org*, December 24, 2015, https://informnapalm.org/en/4723-the-newest-electronic-warfare-systems-borisoglebsk-2-are-noticed-at-the-border-and-in-the-ato-zone/.

11. Lapaiev, Yuri, "Ukraine as Clandestine Testing Ground for Russian Electronic Warfare," *Jamestown*, November 5, 2018, https://jamestown.org/program/ukraine-as-clandestine-testing-ground-for-russian-electronic-warfare/.

12. Gould, Joe, "Electronic Warfare: What US Army Can Learn from Ukraine," *Defense News*, August 8, 2017, https://www.defensenews.com/home/2015/08/02/electronic-warfare-what-us-army-can-learn-from-ukraine/.

13. Аваков, Артур, "Украинские Сайты Разместили Личные Данные Российских Летчиков, Воюющих в Сирии," *Московский Комсомолец*, October 13, 2015, https://www.mk.ru/politics/2015/10/13/ukrainskie-sayty-razmestili-lichnye-dannye-rossiyskikh-letchikov-voyuyushhikh-v-sirii.html.

14. "Песков Назвал 'Враждебными Действиями' Появление Сайтов с Данными Пилотов ВКС," *Московский Комсомолец*, October 15, 2015, https://www.mk.ru/politics/2015/10/15/peskov-nazval-vrazhdebnymi-deystviyami-poyavlenie-saytov-s-dannymi-pilotov-vks.html.

15. Ling, Justin, "A Ukrainian Website Is Outing Russian Soldiers, and Moscow Wants Canada to Stop It," *VICE*, December 17, 2015, https://www.vice.com/en/article/bjk7ea/a-ukrainian-website-is-outing-russian-soldiers-and-moscow-wants-canada-to-stop-it.

16. Ling, Justin, "A Ukrainian Website Is Outing Russian Soldiers, and Moscow Wants Canada to Stop It," *VICE*, December 17, 2015, https://www.

vice.com/en/article/bjk7ea/a-ukrainian-website-is-outing-russian-soldiers-and-moscow-wants-canada-to-stop-it.

17. Pugliese, David, "Canada-Linked Website Exposing Pilots' Identities to Extremists, Russians Say," *Ottawa Citizen*, June 3, 2020, https://ottawacitizen.com/news/politics/canada-linked-website-exposing-pilots-identities-to-extremists-russians-say.

18. Перевозкина, Марина, "Украина Слила Личные Данные Российских Пилотов Террористам ИГИЛ," *Московский Комсомолец*, October 28, 2015, https://www.mk.ru/politics/2015/10/28/ukraina-slila-lichnye-dannye-rossiyskikh-pilotov-terroristam-igil.html.

19. Belvpo.com, December 10, 2021, https://www.belvpo.com/.

20. Yurchenko, Grigory, "Informnapalm - Проект Специальных Структур Минобороны Украины (ДОКУМЕНТЫ)," *Русская весна*, August 4, 2016, https://rusvesna.su/recent_opinions/1454880002.

21. Strubinger, Lee Michael, "What Is Burning the Ministry of Defence of the Russian Federation? Informnapalm to Start Series Based on Leaked Information," *InformNapalm*, May 14, 2016, https://informnapalm.org/en/burning-ministry-defence-russian/.

22. Yaresko, Kateryna, and Mikhail Kuznetsov, "Russia Opens Visas for Terrorists Operating in Ukraine - Leaked Passport Data of Mercenaries," trans. Artyom Velichko, *InformNapalm*, May 14, 2016, https://informnapalm.org/en/russia-opens-visas-terrorists-operating-ukraine/.

23. "Ukrainian Hackers Defacing the Russian Propaganda Site Anna News (Video)," *InformNapalm*, May 14, 2016, https://informnapalm.org/en/ukrainian-hackers-anna-news/.

24. Большаков, Михаил, "Горелый Запах 'Информнапалма': 'Волонтеры', Которых Кормит Минобороны Украины," *Федеральное агентство новостей*, No.1, September 9, 2016, https://riafan.ru/553573-gorelyi-zapah-informnapalma-volontery-kotoryh-kormit-minoborony-ukrainy.

25. "SurkovLeaks: 1GB Mail Cache Retrieved by Ukrainian Hacktivists," *InformNapalm*, November 2, 2016, https://informnapalm.org/en/surkovleaks/.

26. "SurkovLeaks (Part 2): Hacktivists Publish New Email Dump." *InformNapalm*, November 3, 2016, https://informnapalm.org/en/surkovleaks-part2/.

27. Barbashin, Anton, and Hannah Thoburn, "Putin's Brain," *Foreign Affairs*, April 4, 2014, https://www.foreignaffairs.com/articles/russia-fsu/2014-03-31/putins-brain.

28. Egutkina, Anna, "Hybridiosaamiskeskuksen Perustamisasiakirja Allekirjoitettiin - Bäckmanin Kutsuma Dugin Kuumensi Tunteita," *Iltalehti*, April 11, 2017, https://www.iltalehti.fi/uutiset/a/201704112200101198.

29. "In Estonia, NATO Trains Personnel for the Occupation of Russia," *Evrazia.org*, October 28, 2016, http://evrazia.org/news/47013.

30. "Kremlin Financing Polish Radicals: Tasks, Payments, and Reporting to Moscow," *InformNapalm*, March 18, 2017, https://informnapalm.org/en/kremlin-financing-polish-radicals-tasks-payments-reporting-moscow/.

31. "Private Military Companies in Russia: Carrying out Criminal Orders of the Kremlin," *InformNapalm.rocks*, n.d., http://informnapalm.rocks/private-military-companies-in-russia-carrying-out-criminal-orders-of-the-kremlin.

32. "Russian Citizen Making Hoax Bomb Threats against Ukrainian Infrastructure with FSB Support," *InformNapalm.org*, August 10, 2017, https://informnapalm.org/en/russian-citizen-making-hoax-bomb-threats-against-ukrainian-infrastructure-with-fsb-support/.

33. "UCA: Hunting down Russian Propagandists on an Industrial Scale," *InformNapalm.org*, March 24, 2017, https://informnapalm.org/en/uca-hunting-russian-propagandists-industrial-scale/.

34. "Alexander Usovsky Archives," *InformNapalm.org*, https://informnapalm.org/en/tag/alexander-usovsky/.

35. Velichko, Artem, ed., "Kremlin Is behind Anti-Ukrainian Protests in Poland: Analysis of the Hacked Correspondence," trans. Victor Danilchenko, *InformNapalm.org*, March 7, 2017, https://informnapalm.org/en/kremlin-behind-anti-ukrainian-protests-poland-analysis-hacked-correspondence/.

36. Velichko, Artem, ed., "Kremlin Is behind Anti-Ukrainian Protests in Poland: Analysis of the Hacked Correspondence," trans. Victor Danilchenko, *InformNapalm.org*, March 7, 2017, https://informnapalm.org/en/kremlin-behind-anti-ukrainian-protests-poland-analysis-hacked-correspondence/.

37. "Monuments of Contention: A Study into Russia's Interference in Ukrainian-Polish Relations (Video)," *InformNapalm.org*, December 5, 2017, https://informnapalm.org/en/monuments-of-contention-a-study-into-russias-interference-in-ukrainian-polish-relations-video/.

38. "Kremlin Financing Polish Radicals: Tasks, Payments, and Reporting to Moscow," *InformNapalm.org*, March 18, 2017, https://informnapalm.org/en/kremlin-financing-polish-radicals-tasks-payments-reporting-moscow/.

39. France-Presse, Agence, "Poland Detains pro-Kremlin Party Leader for 'Spying'," *The Guardian*, May 19, 2016, https://www.theguardian.com/world/2016/may/19/poland-detains-pro-kremlin-party-leader-mateusz-piskorski-spying.

40. "MIP and InformNapalm Volunteers Present Evidence of Involvement of the Kremlin's Private Military Companies in Aggression in Donbas," *Ministry of Information Policy of Ukraine*, August 31, 2017, https://mip.gov.ua/en/news/1947.html.

41. Lapayev, Yuriy, "Ivan Lishchyna: 'The ECHR Is One of the Best International Institutions to Help Ukraine Establish Russia's Aggression,'" *PressReader.com*, February 15, 2018, https://www.pressreader.com/.

42. "Proofs of the Russian Aggression: Informnapalm Releases Extensive Database of Evidence," *InformNapalm*, March 12, 2021, https://informnapalm.

org/en/proofs-of-the-russian-aggression-informnapalm-releases-extensive-database-of-evidence/.

43. Shandra, Alya, "Ukrainian OSINT SLEUTHS Release Largest Existing Database of Evidence of Russian Aggression in Ukraine," *Euromaidan Press*, April 26, 2018, http://euromaidanpress.com/2018/04/25/informnapalm-release-huge-osint-database-of-evidence-of-russian-aggression-in-ukraine/.

44. Facebook, March 25, 2018, https://m.facebook.com/story.php?story_fbid=1744863948935284&id=920861058002248.

45. "Facebook Muzzles Free Media," *InformNapalm*, May 26, 2018, https://informnapalm.org/en/facebook-muzzles-free-media/.

46. "44 People Disappeared in Crime during the Annexation—CrimeaSOS," *Zmina*, August 31, 2017, https://humanrights.org.ua/en/material/u_krimu_a_chas_aneksiji_znikali_44_ljiudini__krimsos.

5. Millions of Views

1. RighteousWrath17, "Ukrainian Prisoners of War with Givi," YouTube video, 6:07, April 29, 2017, https://www.youtube.com/watch?v=H2NeXrUgfco.

2. RT. "Deadly Thunder: Exclusive Close-up Footage of GRAD Missile Launcher in Action (Ukraine, 02.09.2014)," YouTube Video, September 5, 2014, https://www.youtube.com/watch?v=_KCzUCJzpig.

3. Grishanov, "Артём Гришанов – Мобилизационный Ролик / Mobilization Video / War in Ukraine (English Subtitles)," YouTube video, 5:45, February 2, 2015, https://www.youtube.com/watch?v=bIPCvCERghQ

6. The Businessman

1. Higgins, Andrew, "Efforts to Expose Russia's 'Troll Army' Draws Vicious Retaliation," *New York Times*, May 30, 2016, https://www.nytimes.com/2016/05/31/world/europe/russia-finland-nato-trolls.html

2. Chazan, Guy. "Hermitage Management Capital Runs Into Trouble in Russia." *Wall Street Journal*, April 4, 2008, https://www.wsj.com/articles/SB120725601229787559

3. Buckley, Neil and Catherine Belton, "Hermitage in Russian Fraud Claim," *Financial Times*, April 3, 2008, https://www.ft.com/content/da0bbffe-01b7-11dd-a323-000077b07658

4. Knight, Amy, "Russia's Magnitsky affair and how it comes closer to Donald Trump," *Financial Review*, February 15, 2018, https://www.afr.com/world/europe/russias-magnitsky-affair-and-how-it-comes-closer-to-donald-trump-20180212-h0vx5a

5. Ibid.

6. "Sanctions Programs and Country Information," *U.S. Department of*

the Treasury, November 22, 2021, https://home.treasury.gov/policy-issues/financial-sanctions/sanctions-programs-and-country-information.

7. Herszenhorn, David M. and Erik Eckholm, "Putin Signs Bill that Bars US Adoptions, Upending Families," *New York Times*, December 27, 2012, https://www.nytimes.com/2012/12/28/world/europe/putin-to-sign-ban-on-us-adoptions-of-russian-children.html

8. Gray, Rosie, "Bill Browder's Testimony to the Senate Judiciary Committee," *The Atlantic*, July 26, 2017, https://www.theatlantic.com/politics/archive/2017/07/bill-browders-testimony-to-the-senate-judiciary-committee/534864/.

9. Список Браудера, NTV Video, 23:35, June 3, 2013, https://www.ntv.ru/peredacha/proisschestvie/m4001/o149336/video/.

10. Tsvetkova, Maria and Steve Gutterman, "Russia Convicts Lawyer Magnitsky in Posthumous Trial," *Reuters*, https://www.reuters.com/article/us-russia-magnitsky/russia-convicts-lawyer-magnitsky-in-posthumous-trial-idUSBRE96A09V20130711

11. "Designation of Eighteen Individuals Pursuant to the Sergei Magnitsky Rule of Law Accountability Act of 2012," *The Federal Register*, April 22, 2013, https://www.federalregister.gov/documents/2013/04/22/2013-09369/designation-of-eighteen-individuals-pursuant-to-the-sergei-magnitsky-rule-of-law-accountability-act

12. Heintz, Jim, "Russia Bans 18 Americans after similar US move," Associated Press, April 13, 2013, https://apnews.com/article/5595e7134d5e4594808ddcd48e0c5302

13. Gordon, Michael R., "U.S. Imposes New Sanctions on 12 Russians," *New York Times*, May 20, 2014, https://www.nytimes.com/2014/05/21/world/europe/us-imposes-new-sanctions-on-12-russians.html

14. "Глазами Шерлока Холмса, Литера 'М,'" NTV Video, 20:10, November 16, 2014, https://www.ntv.ru/peredacha/Litera_M/m80980/o307456/video/.

15. Browder, Bill, *Red Notice: A True Story of High Finance, Murder, and One Man's Fight for Justice,* New York: Simon & Schuster, 2015.

16. "Chaika: An investigative documentary by the Anti-Corruption Foundation," January 16, 2016, https://www.youtube.com/watch?v=3eO8ZHfV4fk.

17. Radu, Paul, "Russia: The Cellist and the Lawyer," *Organized Crime and Corruption Reportingn Project*, April 26, 2016, https://www.occrp.org/en/panamapapers/russia-the-cellist-and-the-lawyer.

18. Eckel, Mike, "In U.S. Money-Laundering Case, Shades Of Russian Corruption," Radio Free Europe, January 18, 2016, https://www.rferl.org/a/us-money-laundering-case-russian-corruption-browder-magnitsky-prevezon-katsyv/27494612.html

19. Weiss, Michael, "Russian Oligarch or FBI Rat?" *The Daily Beast*, December 11, 2015, https://www.thedailybeast.com/russian-oligarch-or-fbi-rat.

20. "Manhattan U.S. Attorney Announces Civil Forfeiture Complaint Against Real Estate Corporations Allegedly Involved In Laundering Proceeds Of Russian Tax Refund Fraud Scheme," Department of Justice, U.S. Attorney's Office Southern District of New York, September 10, 2013, https://www.justice.gov/usao-sdny/pr/manhattan-us-attorney-announces-civil-forfeiture-complaint-against-real-estate.

21. Macfarquhar, Neil, and Andrew E. Kramer. "Natalia Veselnitskaya, Lawyer Who Met Trump Jr., Seen as Fearsome Moscow Insider," *New York Times*, July 12, 2017, https://www.nytimes.com/2017/07/11/world/europe/natalia-veselnitskaya-donald-trump-jr-russian-lawyer.html.

22. Moscow Project Research Staff, "Everything You Need to Know about Natalia Veselnitskaya, Contextualized," *The Moscow Project*, October 24, 2018, https://themoscowproject.org/explainers/everything-need-know-natalia-veselnitskaya-contextualized/index.html.

23. BakerHostetler, "About Us," Last modified 2021, https://www.bakerlaw.com/AboutUs/Overview.

24. "Acting Manhattan U.S. Attorney Announces $5.9 Million Settlement Of Civil Money Laundering And Forfeiture Claims Against Real Estate Corporations Alleged To Have Laundered Proceeds Of Russian Tax Fraud," Department of Justice, U.S. Attorney's Office, Southern District of New York, May 12, 2017, https://www.justice.gov/usao-sdny/pr/acting-manhattan-us-attorney-announces-59-million-settlement-civil-money-laundering-and.

25. Released 13 April 2016, name "Browder Effect," distributor Russia Channel One, production company not known, likely the troll factory in St. Petersburg.

26. "The Magnitaky Act—Behind the Scenes," https://www.youtube.com/watch?v=snbepDSmA-4.

27. Nekrasov, Andrei, "A Spectre is haunting Europe—the Spectre of Magnitsky," November 26, 2020, https://rebelheldblog.medium.com/a-spectre-is-haunting-europe-the-spectre-of-magnitsky-dab601ce548e.

28. RFE/RL, "U.K. Imposes First Sanctions from Magnitsky Law, Including 14 Russians," *RadioFreeEurope/RadioLiberty*, April 27, 2021, https://www.rferl.org/a/uk-first-magnitsky-sanctions-include-14-russians/31224946.html.

29. "European Parliament Cancels Show of Film about Magnitsky on Browder's Order - Lawyer," *Russian News Agency*, April 27, 2016, https://tass.com/politics/872893.

30. Ibid.

31. "В Брюсселе Сорван Показ Фильма о Смерти Сергея Магнитского," *Пятый канал, Пятый канал*, April 28, 2016, https://www.5-tv.ru/news/106468/.

32. Sirén, Vesa, "Andrei Nekrasovin Kohudokumentista Tuli Massiivinen Poliittinen Puheenvuoro," *Helsingin Sanomat*, September 21, 2016, https://www.hs.fi/kulttuuri/art-2000002921959.html.

33. Satter, Raphael, "Emails: Lawyer who met Trump Jr. tied to Russian officials," Associated Press, July 27, 2018, https://apnews.com/article/moscow-donald-trump-ap-top-news-international-news-russia-d093a02a3d8a4e1b8dc7f5d19475899b.

34. "Lobbyist who met Trump team says he's not with Russian intel," *PBS News Hour*, July 15, 2017, https://www.pbs.org/newshour/politics/lobbyist-met-trump-team-says-hes-not-russian-intel.

35. Arnsdorf, Isaac, and Benjamin Oreskes, "Vladimir Putin's Favorite US Congressman," *Politico*, November 25, 2016, https://www.politico.eu/article/vladimir-putin-favorite-us-congressman-dana-rohrabacher-magnitsky-act-russia/.

36. Weiss, Michael, "Putin's Dirty Game in the U.S. Congress," *The Daily Beast*, April 13, 2017, https://www.thedailybeast.com/putins-dirty-game-in-the-us-congress.

37. Hines, Nico, "GOP Lawmaker Got Direction from Moscow, Took It Back to DC," *The Daily Beast*, July 19, 2017, https://www.thedailybeast.com/gop-lawmaker-got-direction-from-moscow-took-it-back-to-dc.

38. Goodman, Alana, "Russian Lawyer Who Met Don Jr Pictured with the D.C. Elite," *Daily Mail Online*, July 14, 2017, https://www.dailymail.co.uk/news/article-4694566/Russian-lawyer-met-Don-Jr-pictured-D-C-elite.html.

39. Eckel, Mike, "Russian 'Gun-for-Hire' Lurks in Shadows of Washington's Lobbying World," *RadioFreeEurope/RadioLiberty*, November 5, 2019, https://www.rferl.org/a/rinat-akmetshin-russia-gun-for-hire-washington-lobbying-magnitsky-browder/27863265.html.

40. "Украина, Санкции, США: Большое Интервью Сергея Лаврова," *RT*, May 31, 2016, https://russian.rt.com/article/305390-sergei-lavrov.

41. "Чайка Назвал Фильм 'Акт Магнитского, За Кулисами' 'Приговором Браудеру,'" *РИА Новости*, March 2, 2020, https://ria.ru/20160615/1447921648.html.

42. "United States Senate Committee on the Judiciary," April 4, 2017, https://www.judiciary.senate.gov/imo/media/doc/2017-04-04%20CEG%20to%20DHS%20%28Akhmetshin%20Information%29%20with%20attachment.pdf.

43. "We Demand That the U.S. Congress Repeals the Magnitsky Act," *National Archives and Records Administration*, April 23, 2016, https://petitions.obamawhitehouse.archives.gov/petition/we-demand-us-congress-repeals-magnitsky-act/.

44. Solomon, John, and Jonathan Easley, "Trump Jr. Pitch Was Part of Broad Russian Effort," *The Hill*, July 15, 2017, https://thehill.com/homenews/administration/341946-trump-jr-pitch-was-part-of-broad-russian-effort.

45. Delk, Josh, "Rohrabacher Aide Fired over Russia Connections," *The Hill*, July 20, 2017, https://thehill.com/homenews/house/342917-rohrabacher-aide-fired-over-russia-connections.

46. Kramer, Andrew E. and Sharon LaFraniere, "Lawyer Who Was Said to

Have Dirt on Clinton Had Closer Ties to Kremlin Than She Let On," *New York Times*, April 27, 2018, https://www.nytimes.com/2018/04/27/us/natalya-veselnitskaya-trump-tower-russian-prosecutor-general.html

47. "Trump Jr. Scandal: Russian Lawyer Veselnitskaya Ready 'to Share Everything' with Senate," *RT*, July 18, 2017, https://www.rt.com/news/396728-russian-lawyer-scandal-america/.

48. Gray, Rosie, "Bill Browder's Testimony to the Senate Judiciary Committee," *The Atlantic*, July 26, 2017, https://www.theatlantic.com/politics/archive/2017/07/bill-browders-testimony-to-the-senate-judiciary-committee/534864/.

49. "Testimony of NATALIA VESELNITSKAYA Before the United States Senate Committee on the Judiciary," November 20, 2017, https://www.judiciary.senate.gov/imo/media/doc/2017-11-20%20Veselnitskaya%20to%20CEG%20(June%209%20Meeting).pdf.

50. Ibid.

51. Ibid, 33.

52. "Interview of: Glenn Simpson," United States Congress, August 22, 2017, https://www.documentcloud.org/documents/4345537-Fusion-GPS-Simpson-Transcript.html.

53. Baker, Stephanie, "Russia-Funded Adoption Group Is Said to Draw Mueller Scrutiny," *BloombergQuint*, December 21, 2017, https://www.bloombergquint.com/politics/russia-funded-adoption-group-is-said-to-draw-mueller-scrutiny.

54. "Russia Asks Interpol To Arrest Kremlin Critic Bill Browder Again," *Reuters*, April 9, 2019, https://www.reuters.com/article/russia-browder/russia-asks-interpol-to-arrest-kremlin-critic-bill-browder-again-letter-idUKL8N21Q5ZK?edition-redirect=uk.

55. "Interview of: Glenn Simpson," United States Congress, August 22, 2017, https://www.documentcloud.org/documents/4345537-Fusion-GPS-Simpson-Transcript.html.

56. "Interview of: Rinat Akhmetshin," United States Congress, November 14, 2017, https://www.judiciary.senate.gov/imo/media/doc/Akhmetshin%20Transcript_redacted.pdf.

57. Butler, Desmond, and Chad Day, "Russian-American Lobbyist Joined Trump's Son's Meeting, Too," *Associated Press*, July 15, 2017, https://apnews.com/dceed1008d8f45afb314aca65797762a.

58. Weiss, Michael, "US Congressman Talks Russian Money Laundering with Alleged Ex-Spy in Berlin," *CNN*, May 4, 2017, https://edition.cnn.com/2017/05/04/politics/rohrabacher-prevezon/index.html.

59. "Treasury Targets Individuals Involved in the Sergei Magnitsky Case and Other Gross Violations of Human Rights in Russia," *U.S. Department of the Treasury*, December 20, 2017, https://home.treasury.gov/news/press-releases/sm0240.

60. "United States Sanctions Human Rights Abusers and Corrupt Actors

across the Globe," *U.S. Department of the Treasury*, June 4, 2018, https://home. treasury.gov/news/press-releases/sm0243.

61. "Moscow Court Sentences US-Born Investor Browder to 9 Years for Massive Tax Fraud," *RT International*, December 29, 2017, https://www.rt.com/russia/414540-moscow-court-sentences-us-investor/.

62. Townsend, Mark, "Putin Accuses British Anti-Corruption Campaigner Browder of Three Murders," *The Guardian*, November 19, 2017, https://www.theguardian.com/world/2017/nov/19/bill-browder-putin-accuses-three-murders-campaigner-sergei-magnitsky.

63. Breuninger, Kevin, "Russian Lawyer from Infamous Trump Tower Meeting Admits to Being an Informant for the Kremlin: Report," *CNBC*, April 27, 2018, https://www.cnbc.com/2018/04/27/emails-show-new-ties-between-trump-tower-russian-and-kremlin-nbc.html.

64. "Russian Lawyer Who Met with Donald Trump Jr. in Trump Tower Says Mueller Hasn't Contacted Her, Accuses Him of 'Not Working to Discover the Truth'," *Business Insider*, April 22, 2018, https://www.businessinsider.com/ap-russian-lawyer-questions-why-mueller-hasnt-contacted-her-2018-4?r=US&IR=T.

65. *Akhmetshin v. Browder*, No. 19-7129 (D.C. Cir. Apr. 13, 2021). https://casetext.com/case/akhmetshin-v-browder-2.

66. Ibid.

67. United States Senate Select Committee on Intelligence, "Report on Russian Active Measures Campaigns and Interference in the 2016 Election," 116th Congress, 1st session, Report 116-XX, Vol. 5, p. ix, August 8, 2020, https://www.intelligence.senate.gov/sites/default/files/documents/report_volume5.pdf.

68. United States of America v. Viktor Borisovich Netyksho et. al., No. 1:18-cr-00215-ABJ (D.C. Cir. July 13, 2018), https://www.justice.gov/file/1080281/download.

69. Neufeld, Jennie, "Read the Full Transcript of the Helsinki Press Conference," *Vox*, July 16, 2018, https://www.vox.com/2018/7/16/17576956/transcript-putin-trump-russia-helsinki-press-conference.

70. "Russia Ready to Send Request to US over Questionings in Browder Case," *Russian News Agency*, July 17, 2018, https://tass.com/world/1013707.

71. Mueller, Eleanor, "White House: Trump Will Consider Letting Russia Question Investor, Former Ambassador," *Politico*, July 18, 2018, https://www.politico.com/story/2018/07/18/trump-russia-browder-mcfaul-questioning-731616.

72. Rodriguez, Jesus, "State Dept: Russia's Allegations about American Citizens 'Absolutely Absurd'," *TheHill*, July 18, 2018, https://thehill.com/homenews/administration/397763-state-dept-russias-allegations-about-american-citizens-absolutely.

73. Staff, "Russian Prosecutors Seek Ex-U.S. Ambassador Mcfaul for

Questioning in Browder Case," *The Moscow Times*, July 18, 2018, https://www.themoscowtimes.com/2018/07/18/russian-prosecutors-seek-ex-us-ambassador-mcfaul-for-questioning-in-browder-case-a62280.

74. Kramer, David J., "I'm on Putin's Hit List but I'm Not the Real Victim," *Politico*, April 18, 2019, https://www.politico.eu/article/vladimir-putin-william-browder-the-real-victims-of-putins-enemies-list/.

75. "Bill Browder: Vladimir Putin is Obsessed With Me," Fox News, July 22, 2018, https://www.youtube.com/watch?v=YTuLb7Rl2sY

76. Loop, Emma, Anthony Cormier, Jason Leopold, John Templon, and Tanya Kozyreva, "A Lobbyist at the Trump Tower Meeting Received Half a Million Dollars in Suspicious Payments," *BuzzFeed News*, April 17, 2019, https://www.buzzfeednews.com/article/emmaloop/trump-tower-meeting-russian-lobbyist-akhmetshin-suspicious-p.

77. Barr, William P., *Letter to House and Senate*, March 24, 2019, https://vi.m.wikipedia.org/wiki/T%E1%BA%ADp_tin:AG_March_24_2019_Letter_to_House_and_Senate_Judiciary_Committees.pdf?page=4.

78. Palmeri, Tara, "Russian lobbyist at Trump Tower meeting 'happy and relieved' Mueller probe over," *ABC News*, March 26, 2019, https://abcnews.go.com/Politics/russian-lobbyist-trump-tower-meeting-happy-relieved-mueller/story?id=61943196https.

79. Mueller, Robert S., "Report on the Investigation into Russian Interference in the 2016 Presidential Election, volumes I and II," *United States Department of Justice*, March 2019, https://justice.gov/archives/sco/file/1373816.

80. Becker, Jo, Mark Mazzetti, Matt Apuzzo, Maggie Haberman, "Mueller Zeros In on Story Put Together about Trump Tower Meeting," *New York Times*, January 31, 2018, https://www.nytimes.com/2018/01/31/us/politics/trump-russia-hope-hicks-mueller.html.

81. "Russian Senator Suggests Compiling 'Browder's List' of Politicians Lying about Russia," *Russian News Agency*, December 25, 2018, https://tass.com/politics/1037889.

82. "Russian Attorney Natalya Veselnitskaya Charged With Obstruction Of Justice In Connection With Civil Money Laundering And Forfeiture Action," *United States Department of Justice*, January 8, 2019, https://www.justice.gov/usao-sdny/pr/russian-attorney-natalya-veselnitskaya-charged-obstruction-justice-connection-civil.

83. France-Presse, Agence, and Guillaume Lavallee, "Moscow Demands 'Clear Explanation' of US Charges against Russian Lawyer," *Rappler*, January 11, 2019, https://www.rappler.com/world/europe/moscow-demands-explanation-of-charges-against-russian-lawyer.

84. Neumann, Jeanette. "Last Stop for Some of Danske Bank's Dirty Money: Spanish Real Estate," *Bloomberg*, April 10, 2019, https://www.bloomberg.com/news/articles/2019-04-10/last-stop-for-some-of-danske-s-dirty-money-spanish-real-estate.

85. Springe, Inga, and Karina Shedrofsky, "Mega-Donor to pro-Russian Party Benefits from Magnitsky and Azerbaijani Laundromats," *re:baltica*, March 20, 2019, https://en.rebaltica.lv/2019/03/mega-donor-to-pro-russian-party-benefits-from-magnitsky-and-azerbaijani-laundromats.

86. "Russia Asks Interpol to Arrest Kremlin Critic Bill Browder Again - Letter," *Reuters*, April 9, 2019, https://www.reuters.com/article/russia-browder/russia-asks-interpol-to-arrest-kremlin-critic-bill-browder-again-letter-idUKL8N21Q5ZK?edition-redirect=uk.

87. Mendick, Robert, "Interpol's Integrity at Risk over Russia's Attempts to Force the International Arrest of Bill Browder," *The Telegraph*, April 13, 2019, https://www.telegraph.co.uk/news/2019/04/13/interpols-integrity-risk-russias-attempts-force-international.

88. Browder, Bill (@Billbrowder), "I'm feeling good today...," Twitter post, May 15, 2019, 8:45 AM, https://twitter.com/Billbrowder/status/1128642653434929153?s=20

89. Russia In Australia (@RusEmbAu), "#BillBrowder stole...," Twitter post, May 15, 2019, 4:23 AM, https://mobile.twitter.com/rusembau/status/1128576523600928768.

90. "Treasury Targets Additional Individuals Involved in the Sergei Magnitsky Case and Gross Violations of Human Rights in Russia," *US Department of The Treasury*, May 16, 2019, https://home.treasury.gov/news/press-releases/sm691.

91. Browder, Bill (@Billbrowder). "So far 42...," Twitter post, May 16, 2019, 2:25 PM, https://twitter.com/Billbrowder/status/1129090531378835456

92. Engel, Richard, and Aggelos Petropoulos, "Lawyer Probing Russian Corruption Says His Balcony Fall Was 'No Accident'," *NBCNews.com*, July 8, 2017, https://www.nbcnews.com/news/world/lawyer-probing-russian-corruption-says-his-balcony-fall-was-no-n780416.

7. Special Courses at Moscow State University

1. Илларионов, Андрей, "В.Яковлев. Методы Боевой Спецпропаганды," Web log. LiveJournal (blog), August 17, 2015, https://aillarionov.livejournal.com/846809.

2. Zabrisky, Zarina, "Big Lies and Rotten Herrings: 17 Kremlin Disinformation Techniques You Need To Know Now," *Byline Times*, March 4, 2020, https://bylinetimes.com/2020/03/04/big-lies-and-rotten-herrings-17-kremlin-disinformation-techniques-you-need-to-know-now/.

8. The Reporters

1. *The Independent Barents Observer*, https://thebarentsobserver.com/en.

2. Ibid.

3. "Promoting Norwegian-Russian Relations in the North," *Barents Secretariat*, May 23, 2016, https://barents.no/en/promoting-norwegian-russian-relations-north.

4. "Statoil to Change Name to Equinor - Statoil to Change Name to Equinor," *Equinor*, March 15, 2018, https://www.equinor.com/en/news/15mar2018-statoil.html.

5. "Russia Running out of Oil? Profitable Reserves May Last Only Another 20 Years, Moscow Says, Citing Improved Tech as Only solution2021," *RT International*, September 15, 2021, https://www.rt.com/russia/534890-oil-depozits-running-dry/.

6. Farchy, Jack, "Igor Sechin: Russia's Second Most Powerful Man," *Financial Times*, April 28, 2014, https://www.ft.com/content/a8f24922-cef4-11e3-9165-00144feabdc0.

7. "Sechin Igor," Putin's List, The Database of Free Russia Forum, November 19, 2021, https://www.spisok-putina.org/en/personas/sechin-2/.

8. "Federal Security Service—Cheka 2.0," *Warsaw Institute*, February 6, 2018, https://warsawinstitute.org/fsb-cheka-2-0-2/.

9. Digges, Charles, "Son of FSB Director Patrushev to Be Advisor to Chairman of Oil Giant Rosneft," *Bellona*, June 11, 2015, https://bellona.org/news/fossil-fuels/oil/2006-09-son-of-fsb-director-patrushev-to-be-advisor-to-chairman-of-oil-giant-rosneft.

10. Galeotti, Mark, "Stolypin: Adding Spooks to Companies Creates Stagnation," *bne IntelliNews*, April 20, 2017, https://www.intellinews.com/stolypin-adding-spooks-to-companies-creates-stagnation-119924/.

11. Nilsen, Thomas, "Sanctions No Obstacle for Rosneft's Deal with Norwegian Seadrill," *Barents Observer*, August 24, 2014, https://barentsobserver.com/en/energy/2014/08/sanctions-no-obstacle-rosnefts-deal-norwegian-seadrill-24-08.

12. Aro, Jessikka, Personal interview with Thomas Nilsen and Atle Staalesen, n.d.

13. Pettersen, Trude, "Russia Sends Aircraft Carrier to Lebanon, Syria," *Barents Observer*, November 28, 2011, https://barentsobserver.com/en/articles/russia-sends-aircraft-carrier-lebanon-syria.

14. Nilsen, Thomas, "Barents Cooperation in Putin's Dangerous New Era," *Barents Observer*, April 11, 2014, https://web.archive.org/web/20151002175914/http://barentsobserver.com/en/opinion/2014/04/barents-cooperation-putins-dangerous-new-era-11-04.

15. Pedersen, Ole-Tommy, "– Neinei, Hva Mener Du? Ukrainerne Dro Frivillig," *iFinnmark*, April 29, 2014, https://www.ifinnmark.no/nyheter/neinei-hva-mener-du-ukrainerne-dro-frivillig/s/1-30002-7322052.

16. Mathiesen, Karl, "Russian Intelligence Accused of Silencing Norwegian Newspaper Editor," *The Guardian*, October 6, 2015, https://www.theguardian.com/environment/2015/oct/06/russian-intelligence-accused-of-silencing-norwegian-newspaper-editor.

17. DeGeorge, Krestia, "Norwegian Arctic Journalist Barred from Russia

Is Suing to Overturn the Decision," *ArcticToday*, June 16, 2017, https://www.arctictoday.com/norwegian-arctic-journalist-barred-from-russia-is-suing-to-overturn-the-decision/.

18. Staalesen, Atle, "Barents Observer Editor Thomas Nilsen Is Declared Unwanted in Russia by FSB," *Barents Observer*, March 9, 2017, https://thebarentsobserver.com/en/civil-society-and-media/2017/03/barents-observer-editor-thomas-nilsen-declared-unwanted-russia.

19. Leisti, Tapani, "Venäjän Konsuli Puuttui Norjan Uutissivusto Barentsobserverin Sananvapauteen," *Yle Uutiset*, April 30, 2014, https://yle.fi/uutiset/3-7213624.

20. France-Presse, Agence, "Rosneft Begins Oil Prospecting off Norway despite Sanctions," *IndustryWeek*, August 18, 2014, https://www.industryweek.com/technology-and-iiot/energy/article/21963472/rosneft-begins-oil-prospecting-off-norway-despite-sanctions.

21. "Rosneft and Statoil Start Exploration Operations on the Norwegian Continental Shelf in the Barents Sea," *Rosneft*, August 18, 2014, https://www.rosneft.com/press/news/item/153659/.

22. Pettersen, Trude, "Russia Builds New Airfield on Franz Josef Land," *Barents Observer*, February 16, 2015, https://barentsobserver.com/en/security/2015/02/russia-builds-new-airfield-franz-josef-land-16-02.

23. "Rogozin Tells Japanese to Commit Ritualistic Suicide amid Kuril Island Spat," *The Moscow Times*, August 24, 2015, https://www.themoscowtimes.com/2015/08/24/rogozin-tells-japanese-to-commit-ritualistic-suicide-amid-kuril-island-spat-a49121.

24. France-Presse, Agence, "Russian Official: 'Tanks Don't Need Visas'," *Defense News*, August 8, 2017, https://www.defensenews.com/global/europe/2015/05/25/russian-official-tanks-don-t-need-visas/.

25. Nilsen, Thomas, "Russia's Sanctioned Rogozin Landed on Svalbard," *Barents Observer*, April 18, 2015, https://barentsobserver.com/en/politics/2015/04/russias-sanctioned-rogozin-landed-svalbard-18-04.

26. Ibid.

27. Nilsen, Thomas, "Norway Summons Russian Ambassador," *Barents Observer*, April 20, 2015, https://barentsobserver.com/en/politics/2015/04/norway-summons-russian-ambassador-20-04.

28. Ibid.

29. Pettersen, Trude, "Stronger Control of Visitors to Svalbard," *Barents Observer*, August 3, 2015, https://barentsobserver.com/en/borders/2015/08/stronger-control-visitors-svalbard-03-08.

30. Association of Norwegian Editors, https://www.nored.no/Association-of-Norwegian-Editors.

31. Nilsen, Thomas, Atle Staalesen, Trude Pettersen, and Jonas Karlsbakk, "Owners Clamp down on BarentsObserver," *Barents Observer*,

May 21, 2015, https://barentsobserver.com/en/politics/2015/05/owners-clamp-down-barentsobserver-21-05.

32. Staalesen, Atle, "Owners of Norwegian Arctic Newspaper Fire Editor," *Anchorage Daily News*, September 28, 2016, https://www.adn.com/arctic/article/owners-fire-barentsobserver-editor/2015/09/30.

33. Strand, Tormod, "Kilde Til NRK: – Russisk Etterretning Ba Norge Om Å Bringe Barentsobserver Til Taushet," *NRK*, December 16, 2015, https://www.nrk.no/norge/kilde-til-nrk_-_-russisk-etterretning-ba-norge-om-a-bringe-barentsobserver-til-taushet-1.12583998.

34. Ibid.

35. "Agenttien Värvääminen Suomessa," *Suojelupoliisin vuosikirja*, n.d. https://vuosikirja.supo.fi/agenttien-varvaaminen-suomessa.

36. Aro, Jessikka, Interview with Thomas Nilsen and Atle Staalesen. n.d.

37. Staalesen, Atle, "Researcher Calls to Stand up for Independent Barents Observer," *Barents Observer*, October 27, 2015, https://thebarentsobserver.com/ru/2015/10/researcher-calls-stand-independent-barents-observer.

38. Pettersen, Trude, "Russian Military Instructors Plan to Land on Svalbard," *Barents Observer*, April 7, 2016, https://thebarentsobserver.com/en/security/2016/04/russian-military-instructors-plan-land-svalbard.

39. Balmforth, Tom, "Russian Media Behemoth Set to Launch Wave of Foreign Bureaus," *RadioFreeEurope/RadioLiberty*, October 29, 2014, https://www.rferl.org/a/russia-rossiya-segodnya-expansion-belgrade-dushanbe/26664310.html.

40. Nilsen, Thomas, "Russia's Oslo Embassy: Norway's Selective Approach for Cooperation Is Not Tenable," *Barents Observer*, February 17, 2017, https://thebarentsobserver.com/en/life-and-public/2017/02/russias-oslo-embassy-norways-selective-approach-cooperation-not-tenable.

41. Den Russiske Ambassade Oslo, "Kommentar fra Russlands Ambassade i Norge i forbindelse med innreiseforbud for sjefredaktøren i Independent Barents Observer Thomas Nielsen," March 10, 2017, https://web.archive.org/web/20170320010059/https://norway.mid.ru/press_17_014.html/.

42. Staalesen, Atle, "Supreme Court Sides with FSB, Says Barents Observer Editor Poses Threat to Russia's National Security," *Barents Observer*, May 25, 2018, https://thebarentsobserver.com/en/2018/05/supreme-court-sides-fsb-says-barents-observer-editor-poses-threat-russias-national-security.

43. *Nilsen v. Russia*, No. 58505/18, European Court of Human Rights, March 1 2021, https://polit-x.de/en/documents/5165450.

44. Hofman, Marianne, "From Suicide Attempts to Happiness and Sámi Pride," *Barents Observer*, January 10, 2019, https://thebarentsobserver.com/en/life-and-public/2019/01/suicide-attempts-happiness-and-pride.

45. Hofman, Marianne, "От Попыток Самоубийства к Счастью и Гордости." *Barents Observer*, January 14, 2019, https://thebarentsobserver.com/ru/obshchestvennost/2019/01/ot-popytok-samoubiystva-k-schastyu-i-gordosti.

46. Staalesen, Atle, "Russia's Media Controllers Aim for Blocking the Barents Observer," *Barents Observer*, January 30, 2019, https://thebarentsobserver.com/en/civil-society-and-media/2019/01/russias-media-controllers-aim-blocking-barents-observer.

47. Staalesen, Atle, "The Barents Observer Is Now Blocked in Russia," *Barents Observer*, February 19, 2019, https://thebarentsobserver.com/en/civil-society-and-media/2019/02/barents-observer-now-blocked-russia.

48. Ibid.

49. Staalesen, Atle, "Repressive Authority Steps up Blocking of Independent News Media," *Barents Observer*, February 1, 2019, https://thebarentsobserver.com/en/2019/02/repressive-authority-steps-blocking-independent-news-media.

50. Staalesen, Atle, "Appeal Case 'Barents Observer vs Roskomnadzor' Comes up in Moscow Court," *Barents Observer*, August 18, 2020, https://thebarentsobserver.com/en/civil-society-and-media/2020/08/appeal-case-barents-observer-vs-roskomnadzor-comes-moscow-court.

9. 55 Savushkina Street

1. Alexandra Garmazhapova, Где живут тролли. Как работают интернет-провокаторы в Санкт-Петербурге и кто ими заправляет, *Novaya Gazeta,* September 9, 2013.

2. Aro, Jessikka, and Mika Mäkeläinen, "Yle Kioski Traces the Origins of Russian Social Media Propaganda—Never-before-Seen Material from the Troll Factory," *Yle Kioski*, February 20, 2015, https://kioski.yle.fi/omat/at-the-origins-of-russian-propaganda.

3. Lucas, Ryan, "How Russia Used Facebook to Organize 2 Sets of Protesters," *NPR*, November 1, 2017, https://www.npr.org/2017/11/01/561427876/how-russia-used-facebook-to-organize-two-sets-of-protesters.

4. Bertrand, Natasha, "Russia Organized 2 Sides of a Texas Protest and Encouraged 'Both Sides to Battle in the Streets'," *Business Insider*, November 1, 2017, https://www.businessinsider.com/russia-trolls-senate-intelligence-committee-hearing-2017-11.

10. The Scholar

1. Martin Kragh and Åsberg, Sebastian, "Russia's Strategy for Influence through Public Diplomacy and Active Measures: The Swedish Case," *Journal of Strategic Studies* 40, no. 6, January 5, 2017.

2. Andrew Brown, "Wikileaks and Israel Shamir," *The Guardian*, December 17, 2010, https://www.theguardian.com/commentisfree/andrewbrown/2010/

dec/17/wikileaks-israel-shamir-russia-scandinavia.

3. Aagård, Martin, "Häxjakten Måste Få Ett Slut," *Aftonbladet*, January 9, 2017, https://www.aftonbladet.se/kultur/a/Kgva7/haxjakten-maste-fa-ett-slut.

4. Linderborg, Åsa, "Försvara Det Fria Ordet," *Aftonbladet*, January 9, 2017, https://www.aftonbladet.se/kultur/a/ErWvo/forsvara-det-fria-ordet).

5. Andersson, Tom, "Analysen Liknar Viskningsleken," *Aftonbladet*, January 18, 2017, https://www.aftonbladet.se/kultur/a/kgBL6/analysen-liknar-viskningsleken.

6. Kälvemark, Torsten, "En Välkommen Tillnyktring I Rysslandsdebatten," *Aftonbladet*, June 30, 2017, https://www.aftonbladet.se/kultur/a/4PmKE/en-valkommen-tillnyktring-i-rysslandsdebatten.

7. "HBL: Ex-Suurlähettiläs Pitää Ahvenanmaan Rauhanleiriä Venäjän Vaikuttamisoperaationa," *MTV Uutiset*, June 26, 2017, https://www.mtvuutiset.fi/artikkeli/hbl-ex-suurlahettilas-pitaa-ahvenanmaan-rauhanleiria-venajan-vaik uttamisoperaationa/6485014#gs.h0yxod.

8. Linderborg, Åsa, "Forskarna Duckar Kritiken," *Aftonbladet*, February 22, 2017, https://www.aftonbladet.se/kultur/a/8aqQx/forskarna-duckar-kritiken.

9. Törner, Amanda, "Åsa Linderborg: 'De Här Ryktena Måste Vi Döda,'" *Dagens Media*, January 16, 2017, https://www.dagensmedia.se/medier/dagspress/asa-linderborg-de-har-ryktena-maste-vi-doda-6818363.

10. "Anti-Euromaiden Sweden," Facebook Group, n.d., https://www.facebook.com/groups/757952094312159.

11. "White Helmets Video: Swedish Doctors for Human Rights Denounce Medical Malpractice and 'Misuse' of Children for Propaganda Aims," March 2017, https://theindicter.com/white-helmets-video-swedish-doctors-for-human-rights-denounce-medical-malpractice-and-misuse-of-children-for-propaganda-aims.

12. Katia Patin, "Russia Used A Two-Year Old Video and an 'Alternative" Swedish Group to Discredit Reports of a Syria Gas Attack," May 2, 2017, https://www.codastory.com/disinformation/armed-conflict/a-swedish-alternative-ngo-disputes-a-video-of-syrian-carnage-and-a-russian-fake-news-meme-is-born.

13. Wechselmann, Maj, "Maj Wechselmann: Här Borde Också Huvuden Falla!" *Göteborgs-Posten*, February 6, 2017, https://www.gp.se/kultur/kultur/maj-wechselmann-h%C3%A4r-borde-ocks%C3%A5-huvuden-falla-1.4144487.

14. Asplid, Åsa, "Egor Putilov Har Skaffat Ny Identitet," *Expressen*, February 18, 2018, https://www.expressen.se/nyheter/egor-putilov-har-skaffat-ny-identitet/.

15. Wiman, Erik, Frida Svensson, Frida Sundkvist, and Maria Georgieva, "Här Tränar Svenska Nazister Krig I Ryssland: SVD," *Svenska Dagbladet*, September 29, 2017, https://www.svd.se/har-tranar-svenska-nazister-krig-i-ryssland.

16. Ståhle, Mathias, "Så Styrs Den Svenska Trollfabriken Som Sprider Hat På Nätet Mot Betalning," *SN*, February 17, 2017, https://sn.se/tjanster/sa-styrs-den-svenska-trollfabriken-som-sprider-hat-pa-natet-mot-betalning.

17. "Sweden Caught Peddling Fake News about 'Russian Influence'," *Sputnik International*, April 10, 2017, https://sputniknews.com/20170410/

sweden-russia-fake-news-1052490607.

18. Shamir, Israel, "Вашими Устами Да Мёд Пить," *RT*, February 7, 2017, https://russian.rt.com/opinion/356770-shamir-shveciy-usa-rt.

19. Brown, Andrew, "Wikileaks and Israel Shamir," *The Guardian*, December 17, 2010, https://www.theguardian.com/commentisfree/andrewbrown/2010/dec/17/wikileaks-israel-shamir-russia-scandinavia.

20. Kishkovsky, Sophia, "Russian Publisher Rewrites Books on Putin without Western Authors' Consent," *New York Times*, August 14, 2015, https://www.nytimes.com/2015/08/15/world/europe/russian-publisher-rewrites-books-on-putin-without-western-authors-consent.

21. АСЛАМОВА, Дарья, "Оппозиционер Сахнин: В Швеции Меня Привечали, Пока Выступал Против Путина, А Когда Написал Правду Об Украине, Объявили 'Агентом ГРУ,'" *kp.ru*, June 22, 2017, https://www.kp.ru/daily/26667.5/3688877.

22. Edwards, Jim, "What it's like when the Russians hack your company and turn you into a fake news conspiracy story on state TV," *Insider*, December 23, 2019, https://www.insider.com/russia-hack-on-institute-for-statecraft-tactics-in-west-2019-12.

23. "UK Psyops Bigwig Pushed Plan to 'Mine Sevastopol Bay' during 2014 Crimea Crisis – Leaked Documents," *RT International*, December 17, 2018, https://www.rt.com/news/446728-uk-psyops-mine-crimea/.

24. Сахнин, Алексей, "Novayagazeta.ru," *Новая газета*, February 5, 2019, https://novayagazeta.ru/articles/2019/02/05/79440-vas-zastavyat-pomenyat-svoe-mnenie.

25. Linderborg, Åsa, "Martin Kragh Är Ett Demokratiskt Problem," *Aftonbladet*, February 21, 2019, https://www.aftonbladet.se/kultur/a/0E1nm6/martin-kragh-ar-ett-demokratiskt-problem.

26. Linderborg, Åsa, "Karin Olssons Utbrott Döljer Sakfrågan," *Aftonbladet*, February 12, 2019, https://www.aftonbladet.se/kultur/a/XwX77x/karin-olssons-utbrott-doljer-sakfragan.

27. Samuelsson, Lena K., "Anmälan Om Brott (Brådskande P.g.a. Förestående Preskription)," https://static1.squarespace.com/static/550b4d42e4b09d0652882d74/t/5cdc08c6a4222f0418d2b10c/1557924040210/Anm%C3%A4lan+om+brott_version+f%C3%B6r+hemsidan.pdf.

28. "Aftonbladet Klandras För En Artikel Om Forskare," *Aftonbladet*, December 2, 2019, https://www.aftonbladet.se/nyheter/a/zGwXn9/aftonbladet-klandras-for-en-artikel-om-forskare.

11. The Trolls'

1. "Jessikka Aro's Prize-Winning Stories on Russian Propaganda," *Yle Kioski*, June 17, 2016, https://kioski.yle.fi/omat/jessikka-aros-prize-winning-stories-on-russian-propaganda.

2. "Jessikka Aro (Yle), Tutkivan Journalismin Pelle!!" *MV-Lehti*, May 19, 2015. https://mvlehti.net/2015/05/19/jessikka-aro-yle-tutkivan-journalismin-pelle/.

3. "Jessikka Aron Trollijahti" https://www.youtube.com/watch?v=igOa1 EXKzTI.

12. The Think-Tanker

1. "Politico 28 Class of 2017 Ranking," *Politico*, https://www.politico.eu/list/politico-28-class-of-2017-ranking/.

2. Talović, Violeta, "Čepurin: Nećemo da budemo veći Srbi od vas," Novosti, October 17, 2013, https://www.novosti.rs/vesti/naslovna/politika/aktuelno.289.html:459411-Cepurin-Necemo-da-budemo-veci-Srbi-od-vas.

3. "Even Less than the '30 Pieces of Silver' Is More, Mister Chepurin, It." *CEAS, n.d.* https://www.ceas-serbia.org/en/announcements/1691-less-is-also-more-than-the-30-pieces-of-silver-mister-chepurin-it-is-a-pity-that-you-do-not-understand.

4. Rudic, Fillip, "Serbian Far Right Leader Acquitted for Publishing 'Traitor' List," BalkanInsight, November 7, 2017, https://balkaninsight.com/2017/11/07/serbian-right-extremist-acquitted-for-publishing-traitors-list-11-07-2017/.

5. "Eyes Wide Shut - Strengthening of the Russian Soft Power in Serbia—Goals, Instruments and Effects," *CEAS*, July 6, 2016, https://www.ceas-serbia.org/en/ceas-publications/study-eyes-wide-shut.

6. "Conference Serbia and Russia: Russian Influence on Stabilization, Democratization and European Integration of Serbia," *CEAS*, February 22, 2016, https://www.ceas-serbia.org/en/news/ceas-news/4628-conference-serbia-and-russia-russian-influence-on-stabilization-democratization-and-european-integration-of-serbia.

7. Sudar, Vladimir, "Nato Demokrate U Staljinovom Šinjelu (Video)," *Sputnik Srbija*, August 30, 2021, https://rs-lat.sputniknews.com/20160222/nato-ceas-srbija-staljin-1103452465.html.

8. "Suspect in Alleged Montenegrin Coup Plot Pictured with Lavrov in Belgrade," *RadioFreeEurope/RadioLiberty*, December 15, 2016, https://www.rferl.org/a/montenegro-coup-plot-suspect-instagram-lavrov-ristic/28176472.html.

9. "Vencislav the Virgin - Ceas-Serbia.org," *CEAS*, March 2018, https://www.ceas-serbia.org/images/2018/201803_CEAS_Report.pdf.

10. Dragojlo, Sasa, "With Ruling Party Ties, Serbian Right-Wing 'Security' Groups Flourish," BalkanInsight, December 9, 2021, https://balkaninsight.com/2021/12/09/with-ruling-party-ties-serbian-right-wing-security-groups-flourish.

11. Grozev, Christo, "The Kremlin's Balkan Gambit: Part I," *Bellingcat*, November 1, 2019, https://www.bellingcat.com/news/uk-and-europe/2017/03/04/kremlins-balkan-gambit-part/.

12. "Eyes Wide Shut: Russian Soft Power Gaining Strength in Serbia—Goals, Instruments and Effects," *CEAS*, May 2016, https://www.ceas-serbia.org/images/2016/05/CEAS_-_Eyes_Wide_Shut_-_Russian_soft_power_gaining_strength_in_Serbia_-_Executive_summary.pdf.

13. "Who We Are," *Open Society Foundations*, n.d., https://www.opensociety foundations.org/who-we-are.

14. "Vilify and Amplify From Serbian and Russian Trolls Factories to pro Serbian and Russian Governments Mainstream Media," *CEAS*, December 2017, https://www.ceas-serbia.org/images/2016/vilify-and-amplify/CEAS_Vilify_and_Amplify.pdf.

15. Ibid.

16. "CEAS press announcement: The case of the Center for Euro-Atlantic Studies and its Director Jelena Milić confirms that Serbia is not a state with the rule of law," December 28, 2017, https://www.ceas-serbia.org/en/news/announcements/6784-ceas-press-announcement-the-case-of-the-center-for-euro-atlantic-studies-and-its-director-jelena-milic-confirms-that-serbia-is-not-a-state-with-the-rule-of-law.

17. "UN Judges Overturn Acquittal of Serbian Ultra-Nationalist for Role in Wars," *Reuters*, April 11, 2018, https://www.reuters.com/article/us-warcrimes-serbia/u-n-judges-overturn-acquittal-of-serbian-ultra-nationalist-for-role-in-wars-idUSKBN1HI1X3.

18. "CEAS press announcement: The case of the Center for Euro-Atlantic Studies and its Director Jelena Milić confirms that Serbia is not a state with the rule of law," December 28, 2017, https://www.ceas-serbia.org/en/news/announcements/6784-ceas-press-announcement-the-case-of-the-center-for-euro-atlantic-studies-and-its-director-jelena-milic-confirms-that-serbia-is-not-a-state-with-the-rule-of-law.

19. "Announcement: A Warning on the Activities Executed by Vencislav Bujić," *CEAS*, February 27, 2018, https://www.ceas-serbia.org/en/news/announcements/6909-announcement-a-warning-on-the-activities-executed-by-vencislav-bujic-against-ceas.

20. Ibid.

21. Ibid.

22. "Putin's Asymmetric Assault on Democracy in Russia and Europe: Implications for U.S. National Security," *govinfo.gov*, January 10, 2018, https://www.govinfo.gov/metadata/granule/CPRT-115SPRT28110/CPRT-115SPRT28110/mods.xml.

23. "Country Reports on Human Rights Practices: Serbia," *U.S. Department of State*, 2016, https://www.state.gov/reports/2016-country-reports-on-human-rights-practices/serbia/.

13. What the F . . . k??!!

1. "Näistä Epäilyistä 'Rikoksista' Ilja Janitskin on Ollut Vangittuna Yli 8KK - 12 Kohtaa 'Perusteluineen,'" *MV-Lehti*, April 24, 2018, https://mvlehti. net/2018/04/23/naista-epailyista-rikoksista-ilja-janitskin-on-ollut-vangittuna-yli-8kk-12-kohtaa-perusteluineen/.

2. "Fire that broke out in a future reception centre in Rauma was lit on purpose, police confirm," *Helsinki Times*, December 8, 2015, https://www. helsinkitimes.fi/finland/finland-news/domestic/13650-fire-that-broke-out-in-a-future-reception-centre-in-rauma-was-lit-on-purpose-police-confirm.html.

3. "Yle-Toimittaja Jessikka Aro on Tuomittu Huumerikollinen!" *MV-Lehti*, February 22, 2016, https://mvlehti.net/2016/02/22/yle-toimittaja-jessikka-aro-on-tuomittu-huumerikollinen/.

4. "NATO's Information Expert Jessikka Aro Turned out to Be a Convicted Drug Dealer," *MV-Lehti*, December 9, 2018, https://mvlehti.net/2016/02/24/natos-information-expert-jessikka-aro-turned-out-to-be-a-convicted-drug-dealer/.

5. "Päätoimittajien Kannanotto: Luotettavan Median Puolesta," *Yle Uutiset*, February 29, 2016, https://yle.fi/uutiset/3-8709207.

6. "Aro and Kankkonen win Bonnier journalism prizes," Yle, March 3, 2016, https://yle.fi/news/3-8748609.

7. "Jessikka Aro," *Wikipedia*, https://fi.wikipedia.org/wiki/Jessikka_Aro.

8. Gustafsson, Mikko, "Poliisi on Aloittanut Esitutkinnan Johan Bäckmanista Ja MV-Lehden Ilja Janitskinista," *Iltalehti*, March 2, 2016, https://www.iltalehti. fi/uutiset/a/2016030221205667.

9. "MV-Lehdessä Puhutaan Poliisin Ja Syyttäjän Murhasta – Poliisi Hermostui: Tämä Ylittää Kaikki Rajat," *Yle Uutiset*, November 2, 2016, https:// yle.fi/uutiset/3-9267637.

10. "Anti-Immigrant Agitator Janitskin Extradited to Finland, in Police Custody in Helsinki," *Yle Uutiset*, April 14, 2018, https://yle.fi/uutiset/osasto/news/anti-immigrant_agitator_janitskin_extradited_to_finland_in_police_custody_in_helsinki/10160365.

11. https://mvlehti.net/?s=Juha+Molari+jessikka+aro.

12. Paananen, Arja, "Ex-Kirkkoherra Juha Molari Tuomittiin Ehdolliseen Vankeuteen Ja Liki 100 000 Euron Korvauksiin – Vainosi Jessikka Aroa," *Ilta-Sanomat*, October 16, 2020, https://www.is.fi/kotimaa/art-2000006671979.html.

13 Gertsch, Mia. "Ylen Työntekijä Epäiltynä Avunannosta Ylen Toimittajan Vainoamiseen." *Yle Uutiset*, October 11, 2016. https://yle.fi/uutiset/3-9223341.

14. The Investigator

1. Butler, Declan, and Katia Moskvitch, "HIV Community Reels from Losses in MH17 Plane Tragedy," *Nature News*, July 18, 2014, https://www.nature.com/articles/nature.2014.15584.

2. Bosker, Bianca, "Inside the One-Man Intelligence Unit That Exposed the

Secrets and Atrocities of Syria's War," *HuffPost*, December 7, 2017, https://www. huffpost.com/entry/eliot-higgins-syria_n_4269417.

3. Bellingcat, "Home Page," https://www.bellingcat.com/.

4. Paul, Christopher and Miriam Matthews, The Russian "Firehose of Falsehood" Propaganda Model: Why It Might Work and Options to Counter It," Santa Monica, CA: RAND Corporation, 2016. https://www.rand.org/pubs/perspectives/PE198.html.

5. Ofcom, "Home Page," https://www.ofcom.org.uk/home.

6. "The Ofcom Broadcasting Code (with the Cross-Promotion Code and the On Demand Programme Service Rules)," *Ofcom*, July 27, 2021, https://www. ofcom.org.uk/tv-radio-and-on-demand/broadcast-codes/broadcast-code.

7. "Ofcom Broadcast Bulletin," *Ofcom*, February 3, 2014, https://www.ofcom. org.uk/__data/assets/pdf_file/0023/46652/obb247.pdf.

8. "MH17: Conspiracy Theories Swirl over Putin Assassination, War Ploys and Mass Murder," *thespec.com*, July 22, 2014, https://www.thespec.com/news/world/2014/07/22/mh17-conspiracy-theories-swirl-over-putin-assassination-war-ploys-and-mass-murder.html.

9. "MH17 - Forensic Analysis of Satellite Images Released by the Russian Ministry of Defence," *bellingcat*, May 31, 2015, https://www.bellingcat.com/news/uk-and-europe/2015/05/31/mh17-forensic-analysis-of-satellite-images-released-by-the-russian-ministry-of-defence/.

10. "За мгновения до крушения 'Боинга' под Донецком – уникальный кадр в аналитической программе 'Однако' – Первый канал", 1tv.ru (in Russian), 14 November 2014.

11. "The Criminal Investigation by the Joint Investigation Team (JIT)," Public Prosecution Service, Ministerie van Justitie en Veiligheid, March 10, 2020, https://www.prosecutionservice.nl/topics/mh17-plane-crash/criminal-investigation-jit-mh17.

12. Toler, Aric, "The Weird World of mh17 Conspiracy Theories," *bellingcat*, July 11, 2017, https://www.bellingcat.com/news/uk-and-europe/2015/08/07/mh17-conspiracies/.

13. Fleming, Patrick, "Top Russian Officials: Putin's Superweapons Are like Nothing the West Has Ever Seen (Russian TV)," *Russia Insider*, July 25, 2018, https://russia-insider.com/en/military/top-russian-officials-putins-superweapons-are-nothing-west-has-ever-seen-russian-tv/ri24307.

14. Ibid.

15. Cunningham, Finnian, "Is There a British Assassination Campaign Targeting Russian Exiles?" *Russia Insider*, July 24, 2018, https://russia-insider. com/en/there-british-assassination-campaign-targeting-russian-exiles/ri24297.

16. Mercouris, Alexander, "Russia's Chief Intelligence Analyst Comes Out of the Shadows," *Russia Insider*, May 28, 2015, https://russia-insider.com/en/politics/russias-chief-intelligence-analyst-comes-out-shadows/ri7475.

17. Ibid.

18. "The *Wall Street Journal* Thinks Russian Hackers Are Super Smart, and Super Stupid," *Russia Insider*, November 6, 2014, https://russia-insider.com/en/media_watch/2014/11/07/01-12-06pm/wall_street_journal_thinks_russian_hackers_are_super_smart_and.

19. "GPS Enthusiast Eliot Higgins Gets Creamed by Actual Journalist," *Russia Insider*, May 19, 2015, https://russia-insider.com/en/politics/transparent-fraud-eliot-higgins-defends-fake-mh17-evidence/ri7085.

20. "Guardian Corrects Anti-Russian Story Based on 'Research' of Own Reporter," *Sputnik International*, February 19, 2015, https://sputniknews.com/20150219/1018504330.html

21 "Report on Shelling Ukraine by Russia Based on Discredited Source - Experts," *Sputnik International*, February 20, 2015, https://sputniknews.com/20150219/1018513293.html.

22. "British Blogger Takes Pride in Refusing to Defend His Claims on MH17 Crash," *Sputnik International*, June 4, 2015, https://sputniknews.com/20150604/1022932357.html.

23. Czuperski, Maksymilian, John Herbst, Eliot Higgins, Alina Polyakova, and Damon Wilson, "Hiding in Plain Sight: Putin's War in Ukraine," *Atlantic Council*, February 4, 2021, https://www.atlanticcouncil.org/in-depth-research-reports/report/hiding-in-plain-sight/.

24. "Crowdsourced Geolocation and Analysis of Russian Mod Airstrike Videos from Syria," *bellingcat*, October 5, 2015, https://www.bellingcat.com/resources/articles/2015/10/05/crowdsourced-geolocation-and-analysis-of-russian-mod-airstrike-videos-from-syria/.

25. RT UK, "MSM-Source Leicester Citizen Journo Torn to Shreds over MH17," YouTube video, 3:00, October 8, 2015, https://www.youtube.com/watch?v=LqDvTgbgmjg&list=PLPC0Udeof3T48YMaClFdtW16l_D6WDwRW&index=5&ab_channel=RTUK.

26. "Bellingcat Accuses Russia of Faking Videos Showing Jets Dropping Bombs on Isis," *RT International*, October 8, 2015, https://www.rt.com/news/317971-bellingcat-russia-syria-videos-geolocation/.

27. "Hide, It's RT! Amateur Journo behind Bellingcat so Informed on Russian Targets, He Ducks Interview," *RT International*, October 9, 2015, https://www.rt.com/news/318067-bellingcat-higgins-evades-rt/.

28. ThreatConnect, "Home Page," https://threatconnect.com/.

29. "Belling the BEAR," *ThreatConnect*, November 2, 2021, https://www.threatconnect.com/blog/russia-hacks-bellingcat-mh17-investigation/#post_content.

30. "U.S. Charges Russian GRU Officers with International Hacking and Related Influence and Disinformation Operations," U.S. Department of Justice, October 4, 2018, https://www.justice.gov/opa/pr/us-charges-russian-gru-officers-international-hacking-and-related-influence-and.

31. "КиберБеркут Выявил Связь СБУ и Геращенко с Российскими 'Правозащитниками.'" *vesti.ru*, October 29, 2015, https://www.vesti.ru/

article/1727739.

32. Schultz, Robert. "British Citizen Exposed as a Tool of Russia's FSB," *Ukraine: War Log (blog)*, July 14, 2015, https://ukrainewarlog.blogspot.com/2015/07/british-citizen-exposed-as-tool-of.html.

33. "'Because I Work for RT': Graham Phillips Deported from Ukraine," *RT International*, July 25, 2014, https://www.rt.com/news/175676-ukraine-deport-rt-contributor/.

34. "Open Letter from Ambassador of Ukraine to the United Kingdom of Great Britain and Northern Ireland Natalia Galibarenko," *Головна*, September 22, 2016, https://uk.mfa.gov.ua/en/press-center/news/51028-vidkritij-list-posla-ukrajini-u-velikij-britaniji-movoju-originalu.

35. "Ukraine Calls on UK Police to Probe Graham Phillips for 'Terrorist Activity' in Donbas," *UNIAN Information Agency*, August 8, 2018, https://www.unian.info/politics/10217576-ukraine-calls-on-uk-police-to-probe-graham-phillips-for-terrorist-activity-in-donbas.html.

36. "Graham Phillips Youtube Channel," YouTube channel, https://www.youtube.com/channel/UCbwfUqs5Y6_jblWJwMIfRzA.

37. "Sergey Skripal's Home—I visit," June 21, 2019, https://www.youtube.com/watch?v=Dho2uZkf-_c

38. Bright, Sam, "The Communist Soldier Using Charity Sites to Fund His War," *BBC News*, July 24, 2017, https://www.bbc.com/news/blogs-trending-40647061.

39. "Брифинг Официального Представителя МИД России М.В.Захаровой, Москва, 6 Апреля 2016 Года." Министерство иностранных дел Российской Федерации, April 6, 2016, https://www.mid.ru/foreign_policy/news/-/asset_publisher/cKNonkJE02Bw/content/id/2211888#21).

40. "Response from the Russian Ministry of Foreign Affairs to Bellingcat Regarding Fakery Allegations," *bellingcat*, April 15, 2016, https://www.bellingcat.com/resources/articles/2016/04/14/response-from-the-russian-ministry-of-foreign-affairs-to-bellingcat-regarding-fakery-allegations/.

41. Ibid.

42. "MFA Response," *bellingcat*, April 2016, https://www.bellingcat.com/wp-content/uploads/2016/04/MFA_response_1_en.pdf.

43. "MH17 - The Open Source Investigation, Two Years Later," *bellingcat*, July 15, 2016, https://www.bellingcat.com/news/uk-and-europe/2016/07/15/mh17-the-open-source-investigation-two-years-later/.

44. "The Falsification of Open Sources about MH17," *segodnia.ru*, n.d., http://www.segodnia.ru/sites/default/files/pdf/The%20Falsification%20of%20Open%20Sources%20About%20MH17.pdf.

45. "The Falsification of Open Sources about MH17: Two Years Later," *vdocument.in*, n.d. https://vdocument.in/reader/full/the-falsification-of-open-sources-about-mh17-two-years-later.

46. "Anti-Bellingcat," https://www.segodnia.ru/sites/default/files/pdf/Бук%

203_2%20тайна%20потерянной%20цифры.pdf

47. "JIT Presentation of First Results of the MH17 Criminal Investigation," *Public Prosecution Service*, Ministerie van Justitie en Veiligheid, January 15, 2020, https://www.prosecutionservice.nl/topics/mh17-plane-crash/criminal-investigation-jit-mh17/jit-presentation-first-results-mh17-criminal-investigation-28-9-2016.

48. RT, "Debunking 'Arm Chair Blogger' Bellingcat," YouTube video, 1:55, September 28, 2016, https://www.youtube.com/watch?v=V3lwPS_1E2w.

49. Aro, Jessikka, "The Cyberspace War: Propaganda and Trolling as Warfare Tools," *European View* 15, no. 1 (2016): 121–32, https://doi.org/10.1007/s12290-016-0395-5.

50. "Revealed! SouthFront Is Run by 'the Russian Military'," *SouthFront*, December 9, 2020, https://southfront.org/southfront-is-run-by-the-russian-military/.

51. "Whither Bellingcat in the Age of Trump?" *SouthFront*, February 20, 2017, https://southfront.org/whither-bellingcat-in-the-age-of-trump/.

52. "Примеры Публикаций, Тиражирующих Недостоверную Информацию о России," *Министерство иностранных дел Российской Федерации*, n.d. https://www.mid.ru/nedostovernie-publikacii.

53. EU vs Disinformation, July 28, 2021, https://euvsdisinfo.eu/.

54. "Ofcom Fines RT £200,000," *Ofcom*, July 26, 2019, https://www.ofcom.org.uk/about-ofcom/latest/media/media-releases/2019/ofcom-fines-rt.

55. "Russian Claim against Ofcom Dismissed," *BBC News*, March 27, 2020, https://www.bbc.com/news/entertainment-arts-52066359.

56. "RT Loses Appeal over Ofcom's £200,000 Impartiality Fine," *Press Gazette*, November 1, 2021, https://www.pressgazette.co.uk/rt-ofcom-fine-court-of-appeal/.

57. "Update Investigation Jit Mh17 - Press Meeting (24-5-2018)," *Public Prosecution Service*, Ministerie van Justitie en Veiligheid, March 5, 2020, https://www.prosecutionservice.nl/topics/mh17-plane-crash/criminal-investigation-jit-mh17/speakers-text-jit-mh17-press-meeting-24-5-2018.

58. Bloomberg Politics, "Putin, Macron, Abe, Wang, Lagarde Speak at SPIEF," YouTube video, 2:43:14, May 26, 2018, https://www.youtube.com/watch?v=AQh4YztucQU.

59. Ibid.

60. Bellingcat (@bellingcat), "Having asked @Dpol_un for…," Twitter post, June 12, 2018, 11:37 AM, https://twitter.com/bellingcat/status/1006561126535041024

61. Ibid.

62. "Report of the Secretary-General on progress in the implementation of the 31 December 2016 political agreement," *United Nations Security Council*,

February 15, 2018, https://undocs.org/pdf?symbol=en/S/2018/128.

63. Nakashima, Ellen, "Russian hackers harassed journalists who were investigating Malaysia Airlines plane crash," *Washington Post*, September 28, 2016, https://www.washingtonpost.com/world/national-security/russian-hackers-harass-researchers-who-documented-russian-involvement-in-shootdown-of-malaysian-jetliner-over-ukraine-in-2014/2016/09/28/d086c8bc-84f7-11e6-ac72-a29979381495_story.html.

64. Polyanskiy, Dmitry, "Letter to the Editor of the *Washington Post* with Regard to the Article Entitled 'A Dispatch from the Fight against Russian Disinformation and a Place Where Truth Is Winning,'" *Permanent Mission of the Russian Federation to the United Nations*, August 3, 2018, https://russiaun.ru/en/news/letterwp.

65. "Baltic Parliamentary Committee Chairmen Nominate Bellingcat for Pulitzer," *ERR*, February 1, 2019, https://news.err.ee/906652/baltic-parliamentary-committee-chairmen-nominate-bellingcat-for-pulitzer.

66. "Decision on Prosecution MH17," Parliamentary document, *Ministerie van Algemene Zaken*, June 19, 2019, https://www.government.nl/documents/parliamentary-documents/2019/06/19/decision-on-prosecution-mh17.

67. "Identifying the Separatists Linked to the Downing of MH17," *bellingcat*, October 12, 2020, https://www.bellingcat.com/news/uk-and-europe/2019/06/19/identifying-the-separatists-linked-to-the-downing-of-mh17/.

68. "MH17 Trial: What You Need to Know., *DW.COM*, July 6, 2021, https://www.dw.com/en/mh17-trial-what-you-need-to-know/a-52681068.

15. The Trial

1. "Report for: The Cyberspace War: Propaganda and Trolling as Warfare Tools," *Altmetric*, n.d., https://sage.altmetric.com/details/7574376.

2. Chandra, Akshay, "This YouTube Update Can Make YouTubers Super Rich," *Vidooly*, March 19, 2018, https://vidooly.com/blog/this-youtube-update-can-make-youtubers-super-rich/.

3. "Anti-Immigrant Agitator Ilja Janitskin Gets 22-Month Jail Sentence," *Yle Uutiset*, November 8, 2018, https://yle.fi/uutiset/osasto/news/anti-immigrant_agitator_ilja_janitskin_gets_22-month_jail_sentence/10463931.

4. Paananen, Arja, "Venäjän Valtionmedia Löysi Tavan Kertoa Bäckmanin Ja Janitskinin Tuomiosta," *Ilta-Sanomat*, October 20, 2013, https://www.is.fi/ulkomaat/art-2000005871022.html.

16. The Insider

1. Carroll, Rory, "Russia Today News Anchor Liz Wahl Resigns Live on Air over Ukraine Crisis., *The Guardian*, March 5, 2014, https://www.theguardian.

com/world/2014/mar/06/russia-today-anchor-liz-wahl-resigns-on-air-ukraine.

2. DFRLab, "Question That: RT's Military Mission." *Medium*, November 23, 2018, https://medium.com/dfrlab/question-that-rts-military-mission-4c4bd9f72c88.

3. Габуев , Александр, "'Нет Никакой Объективности,'" *Коммерсантъ*, April 7, 2012, https://www.kommersant.ru/doc/1911336.

4. Pilkington, Ed, "Manning Conviction under Espionage Act Worries Civil Liberties Campaigners," *The Guardian*, July 31, 2013, https://www.theguardian.com/world/2013/jul/31/bradley-manning-espionage-act-civil-liberties.

5. Asp, David, "Espionage Act of 1917," *The First Amendment Encyclopedia*, May 2019, https://www.mtsu.edu/first-amendment/article/1045/espionage-act-of-1917.

6. RT America, "Alex Jones: Obama's Executive Order Facilitates Martial-Law," YouTube video, 14:25, 2012.

7. Ibid.

8. Chappell, Bill, "Steven Seagal Is Now a Citizen of Russia, Courtesy of Putin," NPR, November 3, 2016, https://www.npr.org/sections/thetwo-way/2016/11/03/500535943/steven-seagalis-now-a-citizen-of-russia-courtesy-of-putin.

9. "RT Reacts to Anchor Liz Wahl Quitting on Air," *RT International*, March 6, 2014, https://www.rt.com/usa/rt-reacts-liz-wahl-042/.

10. "Brainwash Level - 'Neocons': Staged Liz Wahl Psy-Op Exposure Explodes on Twitter," *RT International*, March 20, 2014, https://www.rt.com/usa/liz-whal-neocons-twitter-101/.

11. Simonyan, Margarita, "About Abby Martin, Liz Wahl and Media Wars," *RT International*, March 6, 2014, https://www.rt.com/op-ed/about-liz-wahl-media-wars-126/.

12. RT, "Full Skripal Case Interview with the UK's Suspects (EXCLUSIVE)," YouTube video, 27:43, 2018, https://www.youtube.com/watch?v=Ku8OQNyI2i0.

13. Watson, Paul Joseph, "The Truth about RT Host Liz Wahl's Resignation," YouTube video, 9:00, March 7, 2014, https://www.youtube.com/watch?v=HIiiwe6TUtY&list=PL4WqBfljt6TjtMG7GwJJrpq5I_KrC3a1S&ab_channel=PaulJosephWatson.

14. "Neocon Con? US right stage media attack on Alternative Views," RT, March 20, 2104, https://www.youtube.com/watch?v=l1ZwDjzga2k&t=80s.

15. "Confronting Russia's Weaponization of Information," House Committee on Foreign Affairs Republicans, April 15, 2015, https://docs.house.gov/meetings/FA/FA00/20150415/103320/HHRG-114-FA00-Transcript-20150415.pdf.

16. Gold, Hadas, "Russia's RT Television Network Will Go Dark in Washington D.C.," *CNNMoney*, March 30, 2018, https://money.cnn.com/2018/03/29/media/russia-rt-washington-dc/index.html.

17. The Return

1. "PS:N Koko Johto Otti Kantaa Ilja Janitskinin Tuomioon," *Verkkouutiset*, October 21, 2018, https://www.verkkouutiset.fi/psn-koko-johto-kauhisteli-ilja-janitskinin-tuomiota/#7fa90140.

2. "Haastattelussa: Ilja Janitskin," *Suomen Uutiset*, May 23, 2018, https://www.suomenuutiset.fi/haastattelussa-ilja-janitskin/.

3. "MV-Lehti Nimitti Tiedotusvastaavan - Tiina Keskimäki," *MV-Lehti*, November 20, 2016, https://mvlehti.net/2016/11/19/mv-lehti-nimitti-tiedotusvastaavan-tiina-keskimaki/.

4. "Site:Mvlehti.net 'Jessikka Aro,'" Google search, Google, n.d., https://www.google.com/search?q=site%3Amvlehti.net%2B%22Jessikka%2BAro%22&oq=site%3Amvlehti.net%2B%22Jessikka%2BAro%22&aqs=chrome..69i57j69i58.8582j0j7&sourceid=chrome&ie=UTF-8.

5. "Eikka Lehtosaari Haastattelee Ilja Janitskinia (Video)," *MV-Lehti*, January 8, 2019, https://mvlehti.net/2019/01/08/eikka-lehtosaari-haastattelee-ilja-janitskinia-video.

6. Secretary of State's International Women of Courage Award, https://www.state.gov/secretary-of-states-international-women-of-courage-award.

7. Wendling, Mike, and Will Yates, "NATO Says Viral News Outlet Is Part of 'Kremlin Misinformation Machine,'" *BBC News*, February 11, 2017, https://www.bbc.com/news/blogs-trending-38936812.

8. Wendling , Mike, and Will Yates, "NATO Says Viral News Outlet Is Part of 'Kremlin Misinformation Machine.'"

9. Gleicher, Nathaniel, "Removing Coordinated Inauthentic Behavior from Russia," *Meta*, January 17, 2019, https://about.fb.com/news/2019/01/removing-cib-from-russia/.

10. Walker, James,"Facebook Removes 364 'Sputnik Employee-Linked' Pages and Accounts for 'Co-Ordinated Inauthentic Behaviour'," *Press Gazette*, January 17, 2019, https://pressgazette.co.uk/facebook-removes-364-sputnik-employee-linked-pages-and-accounts-for-co-ordinated-inauthentic-behaviour/.

11. Aro, Jessikka, "Emilia Seikkanen Worked in a Trendy Video Start-up in Berlin – Tells All about the Kremlin's Global Information Operation," *Yle Uutiset*, March 6, 2021, https://yle.fi/uutiset/3-11820154

12. Wiebe, Von Jan-Henrik, "Wie Russische Medien Mitten in Berlin Meinung Machen," *t-online*, November 16, 2018, https://www.t-online.de/nachrichten/deutschland/id_84584050/mitten-in-berlin-russlands-heimliche-medienzentrale-in-europa.html).

13. "Populistinen Vastamedia Journalismia Haastamassa: Suomalaiset Vastamediat Yleisötutkimuksen Näkökulmasta," n.d., https://www.hssaatio.fi/wp-content/uploads/2020/08/Loppuraportti-Laura-Ahva.pdf.

14. Aro, Jessikka, "Venäjän Valtionmediat Levittävät Koronasta Salaliittoteorioita Länsimaihin – Samat Teoriat Kiertävät Myös Suomenkielisillä

Foorumeilla," *Yle Uutiset*, July 4, 2020, https://yle.fi/uutiset/3-11386660.

15. Newman, Nic, Richard Fletcher, Antonis Kalogeropoulos, David A.L. Lev and Rasmus Kleis Nielsen, "The Reuters Institute Digital News Report 2021," *Reuters*, 2018, https://reutersinstitute.politics.ox.ac.uk/sites/default/files/2021-06/Digital_News_Report_2021_FINAL.pdf.

16. Standish, Reid, and Robbie Gramer, "U.S. Cancels Journalist's Award Over Her Criticism of Trump," *Foreign Policy*, March 7, 2019, https://foreignpolicy.com/2019/03/07/u-s-cancels-journalists-award-over-her-criticism-of-trump-international-women-in-courage-award-state-department/.

17. Kirby, Jen, "State Department Rescinds Award for Finnish Journalist over Trump Criticism: Report," *Vox*, March 7, 2019, https://www.vox.com/world/2019/3/7/18254829/state-department-jessikka-aro-trump-international-women-courage-awards.

18. Menendez, Bob (@SenatorMenendez), "The United States presents this award...," Twitter post, March 7, 2019, 3:25 PM, https://twitter.com/SenatorMenendez/status/1103753480949428225.

19. "Eikka Lehtosaari Haastattelee Ilja Janitskinia (Video)," *MV-Lehti*, January 8, 2019, https://mvlehti.net/2019/01/08/eikka-lehtosaari-haastattelee-ilja-janitskinia-video/.

20. Глумов, Данила. "Финская Журналистка Лишилась Престижной Премии За Критику Трампа в Соцсети Twitter," Федеральное агентство новостей No.1, March 9, 2019, https://riafan.ru/1158868-finskaya-zhurnalistka-lishilas-prestizhnoi-premii-za-kritiku-trampa-v-socseti-twitter.

21. Collins, Ben, and Brandy Zadrozny, "This Man Is Running Russia's Newest Propaganda Effort in the U.S. - or at Least He's Trying To," *NBCNews.com*, June 15, 2018, https://www.nbcnews.com/news/us-news/man-running-russia-s-newest-propaganda-effort-u-s-or-n883736.

22. "News of Politics, Economy. Interviews, Opinions, Reports," *USA Really*, December 11, 2021, https://usareally.com/.

23. Vankin, Jonathan, "Russian 'Election Observer' and Internet 'Troll,' Alexander Malkevich, Detained and Questioned by FBI," *Yahoo! News*, November 11, 2018, https://news.yahoo.com/russian-election-observer-internet-troll-054212674.html.

24. "Treasury Escalates Sanctions Against the Russian Government's Attempts to Influence U.S. Elections," *U.S. Department of the Treasury*, April 15, 2021.,https://home.treasury.gov/news/press-releases/jy0126.

25. "Engel Decries Reported State Department Retaliation Against Journalist for Criticizing Trump," *House Foreign Affairs Committee,* March 8, 2019, https://foreignaffairs.house.gov/2019/3/engel-decries-reported-state-department-retaliation-against-journalist-for-criticizing-trump.

26. Trump White House Archive, "First Lady Melania Trump at the 2019 International Women of Courage Awards," YouTube video, 0:58, March 8,

2019.,https://www.youtube.com/watch?v=Tbc_syd8jz8.

27. "Examining the State Department's Claims about the International Women of Courage Award and Jessikka Aro," *senate.gov*, March 2019, https://www.foreign.senate.gov/imo/media/doc/SFRC%20Dem%20staff%20report%20on%20Aro%20-%203-28-19.pdf).

28. "Following IG Report, Eight Democratic Senators Demand Secretary Pompeo Answer for Department's Lies about Rescinding Award to Journalist: U.S. Senator Bob Menendez of New Jersey," October 2, 2020, https://www.menendez.senate.gov/newsroom/press/following-ig-report-eight-democratic-senators-demand-secretary-pompeo-answer-for-departments-lies-about-rescinding-award-to-journalist.

29. "Tähän Loppui Foliohattuilu Ja Arvailu Jessikka Aron Touhuista -Katso!" *MV-Lehti*, March 31, 2019, https://mvlehti.net/2019/03/31/tahan-loppui-foliohattuilu-ja-arvailu-jaessikka-aron-touhuista-katso/.

30. "Lännen Trollitehdas Rakensi Tubettajaverkoston Venäjälle Mielipidevaikuttamiseen - Rahoituksen Jäljet Peitelty," *MV-Lehti*, March 31, 2019, https://mvlehti.net/2019/03/31/lannen-trollitehdas-rakensi-tubettajaver koston-venajalle-mielipidevaikuttamiseen-rahoituksen-jaljet-peitelty/.

31. Haynes, Deborah, "'Highly Likely' GRU Hacked UK Institute Countering Russian Fake News," *Sky News*, March 6, 2019, https://news.sky.com/story/highly-likely-moscow-hacked-uk-agency-countering-russian-disinformation-11656539.

32. "Finnish Reporter Jessikka Aro Says Fake News Stories about Her Have Led to Real Threats," *The Washington Post*, April 18, 2018, https://www.washingtonpost.com/video/postlive/finnish-reporter-jessikka-aro-says-fake-news-stories-about-her-have-led-to-real-threats/2019/04/18/8b269948-be64-4d21-9085-2de5fd48ef11_video.html.

33. "Read and Search the Full Mueller Report," *CNN*, July 21, 2019, https://edition.cnn.com/2019/04/18/politics/full-mueller-report-pdf/index.html.

34. "Putin: Trump 'Unquestionably Talented' Person, 'Absolute . . . ," *RealClear Politics*, December 17, 2015, https://www.realclearpolitics.com/video/2015/12/17/putin_trump_unquestionably_talented_person_absolute_leader.html#!

35. Parker, Ned, Jonathan Landay, and John Walcott, "Putin-Linked Think Tank Drew up Plan to Sway 2016 US Election – Documents," *Reuters*, April 19, 2017, https://www.reuters.com/article/us-usa-russia-election-exclusive-idUSKBN17L2N3.

36. Parliamentlive.tv, June 11, 2019. https://parliamentlive.tv/Event/Index/385a6d4c-3764-4570-8796-54f873a054aa.

37. House Foreign Affairs Committee, "Russian Disinformation Attacks on Elections: Lessons from Europe (EventID=109816)," YouTube video, 1:58:06, 2019, https://www.youtube.com/watch?v=

U3heju1HIQE&ab_channel=HouseForeignAffairsCommittee.

38. Jamieson, Kathleen Hall, *Cyberwar: How Russian Hackers and Trolls Helped Elect a President—What We Don't, Can't, and Do Know,* New York: Oxford University Press, 2020.

39. Singh, Maanvi, Joan E Greve, Lauren Gambino, Julia Carrie Wong, Amanda Holpuch, Oliver Laughland, and David Smith, "Mueller Warns of Russian Meddling in 2020: 'They're Doing It as We Sit Here'—as It Happened," *The Guardian*, July 25, 2019, https://www.theguardian.com/us-news/live/2019/jul/24/mueller-testimony-live-stream-trump-news-today-russia-obstruction-report-latest-updates-hearing?page=with%3Ablock-5d38a9368f0845f89e313b79.

Acknowledgments

Thank you to Pupsu, Renatas, Bill, Liz, Eliot, Martin, Jelena, Thomas, Atle, Roman Patrik Oksanen, Jukka Mallinen, Arja Paananen, Saara Jantunen, Imbi Paju, Paul Hacker, Jakub Kalensky, Jakub Janda, Rosa Guevara, Christina Forsgård, Janne Huuskonen, Atte Jääskeläinen, Markku Mantila, Petri Tuomi-Nikula, Matti Ridanpää, Marko Enqvist, Jussi Tuovinen, Torsti Sirén, Aki-Mauri Huhtinen, Kari, Jussi, Jukka, Virve, CC, Saleem Khan, Aki Kuosmanen, Sam Kingsley Thomas, Miikka, Satjiv, Antti Suhone, Jaakko Vuorinen, Timo Kämäräinen, Teri Schultz, Kari Nissinen, Mika Rahkonen, Kjetil Stormark, Pasi Eronen, Jarno Limnéll, Janne "Rysky" Riiheläinen, Aki Heikkinen, Antti Hirvonen, Timo Knuutila, Tomi Huhtanen, Pekka Virkki, Ben Nimmo, Marjaana Toiviainen, Juho Pylvänäinen, Mika Mäkeläinen, Jyri Rantala, Irina Tumakova, Rebekka Härkönen, Laura Saarikoski, Nanne Husman, Juha-Antero Puistola, James Mashiri, Ana Mitrunen, Jaakko Pietiläinen, Timo Ernamo, Timo Julkunen, Marko Lavikkala, Kaikki Ylen tyypit, Kai Kotiranta, Seppo, Mikko, Harri, Ari Martina Kronström, Katleena Kortesuo, Rhea Lyons, Elina Ahlbäck, Niko, Anna.

Special thanks to the courageous Russian journalists who originally exposed the troll factory.

Thank you every known and unknown individual who has sent me encouraging messages during the years.

Thank you also to the organizers of conferences and trainings, as well as to my home university, University of Tampere.

Thank you for the writing grants:
Finnish Ministry of Education and Culture: The Committee for Public Information (TJNK)
Kone Foundation

Thank you to all the crowdfunders!